ISRAEL'S CONCEPT OF THE BEGINNING

ISRAEL'S CONCEPT
OF THE BEGINNING

The Theology of Genesis 1–3

HENRICUS RENCKENS S.J.

HERDER AND HERDER

1964
HERDER AND HERDER   NEW YORK
232 Madison Avenue, New York 16, N.Y

Translated from *Israels Visie op het Verleden*
(Tielt: Lannoo) by Charles Napier.

Contents

Introduction

THIS book brings together in one volume, virtually unchanged and with only a few omissions and additions, a series of articles which originally appeared in four successive volumes of *Verbum* (1950–1953), a review concerned with the teaching of religious knowledge which is under the direction of the *Canisianum* Catechetical Center at Maastricht.

The only objection that has been increasingly made against this series is that by the fact of its being spread over the successive yearly volumes of a review destined for a comparatively limited public, it is difficult to refer to and to use. I am therefore grateful for the opportunity of making generally available what I have written down in a somewhat piecemeal fashion.

The fact that this book thus bears the traces of its origin is perhaps rather an advantage than otherwise. It is at the same time more compelling and more instructive to follow an exegetical line of investigation step by step, rather than to have to listen to someone who from the beginning already knows what his conclusions are going to be, and has an answer ready for everything. Moreover the additional fact that each chapter is distinct in itself does not prevent the book as a whole from having a proper internal unity. This unity is simply that of the contemporary approach to the exegesis of Holy Scripture, as it is put into practice today. It is therefore to be hoped that this book may not only be a help toward the forming of a coherent understanding of the opening pages of the Bible, but that it may also serve as a general introduction to the whole of the Old Testament revelation.

The reader must therefore realize from the start that he is being taken on an adventure—an adventure that will however be worth the trouble inevitably involved, and also a certain risk. For our subject is full of problems, and yet fuller still of God's mystery. The last word about it has by a very long way not yet been said, and certainly not in this book; but our time will not have been wasted if by the end of it we have been able to see a little more light here and there, and to make out something more of the full reality.

ISRAEL'S CONCEPT OF THE BEGINNING

1

The "Biblical Question"

A FEW words, by way of explanation, may serve to give both an indication of the method which will be used in this book, and a first overview of the present state of the question. In the book of Genesis we are presented with Israel's understanding of an already *distant* past: in Genesis 1–11 we find what Israel knew and thought of the beginning of the history of the human race, whereas the rest of the book contains the picture that it had of the dawn of its own national history as a people. The limits of our investigation are thus on the one hand, Israel's understanding, or concept, and on the other, the past itself.

1) The understanding is that of Israel, as a particular people. What does this imply? 2) What does Israel know about the past? In other words, what is the value of this understanding? Its religious value is beyond any question, but what of its historical significance? What, if any, are the limits of the guarantee of inspiration?

Genesis Is Israel's Spiritual Inheritance

We need to keep constantly in mind the fact that the first Bible narratives, in the form in which they have come down to us, originate within Israel itself.

Because the events of the dawn of history took place such an immeasurably long time before the people of Israel came into being, we have a constant tendency to think of the origin

11

of these eleven chapters as being also before Israel's time. This is a mistake. The Old Testament is Israel's national literature; its first pages were composed by Israel and for Israel, and they are even, in their final form, to be dated in a period which was one of considerable maturity and reflective capacity. For it is undeniable that behind these passages there lies a mind in which both the deep religiosity of the preaching of the prophetic period and the depth of understanding of Israel's great seekers after wisdom came together.

This fact, that even in Genesis it is with Israel that we are concerned, will mean more to us if we look at it in the light of the doctrine of inspiration. For through this Israelite speaking to his compatriots, God is speaking—to them and to us. He is not saying more to us than He was saying to them, though we can of course understand more, and better, than they could, now that He has spoken fully in Christ. And so if we wish to know what God's intentions were in speaking to Israel, we must ask ourselves what it was that that Israelite intended to say to his own people, and therefore what he was able to say to them. For in Holy Scripture the words of God and those of men are bound up together in a homogeneous, living unity, so that they interpenetrate and cover each other entirely. God's communication is made known and determinate by the human communication in which it comes, and it is defined and limited by it. Hence the "supreme principle of interpretation . . . : to search out and to determine what the writer intended to say." For "in Scripture divine things are communicated to us by the means that are common to men."[1]

A Realistic Notion of Inspiration

As a means of solving biblical problems, speculative deductions, however dogmatically impeccable their premises may be,

[1] Pius XII, *Divino afflante Spiritu,* Denzinger, *3830.

are insufficient. A theory can all too easily be understood in too static a manner, and then applied mechanically. In other words, speculative thinking needs to find its indispensable fulfillment of concreteness, nuance, and suppleness—in short of workability —through the positive investigation of reality. Our understanding of Holy Scripture must be the result both of a theory which will tell us a priori what kind of conclusions we ought to be reaching (e.g., on the basis of the dogmatic truth that Scripture is God's word), and of the experimental knowledge which will tell us what the reality in fact appears to be. During the last half century we have gained a very much more carefully defined notion of inspiration and of its consequences precisely as the result of a closer contact with the mystery of inspiration as a fact in Scripture. This contact has had a really beneficial effect on the way in which the notion of inspiration has been approached and thought out speculatively, to such an extent that it is described by Pius XII as being among the *new* supports and instruments of present-day exegesis.[2]

Thus the notion of inspiration, as it is now understood, would appear to be in full agreement with the reality as we find it: Israel stood for long centuries under God's particular supernatural guidance, which we express in terms of the notions of inspiration and of revelation, and Scripture is the result of it all—a reality which is wholly divine, but also wholly Israelitic, from its most sublime thoughts up to and including its quaintest details. We cannot understand God in Scripture, if we do not first understand Israel, for the living and historical Israel is presented to us entirely intact under the operation of God's activity. God's message to men has taken a clearly determined and historically conditioned form—characteristically that of Israel—which henceforth lies forever open for further investigation. It is not only the language and the forms of speech that

[2] *Ibid.*

13

are Israelitic: Everything is included, also and above all the whole world of ideas which lies behind the language, ideas about religion and morals not excepted.

Israel's Religious Genius?

In all this, Israel remains wholly a child of its time. And yet, while remaining of its own time, it transcended the latter's limitations in the things that essentially concern God and religion and the crucial questions about man and his life on earth. For the unbeliever, this is precisely the great riddle or mystery of Israel's genius, the inexplicable, nonrational element in Israel as an historical phenomenon. For the believer on the other hand, it constitutes an impressive and deeply persuasive internal argument for the fact of God's intervention in human affairs, as the Bible bears witness of it in Israel. For him this divine intervention is the prelude to the coming of Christ, the gradual unfolding and working out of the plan of salvation which is centered in Christ. In such a perspective, it is a priori unlikely that God should have had the intention of communicating to us things that are "of no value for salvation."[3] And it is indeed clear from Scripture that such is the case. In the whole of the profane sphere Israel remains intact, and yet by the mysterious working of inspiration and revelation God has brought this people's understanding and capacity in religious matters to a stage of fuller and higher activity. Thus Israel's consciousness of divine things achieved a depth of perception such that Christendom, too, continues to be nourished by it: In the best of its children it attained a religious attitude, that of the self-giving of faith and obedience, which will always remain the pattern of man's attitude toward the Kingdom of God.

[3] *Nulli saluti profutura*—the expression is Augustine's, quoted by Leo XIII in *Providentissimus Deus* and by Pius XII in *Divino afflante Spiritu.*

14

Inspiration Not Affected by the Limitations of Israel's Profane Culture

These religious values and realities, however, form a concrete whole with the rest of Israel's understanding of the entirety of human and earthly life in all its variety, which it judged just as did the other peoples of that time. We now know that these peoples had relatively primitive and sometimes erroneous conceptions about many things, and these conceptions were shared by Israel as a whole and by the biblical authors in particular.

And yet it remains that these conceptions, for all their inadequacy, were the indispensable vehicle of religious truth. Indispensable indeed, for if in reality God *had* caused the inspired writers to speak with complete scientific accuracy, the people of Israel would not have understood the saving truth which it was their purpose to convey, any more than it could have grasped their scientific teaching.

We thus come to the conclusion, both on theoretical and on historical grounds, that there was no reason why God should have rectified the inadequacies of Israel's profane knowledge, and that in fact He did not do this. It is only comparatively recently that we have dared to accept, as the fruit of hard experience, the liberating consequences of this never wholly forgotten truth. And we still need to be on our guard in this respect, especially when we are faced with problems whose very existence would, in former times, not have been imagined. The deeply rooted tendency to try to use the Bible as a means of solving some form or other of modern scientific problems is still with us.

It is true that we are by now quite accustomed to recognize that the Bible contains erroneous conceptions in the field of natural science. The principle stated by Cardinal Baronius, that "the purpose of Holy Scripture is to teach us how we may go to heaven, and not how the heavens go,"[4] is nowadays very generally grasped. But what is much less widely realized is that we owe this piece of progress in the science of exegesis to the application, in a particular sort of case, of a principle which is of far more general validity. Provided that we remember that it needs to be more accurately re-defined according to each particular type of question to which it is applied, we may formulate this principle as follows: That God's supernatural influence leaves Israel's profane knowledge intact, without rectifying any of its inadequacies or correcting any of its errors. We are, of course, treading here on delicate ground, and must hasten to add the restriction that where profane knowledge is so closely bound up with the saving message itself that it really forms part of the teaching of the sacred writer, and thus also of God Himself, in such a case error is excluded. Moreover, wherever it is clear that this kind of knowledge is humanly speaking unattainable, and yet is necessary for the communication of the saving history, then, too, God does supply for inadequacies. But even here the original principle retains its value inasmuch as, in such cases, God does not supply any knowledge of a profane kind such as, for example, would be capable of verification by means of scientific investigation or discovery. The reader may well feel that this is all somewhat imprecise; but it will shortly be illustrated from concrete exegetical problems, of which what now follows is already a first example.

Natural Science and History

It will already be clear from what has been said that the above general principle applies to the whole of profane knowledge, and not only to the particular domain of natural science.

---

[4] "L'intention de l'Ecriture sainte est de nous apprendre comment on va au ciel, et non pas comment va le ciel," quoted by Lenormant, *Les origines de l'histoire* (Paris, 1880), Preface, viii. This latter book is a classic of the early days of the drama known as *La question biblique*.

Lenormant completes Baronius as follows: " . . . and still less how the things of the earth go in all their vicissitudes. The Holy Spirit was not concerned to reveal scientific truths, or a universal history of the world. About all these matters, He has left men to dispute among themselves, 'tradidit mundum disputationibus eorum.' "[5] Lenormant thus has no qualms about taking the step from applying this principle to questions of natural science to applying it to history, and there are many exegetes who have enthusiastically followed him in this. And why indeed not? Why should we suppose that Israel should not also have been a child of its time in its understanding of history? This would seem to be confirmed by the undeniable fact that Israel's chronology and ethnology, for example, which are spheres which to some extent impinge upon the domain of history, correspond only distantly or not at all to the actual state of affairs.

And yet there was in reality fierce opposition to this manner of resolving the historical difficulties in the Bible. Holy Scripture offers us a history of salvation. The religious teaching is dependent on the facts, which is indeed precisely why they are given. If the objectivity of these facts is not guaranteed, then the whole basis of Israel's religion disappears. Or we may put it another way: Israel's knowledge of history cannot be defined simply as a matter belonging to the sphere of profane knowledge —revelation and inspiration are involved, and we must, therefore, a priori approach it with confidence as being true, and not vice versa.

In his biblical encyclical, *Spiritus Paraclitus*,[6] Benedict XV declared that it is not permissible, on the authority of *Providentissimus*[7], to lump the two questions of Israel's knowledge of

[5] " . . . à plus forte raison comment vont les choses de la terre, et quelles vicissitudes s'y sont succédées. L'Esprit saint ne s'est pas préoccupé de révéler des vérités scientifiques, non plus qu'une histoire universelle. Pour tout ceci, il a abandonné le monde aux disputes des hommes, 'tradidit mundum disputationibus eorum.' "

[6] Denzinger, *3653.

[7] *Ibid.*, *3290.

17

matters of natural science and of its knowledge of history together. The existence of some relationship between the two kinds of problem is not denied,[8] but each demands an approach that is specifically different.

In the field of natural science, the sacred writers describe things as the senses perceive them. In most cases it is likely enough that they drew from these perceptions the same erroneous conclusions about the objective structure and nature of these things as did their contemporaries; but this is beside the point since their purpose was not to give teaching about these matters. The historical difficulties, however, cannot be thus simply disposed of by saying that the writer, in describing the past, was relating what he as it were perceived, i.e., what the men of his time thought about the past, and that he himself could not know any better than they whether the events did in fact take place as he describes them. Thus according to this interpretation the sacred writers partook of the errors of their time just as much in the field of history as in that of natural science. As we have said, this approach is unsound and is to be rejected, because of the fact that while these writers did not intend to teach anything about the objective structure of natural phenomena, they *did* intend to teach something about certain events which had objectively taken place in the past. Thus the particular principle which is applicable to the one kind of problem, does not work for the other.

As has so frequently been the case in the history of exegesis during the last century, the intervention of the magisterium in this connection has been salutary in its effect on exegetical research in general. Once the solution which had at first appeared to be the simplest and easiest one had been excluded, the exegetes were obliged to seek in another direction, and it soon became clear that this first solution had been of far too simplistic and massive a nature. In reality, the correct solution has to such

[8] *Ibid.*, *3287 ff.

a degree to be carefully re-defined in each case, that it becomes extremely difficult to formulate it in the abstract.

It will however always be found by means of an investigation of the literary genre of the book in question (Genesis, for example) and of the literary procedure according to which it has come into being, as a whole and in its greater or smaller parts.

From such an investigation it will become clear that in cases where an author is not well informed about the past, his intention is not that of communicating the exact objective course of events. In such a case it may perfectly well be possible that he was inwardly convinced of what we should describe as an historical error, in the same way that we can accept without difficulty that he firmly believed in the existence of a metallic dome in the sky that prevented the waters of heaven from falling in on the earth. Such a belief is then to be classed among the many things that the writer says (*dicit*) without in fact teaching them (*docet*). There are moreover many different ways in which historical truths may be affirmed in Holy Scripture; in other words, within the historical genre there are a number of different literary genres.

19

2

Biblical History

THE purpose of this chapter is to form a bridge between the foregoing very general introduction to our subject, and the real theme of this book, which is the opening pages of Genesis.

To this end we shall first have to take a brief glance at the question of the nature of Israel's knowledge of history, as we find it in Scripture. We are concerned here with facts. We must take these facts honestly as they stand, and, with a view to avoiding overhasty conclusions and to softening certain inevitable shocks, we shall begin by setting up a suitably elastic buffer and underline the essentially reliable character of the oldest biblical recitals taken as a whole.

The Vital Importance of the Past

Israel lived, as no other people did, in the future. Expectancy is a constituent part of the very national character of this people whose whole life was grounded in a future hope. Israel knew itself to be the privileged subject of God's promises, and it was just for this reason that it took the past so seriously. How often do we not read that Israel may not forget something, must always remember, recount something to children and to children's children: "And it shall be as a sign in thy hand, and as a memorial before thy eyes" (Ex 13:9–16). The past is reiterated, dwelt and reflected upon, and relived. It is always there to be appealed to: "Remember the days of old." In short, it was equally characteristic of Israel to live on the past as it was to hope in the future.

There is nothing strange in this, since past and future are intimately bound up together, and between them constitute the present. The past is the great guarantee of the future. It is in the past that the promises are given; the great deeds of Jahweh, which are the very foundation stone of Israel's existence as a people and of her national vocation, and which give to these their meaning, are facts of the past. It is just because Israel lives in the hope of a future that has been promised in the past by word and deed, that the reality of that past is a matter of life or death.

Thus both from the national and from the religious point of view, Israel's ever-advancing present was lived under the sign and as the product of both past and future. From day to day, year in year out, between past and future, Israel sought to partake in the salvation which Jahweh offered through the sacramental observances of feasts and ceremonies. For such was the means provided by which Jahweh's ever-active will to save, which had once brought redemption to the Patriarchs, was made present to their children of today. It was by this means that there began to be formed, in the midst of the sinful Israel of that "today," the germ of the holy generation of the future, to whom it would be given to experience the full revelation of Jahweh's salvation.[1]

In the measure that as time went on Jahweh's promises came to appear ever more immense and improbable, and as at the

[1] The analogy with our own Christian experience of salvation, in which, in a far more sublime manner, past and present redemption becomes a living reality in its sacramental celebration, is clear enough. Here, however, there is another analogy which should be emphasized: just as Christianity stands or falls with the historical fact of Christ, so too for Israel the past was a matter of crucial importance.

same time Israel came to feel itself to be ever more unworthy and abandoned by God, in the same degree Israel's thought became more deeply rooted in the past. The more difficult it becomes to go on believing in the future, the more tenaciously faith hangs on to its footing in the past.

We find all this summed up in the thought of the greatest of Israel's prophets, Isaias 40–55. Jahweh has done great things, as the fathers have seen with their own eyes, and of which the story has been handed on from generation to generation. As the almighty Creator He has formed the elements at the beginning of time, and it is the same mighty God who looked down in mercy on the fathers and saved them with His outstretched arm from all their enemies. And now, "the arm of Jahweh is not cut short." He is not only "the First" who created "all things of old," he is also "the Last," who will create "all things new." Just as it is He that formed "the first things" out of nothing simply and solely for the glory of His great Name, so He lacks neither the power nor the will to bring also "the last things" into existence. There is nothing that can stand against Him, nothing that can shake His faithfulness to His promises and His will to save, not even Israel's sin and its betrayal of the Covenant. That which He promised "in the beginning," He will perform "at the end, in His Day, in those days."

Thus whatever further conclusions one may come to in regard to Israel's knowledge of the past, the seriousness of its pre-occupation with history is beyond question. We have said enough to show that we are justified in taking this as an unshakable certainty from which we may set out on our further inquiries.

The Origin of Historical Genres

It does not follow from the general fact of Israel's preoccupation with history that everything in the Bible is equally historical,

22

or is historical in the same sense. There is history and history, and there are many historical genres, whose possibilities extend far beyond that of the simple legal investigation into events as they occurred. It is, for example, perfectly clear that Genesis 1–11 was not intended to be such a plain summary of past events.

One of the factors which have caused these different historical genres to come into being is the distance in time between the account as written down and the occurrence of the events in question; and secondly, the means by which and the circumstances in which the writer has come to know about this occurrence. Much will depend for example on whether the writer possessed documentary evidence of these past facts, and on the time which has passed between the occurrence and the earliest document relating to it. When the bridge over such an interval has been formed by oral tradition, one must investigate to what extent the particular milieu in question was capable of acting as the bearer of such a tradition, and even whether there did in fact exist a group of persons (in the form of some ethnic, religious or perhaps merely geographical association) which was thus capable. There are therefore many different factors which could have affected the historical writer's raw material in many different ways. All is historical in one way or another, but by no means all is historical in our modern, exact sense of the term. Yet in all the diversity of this process of written and oral transmission, the peculiar character of the supernatural influence of inspiration working through the laws of history remains unaffected.

A biblical writer in the time of the kings of Israel, for example, had many different kinds of historical information at his disposal. Certain events he had experienced himself; others, from which he was separated by an interval of time or place, he would know of from direct eye witnesses or perhaps at third or fourth hand; other things, again, he would know because they lived on in the collective memory of the people, handed down from a distant past. Last but not least, he would have the use of written documents, which again might be of a whole variety of different kinds, from eye witness accounts to the most popular sort of anecdote. When this writer, acting under the influence of inspiration, had recourse to all these various kinds of knowledge in order, for example, to illustrate Jahweh's faithfulness to His people, this material remained, in its historical content, exactly what it was before. This does not mean that it is a matter of indifference whether something is said by such an inspired writer or by some other chance author. The effect of inspiration is that the sacred writer looks at the past from an entirely different point of view: God's point of view. Materially speaking, his knowledge of the facts remains what it was before. It is true that by inspiration this knowledge is guaranteed, but it is guaranteed according to the particular nature of that knowledge: What is obscure in it does not thereby become clear, nor does what is uncertain become certain, let alone infallibly so.

Our Starting Point: The Period of the Kings

We must now begin to allow the facts to speak for themselves. That they may do so in an orderly fashion, we shall start rather far on in our "biblical chronology," in a place where it will be easy to find our footing from the historical point of view, and then work backward toward the beginning. This is the only sound method in difficult questions: To begin with what is clear, and from there proceed to what is less clear.

The factual material of the Second Book of Kings consists of data, of a quite accurate nature, that has been taken from virtually contemporary chronicles. The events in question took place in a complex and highly organized society, in which both court and temple possessed their chancellery and hierarchy of officials, with the scribes and books and archives that go with them. It was in this society, which had only been able to develop in this way since the time of David, that the historical books of the Bible came into being. Our task is therefore as it were to think ourselves back into this Israel of the time of the kings and to ask ourselves how it came to possess the information which it had about the events with which the historical books are concerned. In this way we shall be able to give a practical demonstration of our argument against those who are still possessed with an instinctive conviction that the Bible must form a single, homogeneous, infallible block, and at the same time we shall hope to be able to give some help to any who may have already fallen into the opposite extreme. To this end we shall begin by giving a very approximate arrangement of the historical narratives of the Bible into six groups, classed as follows according to their content: 1) David-Solomon; 2) Samuel-Saul; 3) Josue-Judges; 4) the Exodus-cycle; 5) the Patriarchs; 6) the Creation and Fall.

All these groups of writings were complete, in their main lines, by the time of the kings, and we shall thus be able to look back, from our standpoint in this period, up the very long road which already lies behind. We shall see the different objects which we shall be able to discern from here with very varying degrees of precision and clarity, not only because of the variation in the interval of time by which we are separated from them, but also because of obscurities and obstacles of many different kinds, and because of the varying dimensions of the very facts themselves.

David-Solomon

It is in this group of narratives that our information is at its best, since for David and Solomon we possess contemporary

25

documents and biographies which as far as we can tell are based upon first hand sources. And yet even here there are times when the precise course of events escapes us, as for example over the question of how exactly David came into Saul's service. The tradition about this is not unanimous, and it is indeed to be expected that there should be several different accounts in circulation about a matter of this kind. Here the tradition is a double one. Both of them undoubtedly rest upon objective facts, but a certain shifting has taken place during the process of handing down, and unfortunately the charisma of inspiration did not whisper to the sacred writer which of the two traditions was correct. The truth is most probably that both are simplifications of a more complex reality which was capable of being looked at from more than one point of view. This is certainly the case, in our second group of writings, of the accounts of the institution of the kingly office. Anyone who tries to start with the principle that Holy Scripture presents us, phrase by phrase, with infallible truths, will find himself already hopelessly at a loss in face of these two simple examples. The only possible way out is to recognize that in cases of this sort there exists a gap on the side of the human information, and that it is mistaken to imagine that inspiration should always have been coming to the rescue with the arsenal of divine omniscience. The sacred writers were left to do the best they could with the material that they had available, and they showed their respect for objective fact by handing their information over to us precisely as it stood. The result, no doubt, is that our curiosity to know the exact details must remain unsatisfied—but then that is not what Holy Scripture is there for. And in fact the divergences in matters of detail, which show the independence of the various traditional sources from one another, make the historicity of the main events, about which they agree, all the more unquestionable. There is thus always a factual basis that is sufficiently broad and solid to act

26

as a support for the religious doctrine which is the writer's ultimate concern.

Josue-Judges

It is even truer of our third group of writings than of the
second (Samuel-Saul), that the facts which they relate took
place in a time that was still relatively primitive and agitated.
The second group can thus be thought of as forming a transition
between the first and the third. Here a rough and ready indication of the main characteristics of the Josue-Judges group will
have to suffice.

The period of the judges is one of struggle and of austerity.
Israel has lost her unity, in every domain, and civilization does
not exist. Here we have to remember that while past events
which do not become sufficiently fixed as stories may well continue to be remembered in piecemeal form, when the time
eventually comes for these fragments to be organized into some
kind of synthetic whole it is usually too late, and recourse has
to be had either to some form or other of simplistic schematiza-
tion, or to a relatively unhistorical idealization of the events in
question. Thus a rather naïve traditional image of Josue,
the man of God, may have been formed, but in any case it was
the responsibility of the Israelites of the period of the judges to
preserve for posterity the exact course of the events of the conquest. It is they alone who can inform us, looking back from
the time of the kings, about their own time.

In fact, what we now possess is a varied collection of bits and
pieces which despite their great historical value are hopelessly
incomplete. From the fragments which have been carefully
brought together and added to our books of Josue and Judges
by a later writer, we are able, with some difficulty, to reconstruct the main outlines of the historical events of the conquest
and the confused situation of the period of the judges. This

27

writer has naturally enough made use of blocks of material that already existed before his own time (such as the cycle of Samson for example), and for the rest he strings together everything that he has been able to find in the way of documents, fragments, local traditions, etc., giving it the form of an admonitory sermon. His material is exceedingly precious, and palpitating with life: We have here no fantasy, but the fruit of concrete reality. The author has tried to present his material as well as possible, and even to extend it by the use of stereotyped formulas. Moreover he dramatizes and theologizes it, so that the outline which he achieves of this particular part of the "history of salvation," imperfect as it may be from the point of view of secular history, nevertheless gives an impression of completeness: we can clearly discern, through the half-light of so many human vicissitudes, the steady onward progress of the divine plan of salvation.

Exodus and the Wilderness

The historical character of the Exodus-cycle is again different. What is preserved is much better preserved than in the previous group, most probably because the principal episodes which took place before the dispersal of Israel in Canaan will have been recounted again and again—to the point of weariness—both in the family circles and also by Moses and the leaders whom he inspired. Thus when Israel arrived in Canaan there already existed a repertoire of stories whose central content together with its first prophetic interpretation had already achieved a stable form. And yet we cannot speak of a genre that is historical in the exact and scientific meaning of the word, for out of all the forty years which Israel spent wandering in the wilderness, the only events we are told anything about are some which occurred during the first year, and some from the last. In the previous group of documents, there were many more precise and localized particulars than we have here, even though the general picture is somewhat unclear. Here it is rather the other way round: the main facts are there all right, but the detailed contingencies of the concrete situations have been so to speak rubbed off in the course of a long process of handing down, and by going through the mill of a didactic preaching method to which they were irrelevant.

The Patriarchs

It is probable that the oldest written version of the stories from which the narrative concerning the Patriarchs was later constructed dates from the time of Moses. This is five centuries after Abraham, which is a very considerable interval of time—that between ourselves and the fifteenth century in fact. We must not forget, however, that quite apart from the fact that in those days oral tradition was far more tenacious a thing than we can easily imagine, creatures of books and of newspapers that we are, there existed in this particular case a situation that was ideal for the accurate handing down of such a tradition: A closed social sphere, determined by ties of blood and of religion, that had originally consisted of a single family and later of a numerous people, but always held together by the forces of isolation and of oppression from without. Thus was the story of the peregrinations of the Fathers, and of the giving of the promises handed on. Through these long centuries of oppression, the main factual elements of the story had become indelibly fixed in the collective memory of the people of Israel: the individuals with their different characters and their different relationships with each other, the holy places, the theophanies, and so on. A story that had been cooked up by someone living in the time of the kings would have looked very different from this, and in reality the only possible explanation is that Israel brought the story

29

with it out of Egypt, in the form of a tradition that had already become unassailable.[2]

Thus by the time of the conquest of Canaan Israel was already in possession of this incomparable "epic of the Fathers" in a form that in its main lines was definitive. An epic indeed, for however detailed and precise the form of it may appear to be, it is in fact the outcome of centuries of popular tradition and of the story-telling artistry of a few gifted masters. For this reason we must be careful to distinguish the kind of precision in a narrative that is due to empirical contact with the actual facts, from that which derives from the desire and the necessity of telling in a living and concrete manner a story of which the component facts had in reality only come down in a relatively vague form. It was the sacred writer of the period of the kings, or his immediate predecessor, who set this material in the world of nomads and seminomads that was characteristic of his own time. In its realism, his story gives the impression, at first sight, of being an exact and detailed copy of the past. But at a closer look the tradition can be seen to be wavering in regard to details, and notwithstanding the precision of the style, it is impossible to reconstruct the exact historical bearing of all the facts. The many points of detail which fail to harmonize with each other remind us that we have here facts which have been preserved for posterity in the only way that they could have been preserved in the given circumstances, i.e., in the form of a picturesque folk story, in which the basic need is for concrete detail. Of this the Bible has changed nothing. A folk story does not lose its special characteristics for being inspired. Rather,

[2] It is very likely that Moses played a considerable part in the handing on of the story of the Patriarchs. The factual material was there; he it was in all probability who gave it its providential signification, leaving his mark upon it by setting the whole of this past series of events in the light of the promises and of the Covenant. In this way he was able to show clearly that the very self-same Jahweh, who had now for the first time revealed Himself *as* Jahweh on Mount Sinai, had already been actively at work in the distant past.

30

inspiration makes use of this among the many and various forms in which past facts may be preserved among men. It does not suddenly transform what would otherwise have been a folk story into scientific history.

Conclusion

The Bible is a *single* book, a divine book, unique in its spirit —for it is the work of God's Spirit—but at the same time a book that has come into existence by many and varied forms of human activity, with all the limitations of human mentality and intellectual development which belong to specific times and places, and based upon particular human forms of thought and expression, and the more or less complete information that goes with them.

The history which we find in the Bible shows an unfailing constancy in its content of divine teaching, but this teaching is expressed in terms of a very varied series of historical situations of which one can say that, by and large, the human factors involved tend to become more and more elusive in the measure that the situations which are being written about lie further away in the past.

Thus, without excluding certain special considerations which may have to be considered, we shall also, in the case of our present study of the Genesis story, avoid trying to use inspiration as some kind of easy way out of our problems, just as we should elsewhere in the Bible.

In conclusion, we may say that we must recognize that there exists a particular and different kind of solution for the difficulties presented by each separate group of biblical narratives. It should by now be clear how unreasonable it would be to seek to apply mechanically to other groups that which might only be appropriate to one of them.

3

Israel's Sources

OUR next inquiry must concern the sources—both divine and human—from which Israel drew its religious and historical knowledge about the events of the creation. The result will be of crucial importance for the further exegesis of these first passages of Genesis. We shall find that it will be worth our trouble to seek patiently, and that, in doing so, an unexpected amount of light will be thrown on our subject.

Which Revelation?

We must start from the fact of what is known as "primitive revelation" (*revelatio primitiva*)—that God did reveal Himself to the first men whom He created, and that they responded to this revelation with faith. Despite the Fall, this faith of primitive humanity did not entirely disappear, for it was handed on to their descendants in the form of what may be called "primitive tradition." The point of all this being that primitive men were already living in a stage of the "history of salvation," and had the opportunity, according to their lights, of finding a way to God and His salvation. They were not entirely abandoned to their natural powers and capacities.

This divinely given "primitive tradition," upon which the primitive but nonetheless real faith to which we have referred was founded, was no doubt wrapped around with much that was of purely human origin, and indeed formed a concrete whole together with it. In other words, it was not only the content of their faith that was handed on to their children by Adam and Eve, but also their human experiences and discoveries. And in the same way their children in turn handed on this first traditional material, to some extent enriched with new material, but also, no doubt, to some extent impoverished. Whatever else may appear to be denied in the course of this chapter, there will in any case be no denial of what we have just said. On the contrary, it will be constantly assumed as the background of all else, for it is in our opinion clearly contained in the biblical creation narrative itself. It was in this narrative that Israel learned from God about the originally privileged situation of the first men: It learned that God continued to concern Himself with fallen humanity, that He continued to intervene, and that in and through Israel He continued to work out the fulfillment of His saving purposes. Here, too, Israel read of man's "original" sin, the consequences of which were spreading down through history in an ever-widening circle. It read that there had been terrible backslidings in the handing down of the true religion, and even that the human race had ended by becoming entirely corrupt and had completely lost the way to God.

The witness of Scripture, therefore, is that God revealed Himself to the first men. And its witness is equally striking to the fact that God also revealed Himself in a special way to Israel: He made Himself known to the Patriarchs, and He continued to make Himself known to their descendants, by the mouths of Moses and the prophets.

This second stage of the history of revelation, of which the starting point is the story of the calling of Abraham, is an entirely new intervention, by which God as it were takes in hand anew the building up of His Kingdom among men, starting again from the foundations. King and Lord of the whole earth

33

as He is, He nevertheless chose out for Himself one people from all the nations of the earth to be His holy possession, His own personal royal domain. It is this special revelation that has made Israel what it is—indeed to which it owes its very existence as a people. Because of it, Israel, backward in all other matters, stands far above all the other peoples: These are heights upon which Israel stands alone. We cannot account for this phenomenon, even in part, in terms of the "primitive revelation," which was originally given to the whole of the human race as such and became virtually lost by the fault of the same human race. If we find Israel there alone confessing the true religion in the midst of a heathen world, the explanation is not that the true religion had degenerated everywhere else, but had been preserved unimpaired in a chosen series of generations of which Israel was the last. In other words, the only possible way in which we can account for the phenomenon of Israel's religion is by the special revelation of which Israel was the recipient, and it is a complete and adequate explanation of it. There follows from this a conclusion that is of first importance for our present exegetical task: That the immediate source of the biblical creation narrative is not to be sought in the "primitive revelation," but in the revelation that was given by God to Israel.

For understandable reasons it was formerly the practice, and indeed still is only too often, to have recourse to this "primitive tradition" as the source of the main content and even of the details of the creation narrative. It was thought that this was the only possible way of determining and of defending the historical content of the story. This is not so, and it must be clearly said once and for all that such a recourse can no longer be justified, and should therefore be abandoned for good.

We have already seen above that Scripture itself points in the same direction. But we can say more than this, for there is another text that confirms what we have been saying explicitly: "Thus saith Jahweh the God of Israel: Your fathers dwelt of old on the other side of the river, Thare the father of Abraham and Nachor: and they served strange gods. But I took your father Abraham from the other side of the river . . ." (Jos 24:2; Jud 5:6–9). The implications of this text become clear if we place it in its proper context of all that we know about Israel and the ancient Near East, and of the historical background with which the biblical sources, and, in the first place, the book of Genesis itself, provide us. What Abraham inherited from his forefathers in the way of religion—to which his kinsmen continued to adhere—was unambiguously some form or other of heathenism, about which we are, in fact, not too well informed. Those who were called out by God from this heathenism freed themselves from it only with difficulty, and it is clear that Israel was for long in danger of falling back into it. As was pointed out earlier, the basis of our whole approach must be that it is with *Israel's* understanding of the earliest past that we are concerned. Israel is the only possible starting point. The question of what Israel could possibly know about these primeval facts then becomes all the more crucial for our purpose here. We have to ask therefore: *1)* What could Israel possibly know about these facts, humanly speaking? and then, subsequently, *2)* In what sense did Israel receive a supernatural revelation about these facts?

The Human Sources

Even if we accept that there may be several different approaches to the question of God's part in the process by which the Genesis narratives came into being, that of Israel's human part in it remains in any case of the greatest importance, even if only from the point of view of determining better the part of divine intervention.

We must, therefore, in the first place continue the line of approach begun in the previous chapter and ask ourselves how great, in this case, is the interval between the date of the narrative itself and the events to which it refers? And, secondly, what were the possibilities that in fact existed for the handing down of such a narrative? There can in our opinion be no hesitation about the answer to both of these questions. We are faced with an interval that is immeasurably great, and in the case of the handing on of the narrative, even if we need not say that every conceivable form of tradition is completely out of the question, at least we may exclude any kind of tradition that could be sufficiently specific to explain any part either of the content or of the concrete form of the creation narrative. In other words, we are definitely rejecting the position of those who would affirm that the events and even many of the concrete details of the first Genesis narratives correspond in any way to what actually occurred. This position depends upon the assumption that eye- and ear-witnesses of the events of the creation handed on their own empirical knowledge of these events to their descendants, and that our biblical narratives are nothing other than the carefully preserved end-product of this primitive tradition. Whatever other explanations there may be, this one simply will not do.[1]

Four Thousand Years?

If there is one idea to which we must say goodbye once and for all, it is that of the traditional period of four thousand years between Adam and Christ. It is quite certain that this figure is at least ten times too small, the truth being in terms of tens of thousands of years—whether twenty or eighty makes little

[1] N.B. In regard to this question, as to others, we must not be tempted to treat all the narratives that are to be found in Genesis 1–11 as if they were on the same level. Genesis 4–11 contains (in our opinion) many historical reminiscences, but even these cannot be judged to reflect the events of the actual prehistory in question, but rather events much later in date. In any case, what we are saying here refers, above all, to the first three chapters of the book.

36

difference to the revolution which it represents in relation to the ancient chronology.

A simple addition sum based upon the Hebrew text gives us a round figure of something over four thousand. We may set this out diagrammatically as follows:

From:	To:	Interval in years:
Adam	Flood	1656 (Gn 5)
Flood	Abraham	290 (Gn 11:10–26)
Abraham	Departure into Egypt	290 (Gn 21:5; 25: 26; 47:9)
Sojourn in Egypt		430 (Ex 12:40; Gal 3:17)
Exodus out of Egypt	Foundation of the temple	480 (1 K 6:1)
Foundation of the temple	Departure into Babylon	430 ⎫ 480 (1 & 2 K)
Sojourn in Babylon (587/6–538/7)		50 ⎭
Return from Babylon	Birth of Christ	537
Adam	Birth of Christ	4163

According to the Greek text, the total comes to about 5500; and the Roman martyrology for December 25 yields 5199 years *a creatione mundi*.

It should, in fact, be evident even at a first glance that the purpose of these lists is not in the first place historical in the strict sense, even where the figures do indicate historical periods of time. There is a system behind them, even if it is not all that easy to make out exactly what it is. It would at least appear to be certain that the date of the foundation of the Temple was taken as being the central point of the whole of Israel's history, and it may well be that this date was thought to have been both preceded and followed by twelve generations (12 times 40). Before this, in the prehistoric period, the system adopted is quite uncertain, even though the general intention is clear enough. A bridge has been made, with the only material available, between the time of the ancestors of Israel—the Patriarchs—and those of the whole human race. The purpose of this procedure, among other reasons, is to show that the national God of Israel is also the God of the whole world and of the whole of humanity, and that His power and providential overview was limited neither in time nor in space. The sacred writer has most likely made use of whatever material he found at hand, and there is evidence of this in the unevenness of the composition of the creation narrative itself. This material was no doubt generally familiar and popular in nature, but the author has used it to serve his own particular purpose in a way that clearly gives the impression of a unified and coherent vision.

The various tendentious alterations that occur in the above-quoted figures in the old Samaritan and Greek texts is evidence that they were habitually judged quite differently than in our modern accustomed way of reckoning time. Scientific study in this field has achieved at least a certain number of definite results from which we are now able to deduce a good deal about the particular literary genre of these biblical genealogies and about the biblical system of chronology.

Tradition Nevertheless?

The historical likelihood—and indeed the very possibility—of there having existed any kind of concrete tradition between Adam and Abraham stands or falls with whatever judgment must be made about this ancient chronology.

Previously, before this question arose, it was at least possible to argue as follows: when Adam died, Noah's father was already 56 years old, so that he could well have learned about the events of the creation from Adam himself, and have passed this knowledge on to Noah. And Noah in turn could well have handed the whole account over to Abraham, since the latter was 60 years of age when Noah died.

Now it is certainly true, if this course of events is to be accepted as it stands, that the biblical writers could have been extremely well-informed about the events of the creation story, even down to the smallest details, for both the form and the content of their narratives would in this case have derived from eye-witnesses, whose evidence was handed down intact.

When it began to be realized that the interval which needed to be filled in by this tradition was greater than had been imagined, the difficulty was at first solved by admitting that there might well have been gaps in the genealogies; but it gradually became clear as a result of the progress of scientific discovery that the intervals in question were indeed such as to render the whole idea of a chronological interpretation of the genealogies or of such an unbroken tradition impossible to maintain. This did not prevent one specialist in the subject from claiming as late as 1908 that he was able to distinguish the passages which derived from Adam from those which derived from Noah. He ascribed the evident verbosity of the story of the Flood to the garrulousness of the old man Noah, while he explained the peculiarities of form of the first chapter to the fact that it was the result of a vision which had been vouchsafed to Adam and the details of which he had related to his children!

Such imaginative constructions may be given short shrift. To begin with we can say quite definitely that both the enormous interval of time which would have had to have been covered by such a tradition, and still more the circumstances of life of the prehistoric human race in which this tradition would have had to have been preserved and handed down make the hypothesis of any kind of tradition whatever above the purely instinctive or subconscious level a mere delusion. The question is not only one of the length of time, but of the particular stretch of time with which we are concerned, and here the whole of our modern knowledge of prehistory is relevant. Those who adhered to the old chronological interpretation which we have outlined above knew, of course, nothing of this, and they could hardly have suspected it. The handing down of a tradition over a period of tens of thousands of years is just conceivable in later, historical times, given favorable circumstances such as the existence of a particular cohesive social group, the means of writing things down, the guidance of some teaching authority etc., but it would have been simply unthinkable in prehistoric times. We now know that the age of the human race, even taking the minimum possible figure, is extremely great, and that it was spread far and wide over the earth long before Israel came into existence. Israel's appearance on the scene must be situated at the very end of human history, and it emerges then from a background that is profoundly heathen. Under these circumstances it is really no longer possible to suppose the existence of a connecting thread between Israel and the events of the creation.

What Came From God?

We may safely say therefore that whatever Genesis contains in the way of facts about the creation did not get there by way of any human tradition. Its historical content must therefore be judged in terms of God's providential intervention.

Any blind recourse to the unlimited possibilities of divine Providence has, of course, no place in serious exegesis. What Providence has, in fact, done in this case is precisely what has to be discovered; and the important thing about the way in which Providence works in general is that what may credibly be ascribed to Providence goes together with what may credibly be supposed to have happened from an historical point of view—for God always makes use of whatever natural capacities are already there, and guides them so that they yield far more than they otherwise could. And since a miraculously preserved tradition from Adam to Abraham is quite beyond all historical credibility, serious exegesis may safely put any such idea on one side.

Whatever knowledge Israel possessed about the earliest events of human history, therefore, was the result of revelation.

But here, too, it would be to misjudge the way in which God, in fact, acts, to attempt to explain the first chapters of Genesis as if they had fallen ready-made down from heaven. When we talk about revelation in this connection, it must mean rather that Israel came to its knowledge of these early events as the result, on the one hand, of inspired reflection on the mighty historical experiences of Jahweh's activity and power through which it had passed, and, on the other hand, of centuries of practical and speculative wrestling with the great problems of life, especially the problem of evil.

How Facts Are Known by Revelation

Knowledge by revelation is not comparable with the kind of factual knowledge that can be gained empirically. It is characteristic of the latter kind of knowledge that by it we gain access to the facts in all their concreteness of specific time and place. This kind of factual concreteness cannot be gained by either reasoning or reflection, and the same is true of knowledge by revelation, for these ways of obtaining knowledge are only concerned with essentials, with the substance of the facts in question. The knowledge which Israel possessed about the events of its own historical past remained exactly what it was, humanly speaking, when it became the subject matter of revelation. No additional factual matter was added to it. What was new was a deeper and humanly unattainable insight into the meaning of the facts that were already known.

A still better point of comparison is that of Israel's knowledge of *future* events. For the facts of the creation story are not the only ones referred to in the Bible that were entirely beyond the reach of Israel's human capacities, but of which it did possess knowledge by revelation; indeed in the case of the future, this was a very definite and particular kind of knowledge.

In this insight into the future which was given to Israel from

41

time to time, there are a number of substantial certainties: Certain things *will* undoubtedly take place in due time. There are two things together which anyone who has read something of the prophets will at least have felt, if not directly observed. On the one hand there is the absolute certainty which the prophet has about the future happening, and on the other there is his complete incapacity to express what he sees in concrete terms. He sees indeed that what is to come will be consistent with Jahweh's historic manner of dealing with His people, that they will be new events to an undreamed-of extent, and that their meaning will be universal and definitive. He must of course nevertheless try to speak in a concrete and understandable maner, and in doing so he turns, in a way that is stereotyped and almost conventional, to the familiar concreteness of the historical past.

Man is always curious, whether it is the future or the distant past that he wishes to know about, and in both cases the desire to know in greater exactness of detail returns to him inexorably. But it is obvious that an exegesis that goes to work with such a motive in the forefront of its concern is suspect from the start. It is not in the nature of biblical prophecy to foretell details. Only afterward, when the prophecy has been fulfilled, may it sometimes be legitimate cautiously to bring certain of the details of the prophecy into relation with the facts of the known event.

Man was curious, too, in the ancient East, and about the distant past as well as about the future. He possessed a whole body of profane knowledge about this past, according to his lights, and above all he had an explanation of it, which was based to a greater or lesser degree upon real events or known phenomena. Israel had no need to discover this body of contemporary "science" for itself; it had imbibed it from its fellow peoples of the Mesopotamian basin as time went on.

Thus when it became God's purpose to reveal Himself to Israel, he found it already equipped, so to speak, with a whole world of ideas about all kinds of things, and in revealing the crucial saving events of the past to this people, He had to reckon with a whole set of particular human ideas about the past which they already possessed.

We see here the same thing happening as we find everywhere else in Scripture. The often curious ideas which Israel had built up concerning the earliest times—and often enough we can even trace the sources of the material of which these ideas were composed—became the vehicle, the canvas, and lastly also even the indispensable concrete form which God used to communicate the substance of the saving events which it was His purpose to convey. Israel's inspired ideas about the great religious problems and its repertoire of profane information from many different sources have become welded together in a living unity, to form a single narrative. God has grafted His revelation on to Israel's already existing human knowledge.

4

From Chaos to Cosmos

Factorem Caeli et Terrae

GOD is the Creator of all that is. How great a scope the first
verse of the Bible (Gn 1:1) intends to give to God's act of
creation may perhaps be a matter of doubt. What is certain is
that the first pericope of the Bible (Gn 1:1-2, 4a) only goes
on to elaborate how God (*Elohim*) is the Creator of this world
and all that belongs to it.

Visibilium Omnium

For this truth to be conveyed in a concrete manner, it was
not enough to say that God had made all things in general. It
had to be said also in particular, of all the great and small things
that lie within the normal scope of human experience: This, and
that as well, all is God's work. The subject matter of this chapter
is therefore expressed in terms of the natural objects and realities
which came within the scope of the knowledge and ordinary perception of the normal Israelite; and they are described just as
they would appear to his immediate and unbiased perception,
without further explanation. The material has been arranged by
the author in an orderly and indeed transparent manner, so that
we see the whole rich and varied world, which we know only as
complete, growing, as it were, and being formed in God's hands.

44

From this it follows that the author of this narrative was concerned only with this present world as we know and experience it. The current exegesis includes the first verse too in this judgment, understanding it as a short summary of the whole pericope. It is worth noting that ancient Hebrew has no word for "world," and that the expression "heaven and earth" is thus used here in its place. We need not go any further than this. The meaning of the first verse is general—that God has created this world, as we now know it. This is what is called a "proleptic" form of expression, and it is extremely common in the Bible, whatever solution one may choose to adopt here. Others prefer to say (without prolepsis): God created heaven-and-earth-in-their-original-state. But this is not to be recommended, even if it has the advantage of making the second verse follow on easily.

Et Invisibilium

Formerly, verse 1 was often understood in the wider sense, as can be seen from the chiasmal parallelism of the Creed: "factorem caeli et terrae, visibilium omnium et invisibilium." [1] And indeed even now we would not want to be thought of as rejecting so venerable an exegesis of Genesis 1:1 entirely. Sometimes an overprecise exegesis can deprive the ancient texts of the fuller dimensions of meaning which they may in fact possess just because of their vagueness and lack of precision.

In any case we may notice that here at the beginning of the pericope "heaven and earth" has a wider meaning than later on. From verse 10 onward "earth" means quite specifically "the dry land," i.e., as opposed to the sea, whereas at the beginning it is more global in meaning and certainly includes the sea and perhaps even the lower heavens, or what we should call the atmosphere.

In the same way "heaven" in verse 1 need not be so precisely

[1] Cp. also Denzinger *800.

45

understood as in verse 8, where the reference is clearly and specifically to the "blue dome" of heaven or firmament. In this case we may legitimately understand "heaven" in verse 1 as including "the highest heaven" above which God Himself dwells, and also the whole of the "court of heaven"—both of which concepts belong to the general biblical picture of heaven. Taken thus in a general sense, the word retains its full potentiality, and without denying the very real development of ideas that has taken place, we may recognize a genuine continuity between the teaching of this ancient text, and later revelation which has found its expression in the article of the Creed.

The meaning of these opening words of Genesis would then be as follows: God created all things, both those that are above and those that are below. The author then abstains from going further into a description of the things that are above, since his concern is with those that fall within the scope of ordinary human perception. So he continues: "Now as far as the earth is concerned, it was formless and void . . . etc."

According to this reading of the text, the author is thus applying a principle which we find throughout the whole of the book of Genesis. The method is to give first a short summary of a particular section of the subject matter, and then to eliminate quite briefly any aspect of it that falls outside the scope of his real theme, so that he is then free to go on and treat the latter more fully.

His Eyes Were Open to All Things

The irresistible expressiveness of this narrative is due among other reasons to what we have already referred to as the unprejudiced way in which things are perceived. It is as though the author was contemplating them with the wide, astonished eyes of a child, as if he has in some way managed to make the psychology of the first man his own. He does not at once call things by their name, but describes them first according to the immediate, very dynamic and basic impression which he has of them, which is, however, at the same time not capable of being sharply defined. Every particular thing thus comes as an astonishing discovery. Man for him is still a *tabula rasa,* he is busy receiving his first, brand-new impressions. It is like the astonished awakening of a childlike but richly gifted man among the wonders of nature —the atmosphere is that of the first contact, palpitating with life, between the outside world and a deeply sensitive but as yet uncharted interior world of consciousness.

In this human consciousness, it is the formless and vague impression that has the priority. From it, there then grows the clear and fully conscious knowledge of each thing after its kind, in its own specific nature inasmuch as it is distinct from every other thing. Only then can it be named, and it is in the naming of things that man has them as it were fully before him, that he becomes lord and master over them.

Thus for the sacred writer it is by God's creative word that all things have come into existence, by His naming of them. We are shown them as it were being liberated from anonymity and formlessness and achieving their definitive fullness according to the fixed measure of their being. A thing remains forever what it has become in the act of creation: determinate, finished, good. This is the reason why things are called and are what they now are called and are.

Splendor Ordinis

In this way, following in the steps of primitive man's first perceptions, and without any pretense at system or erudition, our author accounts for the existence of the whole of reality. He does not attempt to set down a long and tiresome list of all the things under the sun, but he nevertheless succeeds in setting them out according to an extremely simple and yet compelling and logical order.

For him it is evident that the Creator went to work in an orderly manner. He sees the orderliness of the world as it now appears to him in all its completeness, and this provides him immediately with a means of giving an account of God's work in creation by orderly phases. Thus the order and the successive stages which are observed to exist in the created world become in the narrative the order and succession of God's creative acts: the actual order becomes in Genesis a genetic order. From the starting point of a particular picture of the world, an account of creation has been constructed that corresponds to this picture: A particular cosmology becomes here a cosmogony.

The narrative is so structured that it corresponds with the structure of the finished creation as it is perceived immediately and uncritically. The question of whether it also corresponds with the actual process of evolution is something that the author never dreamed of. He is indeed conscious that what he is writing is true; but this truth is to be sought not on the level of physics, but on that of metaphysics. The task of the exegete is to elucidate the principles and presuppositions which did in fact lie behind the writing of the book of Genesis. Those who have been so concerned to busy themselves with such things as astronomy, geology, and biology in this connection have been on the wrong road—they would have spent the time better by going walking in God's nature.

The World's Great Spaces

We have thus in Genesis the story of the creation told from start to finish in function of the actual world as it is empirically observed to be. The creation on the one hand, and on the other

48

the actual world of the author's own observation, are completely bound up together in his mind. And his world was the same as our own, so that we may legitimately turn to the facts of our own experience in looking for the structure of his narrative. In this experience, we find a truly inexhaustible variety of things and phenomena thrusting themselves upon us, but among them there are two which present themselves immediately as having to be reckoned with before we can proceed with any further classification. Although they too are "things"—even if it is rather difficult to think of them as such—yet they are different from all other things, for it is by means of their mysterious and, as it were, fluid nature that everything else is determined and clarified. There is nothing that escapes their influence, and it is just because of this that they are different from all the rest. Everything that exists is constantly in either one or other of these two mutually opposed states; it is they who govern the very possibility of perception. It is thus highly appropriate that our author's enumeration should begin as it does with light and darkness. Further classification is only possible when these have been taken into account. And the Creator, too, can now proceed with His work, for work is possible only while the light lasts.

One of the key points of the narrative is the distinction between the things that remain immovably in one place, and those that are able to move from place to place of their own accord. Even today, the distinction between immovable and movable property is a fundamental one in the law of many countries. And if we pay attention to the relationship between these two sorts of things, we shall observe that the immovable things serve as a kind of space or area within which the movable things can exist. Among these "immovable" realities that occur immediately to our observation, there are the three great spheres or spaces: 1) the air space, which is enclosed by the dome of heaven; 2) water; and 3) the dry land together with all that

49

belongs directly to it, in particular the plants and other vegetation. The latter is carefully and indeed accurately enumerated, in terms of the writer's point of view, which is no more directly scientific here than elsewhere. The classification is again purely visual: "seedless" vegetation (the grasses and mosses); "seed-bearing" vegetation (corn); and trees which bear seed contained in some kind of fruit. And in every case is added "each after its kind"; for the wonders of nature find their full and complete explanation in God's original act of creation, so that further special interventions are no longer necessary. Hence the special attention that is given to the manner of propagation.

The Inhabiting of the Spaces

As with the plants, so also the moving things are seen to fall spontaneously into their distinct groups, which again, if they do not correspond to the exigencies of scientific genus and species, are nonetheless accurate in terms of the author's criteria, which are those of popular everyday observation. These groups may be listed as follows: 1) the sun, moon, and stars; 2) the fishes, among which he further distinguishes, on the one hand, the great sea-monsters, and, on the other, everything else that lives and teems in the waters, each after its kind; 3) the land animals, further distinguished into tame and wild, and, for the rest, everything else that lives and creeps and teems in the countryside, each after its kind; 4) men, female as well as male. The fish belong in the waters, and the birds in the air; but we should note that according to the ancient manner of thinking, "air"—for which there is, in fact, no word in Hebrew—forms part of the element "water," so that the somewhat free Latin translation: "Let the water bring forth fishes and birds" corresponds well enough to the biblical world of ideas.

The fact of the creation of men and of the animals does not,

50

however, explain the mystery of their propagation, and for this reason we have a special blessing of God given to the latter.

The above characteristic groups are still those which occur spontaneously to man's observation of the world around him, and this fact is, in itself, a natural and sufficient explanation of the particular classification which we find in the Genesis narrative.

Chaos

Our author's purpose is to show that every one of these things, which he shows as they pass one after the other before the eye of the observer, has been created by God. But he cannot do this effectively without saying something about how God went about it, and, to this end, he starts by showing how things were before God's great creative initiative. He had no knowledge of this either by revelation or from any scientific source—his method is one of contrast. From the starting point of the actual world of his own experience, he describes a state of affairs which is the very antithesis of it, in which things are *not* ordered and clearly distinct from each other, indeed are simply not there at all.

This approach is no different from our own. In trying to think or talk about creation, we begin instinctively from "complete nothingness." This is in reality a concept which is incapable of being thought, let alone imagined in any tangible form, and could not, therefore, in any case, have been used in a narrative written by and for concrete-minded Israelites. But our author is, in the last resort, doing the same as we are with our "complete nothingness" in starting with the idea of "chaos," which is quite logically derived, and built up from his knowledge of the existing world. We may take "water" as an example of his approach. Seas and lakes are fed by rivers, and rivers in turn have their beginnings in springs and streams. If man digs deep enough, he comes to water; and if he walks far enough, he will eventually

51

come to a place where the land comes to an end and water begins. Moreover, all this water has a common origin, and is connected in a more or less mysterious way with the mass of water that appears to surround the whole earth and likewise to be found under the earth (this is what is meant by "the waters beneath"). But the phenomenon of rain makes it appear as if there are also waters above, with the natural conclusion that above the sky there is a great mass of water, held back by the great metal dome of heaven which, at certain times, opens its windows and lets some of this water through, so that the water from the sky becomes mixed with the water from beneath. Thus both below and above we find the same element: water. All of this gives food for thought, and so we have the explanation. It is a typical characteristic of the ordered world that this water should not be spread about everywhere but should be held back and contained in specific places. It was the Creator who said to the primeval ocean: "Thus far and no further"! Before this divine command, all the waters formed but a single mass; there were no divisions or limitations, but a single enormous ocean. According to the same picture of things, there was also before this time no dome of heaven, and no dry land—there could as yet be no question of a distinction between land and sea, which were still hidden in the bottomless womb of the primeval ocean (*tehôm*).

The great spaces of the earth, which are now the dwelling place of every kind of living creature, did not yet exist either in any distinct way, and the same may be said, by and large (for one must not expect too great a degree of local consistency from the biblical authors), of the two sharply distinct, but nevertheless tenuous and elusive, substances in which the whole of space is alternately bathed or penetrated. In the day and the night, light and darkness each have their allotted times. Daily the light gives way to the darkness, and again daily it is born out of the darkness. And so it is here in God's act of creation: in the beginning He called the light out of the darkness. Before this there was nothing but an indeterminate grey mass: darkness over the whole of the face of the primeval ocean—in other words, perfect, utter, and complete "chaos."

It would seem that we may not go on from this to say that the author of Genesis teaches that the chaos as well was created by God. At all events this is not the meaning of verse 1, in which he declares that God has created what now exists. The result of God's creative work is good and well ordered (cp. Is 45:18), and we may therefore safely say that verse 2 is not a further explicitation of verse 1. On the contrary, it is the whole pericope which must be read as the explicitation of verse 1, and of this verse 2 is the necessary and logical starting point.[2]

"Chaos" does not exist, and is not thought of in itself, but solely in function of the existing world. It is not prior to the world chronologically speaking, but logically, and indeed the whole further course of the narrative must be understood in the same way, as being expressed in a logical rather than in a chronological order.

In Genesis 2, in which another author recounts the creation of man and the story of the garden of Eden, we find the same identical structure. The starting point is again an antithetical picture of what is going to come into existence as a result of God's creative activity: neither man nor garden, and thus an abandoned, bare, dry expanse of plain.

[2] It may be asked: Is matter then not also created by God? The answer is that such a question belongs to the scholastic world view, and falls outside the perspective of the author of Genesis. If one's preoccupation is basically scientific, one can read into verse 1 the creation of matter, and this has been done. But in fact such an approach presupposes an explicit and technically scientific concept of creation, and this is only present in Genesis insofar as it is also implied in the popular concept of creation. We must remain satisfied with our author's deep conviction that *everything* that exists has been brought forth by God, and that in a manner that can be compared with no kind of human activity whatever.

53

Cosmos

By this means, then, the author of Genesis 1 gives graphic clarity to his story of God's work of creation.

He starts off with "chaos"—precisely in order that he may then show how God has derived the whole world from it. This "chaos" is simply desolation and emptiness (*tóhu wabóhu*), a form of expression that gives the general impression of "formless disorder" and of "abandonedness": the absence of any definite form, of life, or of any particular thing. God's creative activity, concentrated into the space of a single week and divided into two parallel periods of three days each, transforms this *tóhu wabóhu* into the world as we know it. In the course of the first three days, order is created out of disorder, and, as a result, clearly defined spaces or spheres come into being; in the second part of the week the hollow silence and emptiness is taken away, so that the newly created spaces are peopled with moving things.

The presence of this structure in the narrative is not a recent discovery. St. Thomas Aquinas[3] distinguishes three stages or "works" in the six days of creation: the creation itself (verse 1), the work of separation (*opus distinctionis*), and the work of embellishment (*opus ornatus*). *Ornatus* he has taken from the misleading Latin translation of Genesis 2:1 "Igitur perfecti sunt caeli et terra et omnis ornatus eorum," the meaning of the original being: "So heaven and earth were completed and all the host of them." The Bible itself thus distinguishes, here as elsewhere, two stages only in the work of creation, viz., *1*) heaven and earth, and *2*) their "host," i.e., all that moves in or upon them. Compare for example Nehemias 9:6:

> Thou Jahweh, thou hast made heaven,
> and the heaven of heavens, and all the host thereof:
> the earth and all things that are in it:
> the seas and all that are therein.

[3] *Summa theologica*, I, q. 65, *ante* a. 1.

The familiar word *sabaoth* (= hosts, or armies) is the plural of the word that is always used for "army," i.e., *saba,* which was read by the translators of the Septuagint as *sebi* (= ornament) —hence the Vulgate reading *ornatus.*

St. Thomas was not however misled by this mistake in regard to the meaning, for he explains the verse as follows: It was first necessary, he says, for the different parts of the world to be separated, after which each was embellished, i.e., provided with its appropriate inhabitants.[4] He calls attention, moreover, to the fact that separation and embellishment occur in parallel sequence.

That St. Thomas saw quite clearly that things are allotted to the first or to the second group of three days according to whether they move or not, appears from his answer to the difficulty that plants are, after all, obviously an embellishment and therefore do not belong on the third day. The plants, he says, grow in one place on the earth without moving, and therefore they belong to the earth itself and not to its embellishment.[5] In reality, the plants form an appropriate transition from the one group of three days to the other.

When all this has been said, we must remember that the author's system should be understood flexibly, and should not be expected to follow a rigidly logical pattern. It is not really an objection to say that the first two "works of separation" in fact amount to, or at least go together with, two entirely new acts of creation—of the light, and of the dome of heaven. Again, although the heavenly bodies (the "host of heaven") inhabit the firmament, they are placed on the fourth day; while the fish, on the fifth day, seem rather a strange parallel to the firmament. The author has however enough basis for his parallelism: The givers of light go with the light itself, and the fishes and the birds with the waters and the heavens:

[4] *Ibid.,* I, q. 74, a. 1.
[5] *Ibid.,* I, q. 69, a. 2.

55

day	work	separation	embellishment	work	day
		(creation of the spaces)	(inhabitation of the spaces)		
1	1	light/darkness (by the creation of the light)	sun, moon, stars	5	4
2	2	waters above/waters below (by the creation of the dome of heaven)	fishes, birds	6	5
3	{ 3	land/sea	man ⎫ plants	7 ⎫	6
	{ 4	plants	beasts ⎬ as	8 ⎭	
			of the ⎪ food		
			earth ⎭		

Spirit and Word

Such is the world that has been brought forth from chaos by the creative power of God's Spirit, moving over the whole length and breadth of the primeval waters as the form-giving and life-bringing breath of God. It is with this power that the divine words of creation are filled. And it is by God's Word that the creative force of His Spirit is, as it were, made specific and directed to the bringing forth of particular things. Just as our human words are borne on our breath to which they in turn give meaningful form, so we may think of God breaking in from the unfathomable stillness of eternity into this world, in His operation *ad extra*.

By the *word* of the Lord are the heavens made
and all the host of them by the breath of his mouth (Ps 33:6).

Let all thy creation serve thee.
Thou speakest a *word*, and they were made:
Thou didst send forth thy *Spirit,* and they were created (Jud 16; 17).

5

From Jahweh to Elohim

GENESIS 1 need no longer be described as a problem text. After a long period of conflict it has at last become clear that the apparent problem around which so many struggles raged was dependent upon a theory of inspiration which, while historically understandable, was in fact erroneous. The first chapter of this book has been devoted to setting this theory right as well as may be, and we have in the fourth chapter done our best to allow Genesis to speak for itself apart from all the theories.

The Teaching of Genesis 1

Now that these problems connected with the Genesis story have in principle been solved for good, and are thus essentially out of date, there is no reason why the content, too, of Genesis 1 should not be freed from the various complex systems of interpretation which have been forced upon it from time to time. Digressions about the formation of the earth's strata and about the different kinds of fossils really serve no useful purpose; our attention needs to be focused where it belongs—on the message which is the real purpose of the Bible.

Yet if we are to be honest, this is by no means an easy task. For in our approach to the Bible, it is always very much easier to keep, as it were, moving around it in circles than to make the effort to penetrate through directly into the biblical world of thought.

In the case of Genesis 1 we have perhaps a very typical example of this difficulty. Its real meaning and value—which lies essentially in its monotheism—is well enough known and is comparatively easy to formulate. The fundamental importance of this teaching is evident at once, and it does not even sound like anything very new if we say that in this respect Genesis 1 is unique, and without any parallel in the history of religions; that it is, morally speaking, a great miracle, an entirely original composition, or better still that it is clearly and palpably a revelation, if we consider it against the background of the seekings and strayings of the whole of ancient and modern humanity inasmuch as the latter stands outside the influence of this same revelation.

The point we have to make clear, however, is this: that Israel was monotheistic and so are we; but what may escape us all too easily is that during the interval of 3000 years which has elapsed between this primitive monotheism and our own time, new dimensions have developed. Our task here is to try to listen and pay attention to the particular quality of Israel's own faith in God. We may perhaps be jumping to conclusions in being so ready to make comparisons between the monotheism of Genesis 1 and that of our own time, for it was Israel that, so to speak, discovered monotheism, and there is in fact abundant material in the Bible with which to reconstruct the main stages of Israel's journey of discovery. What we shall now try to do is to set aside all our treatises about the doctrine of God, and in the most ordinary and human way seek to share the experience of this discovery of monotheism. Only so shall we be able to hear the real voice of Genesis 1; only so will it become for us too a relevant and contemporary revelation, the source of our own personal and living faith in God.

The "Misunderstanding"

If ever there was a classical monotheistic passage it is Genesis
1. Whenever there is any talk of God and of His existence, it is
this chapter that springs spontaneously to mind. We immediately,
and rightly, see a direct connection between the biblical Creator
God and the "Supreme Being" at which the human understanding may arrive, say, by one of the *quinque viae*. In addition to
this spontaneous tendency, there is, moreover, the logical structure of our usual apologetical method, which—to put it rather
crudely—tries first to establish that God exists, and only thereafter that He has revealed Himself.

It is, of course, true that monotheism is the basis of everything, for the old Israel no less than for ourselves. And yet there
is one very great difference: for us, at least as far as our reflective consciousness of our experience of God is concerned, monotheism is also the point of departure, while for Israel it came
rather as a conclusion. It was the revelation of God as a living
reality which was first in the order of time, and upon this there
followed, slowly developing, the process of reflection on this
revelation and full consciousness of its implications, and only
then its clear formulation.

The danger is that the real spirit of the Bible's revelation may
escape us if we suppose overhastily that the biblical authors had
our modern, rational approach to religious matters. This is a misunderstanding that has been encouraged by the significance which
Genesis 1 has come to have for us, and also by the fact that it is
the first page of Holy Scripture. It may be the first page, but it
is by no means the oldest; it is indeed of fundamental importance,
but as a climax rather than as a starting point.

No doubt we are told that "God's invisible Being, his eternal
power and divinity are clearly to be seen from the creation of
the world by reflection upon the creation" (Rom 1:20), but it

59

is not in this text that we find the key to Genesis 1. The idea of God which we find there is the result not so much of reflection about the created world, as of reflection about God's supernatural revelation. It is not philosophy but theology. Israel was perfectly well able to learn about God from the created world, but, in fact, it learned far more and far more readily about Him from close experience of His intervention in its own life and history. Jahweh had intervened actively, had revealed Himself to Israel, had caused Israel to experience Him directly. This was indeed something to think about, and Genesis 1 is the result.

Monotheism

The great achievement of Genesis 1 is the formulation which it gives to the monotheistic notion of God. If we are to appreciate this achievement for what it is really worth, we must begin by distinguishing two different aspects of monotheism: *1*) the recognition that there is one God who stands over against all else that exists. In other words, the acknowledgment that there is but one universal God of the whole world, and the decisive rejection of all other gods. Thus monotheism is different from what is known as "henotheism" or "monolatry," according to which there are several gods, but only one who is recognized and worshiped in any particular human society. *2*) a true conception of the relationship existing between God, man and the world, to the exclusion of any form of so-called monotheism in which the creation is either insufficiently distinguished from God or is regarded as in some way independent of Him.

Of the above two points, it is clear from the study of the history of religions that the second is much more difficult for man to achieve than the first, although in reality the two are bound up together to such an extent that to err in the one is at the same time to err in the other. In fact the authenticity of one's idea of God is dependent upon the degree of authenticity of one's manner of conceiving the relationship between God and everything else. And it is precisely here that the undying achievement of Genesis 1 is to be found.

This question of the right relationship, or rather perhaps the right tension between the awareness of God's immanence and of His transcendence—difficult as these concepts are to imagine— is the touchstone of all the varying notions of the divine which men have formed for themselves at different times in the course of the centuries. There is no man in whom the discovery of the world around and within him does not awaken a vague awareness of God. But the moment that he, as *homo religiosus,* goes on to try and give some more definite expression to this vague awareness, he tends to fall into every kind of error. The history of man's understanding of God and of his worship of Him has followed a zigzag course between the extremes of pantheism and materialism, of monism and dualism, of deism and emanationism, of polytheism and atheism. Such are the ever-recurring errors which were condemned one after the other at the First Vatican Council.[1] The miracle of Genesis 1 is, so to speak, that it already contains these anathemas.

We may well ask, how was such an achievement possible for Israel? The answer is that it was possible neither by the force of reasoning nor by any communication of theoretical knowledge by God, but simply by the concrete, practical experience of what it meant that Jahweh was the God of Israel. Thus, as regards our first point above, we may say that it was the very facts of history that brought Israel to the acknowledgement of its national God Jahweh as the utterly One and Unique God of all the earth. And to our second point: The reason why Israel's theology was capable of expressing the relationship between God and the world with such unique authenticity was precisely the fact that this theology was nothing other than the outcome of Israel's reflection on its concrete experience of this relationship

[1] Denzinger, *3021–3025.

61

with Jahweh. Thus we can only hope to understand the teaching of Genesis 1 if we see it in terms of Jahwist religion. A short further explanation of this first point may serve to throw some light on the second as well.

From the Redeemer to the Creator

Israel first came to know God as its own national God, as Jahweh, its Redeemer. And it was through the living experience of His saving acts that Israel then came to know Him also as Creator. Thus it was the facts themselves that brought Israel to the mature realization that Jahweh was not merely Israel's "Elohim," but that the ultimate meaning of the whole history of Israel's election was that He was Elohim *as such.*

"Elohim" is the general Semitic word for the godhead. It is the name of a class, by means of which man can refer to everything that he looks upon as possessing divine characteristics. Where this expression is used in Scripture for the one, true God, the emphasis is on His universality. Elohim is the God of nature, of the human race, of the world, and He is therefore also, as in Genesis 1, the Creator.

The emphasis lying behind the name Jahweh, on the other hand, is quite different. Jahweh is a proper name, the name of a particular individual therefore. He is, in fact, the specific national God of Israel, the God of positive revelation and of the history of salvation. Without pressing the distinction too strictly and absolutely, we may say that Elohim is God as He reveals Himself in creation and in nature, and that Jahweh is God as He reveals Himself in history and in His gracious acts.

We must fact the fact that the one, true God did not shrink from becoming the national God of a particular people. This was an adaptation to a conception that was typical of the ancient East. But it was precisely by means of this adaptation that Israel came eventually to be the bearer of such a true and authentic knowledge of God that the ancient Eastern categories in which its thoughts about God were expressed came to have a content that was wholly original, and quite different from the ideas in relation to which they had been evolved.

In comparison with Jahweh, all the various national deities of the ancient East's pantheon pale first to nonentities, and then speedily simply to nothing at all. From the very outset, He breaks through the limitations of the other national and territorial deities. He makes Himself felt in Egypt, and executes judgment on all the gods of Egypt (Ex 12:12). His power is thus already declared in principle over all the peoples of the world, and at the same time His dominion over the whole of life and of nature loses every possible limitation of space or of time.

It belongs to the essential purpose of the entire biblical creation narrative, and of Genesis 1 in particular, to make it clear to Israel that its own Saviour God is one and the same as the Creator of heaven and earth, that He is the God of the whole world and of the whole human race. Thus in Scripture universal and national history appear as interwoven in a single story, for both indeed are governed by a single hand, that of Israel's God.

The subject of Israel's national history proper was, of course, the attitude of Jahweh to His own people Israel and the Promised Land of Canaan. But the question we have to face is that of how it came about that the preaching of the Jahwist religion came to treat, as it were, *ex professo* of Jahweh's attitude to the rest of the world and to humanity as a whole.

The peoples of the Semitic world have various narratives, among those which have been handed down, which are concerned mainly with their own existence as national entities, and there are also others which are of more general interest, about the existence and the destiny of the gods, of the world, and of the human race as such. Often enough more than one of these themes are combined, as a result, for example, of a narrative about the foundation of some regional capital or national sanctuary being given the form of a creation narrative or cosmogony. In the case of Israel, however, there is no trace of any such inter-mingling of motifs, for the simple reason that Israel's origin as a people is clearly marked and falls entirely within the compass of historical memory.

Israel thus possessed its own national historical narratives, but together with these there must also have existed a series of more ancient and more general stories which it had inherited from the cultural world out of which it was born. What has happened in Holy Scripture is that this later, more general, series of stories has been placed as a kind of introduction to the national series which begins with the account of the calling of Abraham. Behind this result there lies a whole process of development, which may be summarized as follows: It is clear from the whole of the Pentateuch taken together that the Mosaic "Jahwist" religion possessed in fact a literally unlimited capacity for assimilation. As a result it was able, in the course of time, radically to sort out and to reinterpret in terms of the new and all-dominating faith in God the contents of this group of general Semitic narratives which already existed in Israel's own tradition. Not only this, but it also gave birth to a virtually quite new series of narratives, which contain only distant reminiscences of more ancient ma-terial, of which the first three chapters of Genesis is a case in point. The doctrinal consequences of this fusing of the two series of narratives into a single whole on the basis of a single underlying religious vision ought neither to be overlooked nor underestimated. The first of these consequences is that we here see Israel setting forth quite explicitly—in complete accord with the Mosaic and the prophetical preaching—that Israel's own God is the one and only true God of the whole world.

The second consequence is that since this universal God is none other than Jahweh Himself, everything that can be asserted of the relationship between Him and His people is true also of the relationship between Jahweh and the world. His dealings with the world as such are understood in terms of His dealings with Israel. The relationship remains the same: it is simply that in Israel's own awareness Jahweh's sphere of influence has been extended from the merely national plane to being worldwide. This means that in the relationship between God and the world both the separation between the two terms *and* God's intense and personal concern for the world are maintained equally, and balance each other. For it was thus and in no other way that it had been with Israel's own experience of Jahweh.

For in the experience both of particular religious individuals and in that of the people as a whole Jahweh is a God who is at the same time unattainably far off and yet intimately close, whose demands and gracious love are as real and total as they are precisely because He infinitely transcends those to whom He condescends. This is the secret of Genesis 1: The Creator is ineffable—He is before, beyond, and above the whole of His Creation. And it is for this very reason that His active power reaches to the heart of every single thing, and is itself the foundation of all existence. We hope to be able now to make it clear how all this is expressed in the text itself.

6

The Religious Climate

MAN is an *animal religiosum*. He knows surely within himself that there exist higher powers upon whom his welfare ultimately depends, who make certain demands upon him and with whom he can enter into contact in one way or another. Religion in its various forms comes to give closer definition to this vague *sensus religiosus* by giving it concrete expression in a more or less systematic complex of theoretical conceptions and practical observances. The fundamental characteristics of human religiosity are the same everywhere and at all times, for they depend on the same ultimate reality. There are, of course, many forms of religion; and according to whether they participate in this one and indivisible religious truth, or fail to do so, they cause man's true religious sense either to flourish or to degenerate.

How Many Gods?

Man can find traces of this divine reality both in the great universe above and below him, and in the smallest realities of which he is able to take account. And since it is precisely in the multiplicity and the diversity of the phenomena which he finds all around him that this occurs, it is not surprising that when he first tries to define this religious awareness more closely, he concludes that there is multiplicity also in God, in other words *polytheism,* sometimes passing by way of *polydaemonism.*[1]

We are able to make certain conjectures about the way in which the polytheism of the ancient East arose on the basis of our knowledge of how the number of deities increased in historical times, about which we have evidence. We find for example that the diversity of tribes and races, of peoples and languages, of countries and political regions led to a like diversity of gods— blood deities and soil deities, private protector gods and inherited family gods, and gods of particular cities and nations. Each and every human group had to have its own god, who would belong specially to that group and to no other: A god who would be as it were "nationalized," himself a member of the tribe in question. This local and national character of the various divinities is very striking.

In the course of time it inevitably happened that some tribes became absorbed by others, that small states and city-states were combined into larger national groups. Peoples and tribes appeared and disappeared from the scene, and wars were fought and treaties made. The territorial and national gods had their part in each of these eventualities, and often became combined with each other along with the peoples to whom they "belonged." The result of this process was a pantheon which is, among other things, a reflection of the map of the whole of the ancient East:

[1] It is true that the universal human experience of the divine as "wholly other" is generally accompanied by a conviction that it is also "one and unique." This original conviction of the divine unity can be seen in the generic Semitic name for a god, which often enough becomes also a personal name. It can also be seen in the specifically universal function of creator that is attributed to gods who are otherwise highly particularized; and also in the tendency which is found everywhere to give a certain monarchical structure to the pantheon: There are many gods, but there is always one of them who is supreme.

It is also true, of course, that the conscious awareness that there can only be one God often disappeared from view, and even that at times it became entirely lost, though in some cases it is difficult to be sure to what extent a certain idea of unity may have remained, as for example in the case of Baal, who was divided up into many different regional Baals.

The gods have divided the world up among themselves, each has his particular sphere of interest and to each is allotted a specific group of worshipers.

But beyond and above all these national and tribal distinctions there remained the undeniable fact of the *kosmos* itself, the world above and below in all its diversity. Its unity suggested the unity of the godhead, but then again the diversity of the powers of nature provided yet another occasion for multiplication; and, in fact, we find that the most ancient gods of all are often personifications of natural phenomena.

For the rest, there was mythology to fill in the gaps. Mythology is however not to be confused with religion, for it is rather the outcome of a primitive yearning after what we should call scientific knowledge, an attempt to satisfy man's universal curiosity and to find a satisfactory explanation for every sort of phenomenon. It is mythology in the strict sense of the word when this explanation is given in terms of the adventures of the various deities.

What Kind of God?

Thus there arose a whole polytheistic world of deities, which in the last resort came to look suspiciously like a sort of deified duplicate of the world here below. Nationalized and particularized, the idea of "god" was subdivided, cut up and measured off to correspond with all the various human needs and situations, and with particular experiences and forms of expression.

Whenever the idea of god loses its unity in this sort of way, it loses its transcendence at the same time, and the absolute distinction between the creature and the Creator tends to disappear: the divine is deprived of its essential characteristics, and becomes humanized and naturalized. The Semitic gods are so to speak super-Semites. Each tribe had to have its own god, "after its own image and likeness": In these circumstances the divinity becomes simply the expression of human and national sentiments and aspirations, a product of the desire for self-assertion, and of the spirit of pride and of self-glorification.

It is for the same reason that polytheism and the involvement in nature of the divinity are closely connected, as a consequence of the "communion of blood and soil" which is felt to exist between the divinity and his people. He is in fact inseparable from his people, and/or from the phenomenon in relation to which he is determined, and from which he takes his special characteristics and sometimes even his name. And it may be remarked in passing that the process by which kingship was divinized in the ancient East is thus not to be considered as an isolated case, but rather as the culmination of the latent divinizing tendencies of the whole cultural sphere in which it arose.

Above we have made a distinction between two elements which are both characteristic of true monotheism: 1) the recognition of a God who is universal, God of the whole world, and 2) an authentic conception of the relationship between God and the world. The extent to which these two aspects of monotheism do in fact affect and determine each other can be illustrated in reverse, so to speak, by an examination of polytheism. By means of this distinction we can gain a better understanding not only of the truth but also of the error which corresponds to it, for the difference between having one God or many is not merely a question of number—it involves also a radical difference in the way one understands the relationship between the divine as such and everything else. The one implies the other. Where there is true monotheism, then the relationship, too, is correctly understood. Polytheism on the other hand leads of its very nature to a blurring of the frontier between the divine and the human and between the divine and nature, and conversely the blurring of this fundamental distinction leads inevitably to a disintegration of the idea of the godhead, i.e., to polytheism.

Moreover polytheism leads, also of its very nature, to the

69

debasement of true religiosity. The primary concern ceases to be that of a man's religious attitude and his way of life; instead we find a magical and mechanical ritualism, through which the favor or disfavor of the gods is decided. The sphere of the divine becomes entirely capricious, without any ethical characteristic. There is thus an advantage to be gained simply by performing the correct ritual or formula at the correct moment. This is because a relationship is conceived to exist in the natural order between the divinity and the sphere in which it operates; one may thus be master of its special power as soon as one understands the right technique. The purpose of religion, in this perspective, is to teach this technique. Evil consists in divine punishment and anger following upon sin, but the latter lacks the nature of moral guilt, being simply a mistake in the combining of the different factors by means of which certain divine powers are brought into operation.

The same tendency is to be found in polytheistic religion wherever it occurs. And when we do come across true religiosity in the ancient East, it is because human nature has got the better of religious doctrine, and the heart has become better than the head. There are times when the "religious sense" of which we have spoken crawls on its knees when it cannot stand upright, and it may sometimes find expression even through the forms of a deficient religious framework. In any case all such deficient religions must ultimately be understood as parasitic growths having their roots in a partial truth.

The Religion of Revelation

It might appear that what we have just been saying is all very far from Holy Scripture, and further still from Genesis 1. In reality, however, it is this background which lies behind the whole of the Old Testament, for it was to men who grew up in a world dominated by false or misleading ideas of this kind that God did in fact reveal Himself.

One of the most characteristic features of the whole of the Old Testament economy of salvation is that we find at the same time an almost extreme degree of adaptation to the prevailing conceptions of the time, together with a profound transformation and redirection of these same conceptions. The biblical revelation makes full use, for example, of the categories which the peoples of the ancient East used in their thinking about supernatural realities, and yet at the same time it corrects and transcends them. Thus we may say that both by way of adaptation and by way of reaction the Old Testament has been deeply influenced by this religious climate of thought which we have been describing.

Adaptation

Here we can only give a few short indications which may serve to show how the well-known texts can be looked at from a somewhat different angle than is customary. The strongest piece of evidence of the adaptation of which we have spoken is the bare fact that the one, true God of the whole universe, who was until then quite unknown by any sort of positive revelation, allowed Himself to become "the God of Abraham." In this theophany, the sort of reasoning process by which man may be able to conclude to the existence of a single "Supreme Being," plays at the most a very secondary and supplementary role. And it continued to be so for long centuries. The all-important fact was that God had taken the initiative and put Himself in the very center of the lives of those who first believed in Him faithfully, in living Truth and in a supernatural manner. When Abraham wants to describe *his* God he does so as follows: "the God who caused me to wander far from my father's house" (Gn 20:13). Isaac learned to know Him as "the God of my father." Thus it was that Abraham's God became known as "the God whom

71

Isaac feared," and later, "the strong one of Jacob," and so in due course: "the God of Abraham, of Isaac, and of Jacob," "the God of the Fathers." For us, there is something paradoxical in the statement that "God is not ashamed to be called *their* God" (Heb 11:16), and yet such is the way which He in fact chose to establish His Kingdom among men; he made Himself known first of all as the God of a *family*.

And when in the course of time the patriarchal family had grown into a great and numerous people, the God of the fathers revealed Himself in the redemptive interventions to which Israel owed its very existence as a people, as Jahweh, i.e., as the God of that particular people. Jahweh is Israel's own God, who can be compared with no other God: "Who is like unto thee among the Gods, O Jahweh, who is like thee, glorious in holiness, terrible because of thy glorious deeds and because of the wonders thou hast wrought" (Ex 15:11).

Chamos is the god of Moab, but Jahweh is the God of Israel, the God of the Hebrews (Ex 5:3). As the national God of His own people, He demands undivided allegiance, He is a jealous God and will tolerate no strange gods before His face in Israel. And the fact that He is a national God by no means signifies any limitation of the extent of His power: "You shall be my particular possession among all peoples; for the whole earth is mine" (Ex 19:5).

Even as regards Israel's own subjective awareness, any such idea of limitation is very relative. For in this living experience of Jahweh, Israel knows Him as He truly is. He is self-authenticating, since in the very act of experiencing Him as God man knows immediately and instinctively that He is the full and perfect answer to all the great questions which are implied in the very fact of human existence. Man's latent capacity for religious truth recognises the Truth immediately. For this reason, every possible limitation is in principle already broken through in the

living and concrete experience of the true God, even if it is evident enough at the same time that the theoretical awareness of
Jahweh's universality only penetrated through gradually into the
conscious awareness of the ordinary people (Jg 11:24; 1 S
26:19 ff.; 2 K 5:15, 17; 17:26; Jon 1:3).

When the national framework is finally and radically broken
through by the prophets, such a development is no more than the
fulfillment of something that was already contained in Abraham's
own experience of God, for it was clear to him from the beginning that it was unthinkable that any other God could ever have
any meaning at all for him. The special vision of the prophets
is that what had up to that time been the national kingdom of
Jahweh is destined to be extended to the very ends of the earth.
Israel's temple, for them, takes on the cosmic proportions of
heaven and earth, that are full of Jahweh's Glory (Is 6). Israel's
privileges are henceforth to be shared by the Gentiles as well:
"Jahweh the Lord of hosts shall bless them and say: Blessed be
my people of Egypt; Assyria, the work of my hands; Israel my
inheritance" (Is 19:23–25). It is thus perfectly clear that from
the very beginning it was not only Israel's destiny that lay in
Jahweh's hands, but that of all other nations as well: "Certainly, I brought up Israel out of the land of Egypt; but also the
Palestines out of Cappadocia, and the Syrians out of Cyrene"
(Amos 9:7). A paradox indeed for Israel, but no longer one
for us.

Transformation

If it is true that the element of adaptation is demonstrated
above all in the fact that Jahweh chose to be the God of a particular group of people and later even of a particular land
(Canaan is Jahweh's inheritance, His resting place), it is also
true that from the very first moment of the process of revelation

Jahwism has an entirely specific and original character which is a consequence of the special relationship which existed between Jahweh and those who belong to the sphere of His concern.

For Jahweh's appearance as God was not simply an event which was coincident with the appearance of a particular nation upon the scene of history. This is made clear by the fact that those who worshiped Him were obliged for the time being to remain as strangers in the land of their earthly pilgrimage, and also by the fact that Abraham had to break with his blood relations and with the land of his birth, in other words, with the whole of his own social and religious background. Thus from the very beginning a great act of faith was demanded of him, for Jahweh had shown Himself to be a God who addresses Himself to the whole of the human person, and demands him entirely for Himself. It is not a question of a natural relationship, but of election, command, and promise on God's side, and of free self-surrender, obedience, and faith on that of man.

This is a God who is to be found everywhere where His worshipers are, not merely within the bounds of some particular piece of territory of greater or lesser extension. But He is nevertheless also a God who is concerned with human life in all its aspects, and He shows this first of all by His relationship with one individual, and then through him with a whole group. Thus He first appears in the role of a personal protector God, and thereafter as the God of a family, of a people, and then ultimately as the God of the whole world. But at each of these stages we find the same characteristic pattern, with the correlation of divine guidance and man's personal self-surrender, of revelation, and the personal commitment of faith, and of love. In other words, it is a pattern of covenant between God and man.

A covenant is a mutual bond which is made freely on both sides, a relationship between one person and another. This essentially religious, personal, and ethical understanding of the relationship between God and man is already firmly established in the original idea of covenant which is peculiar to Israel: "I will establish my covenant between me and you, and your descendants after you, from generation to generation, as an everlasting covenant: I will be your God, and of your descendants after you." (Gn 17:7).

Jahweh is a God who is infinitely far removed from man's level of existence, and yet at the same time infinitely close. The pious Israelite never ceased for a moment to be aware of this distance between himself and God—hence the emphasis on Jahweh's holiness. And yet at the same time the Holy One of Israel is really and truly concerned with earthly things. He really intervenes in the life both of individuals and of His people, and He expects them to show their response to this intervention in their conduct and way of life—hence the constant and parallel emphasis on Jahweh's righteousness and His faithfulness to His covenant (*misericordia et veritas*), which manifests that aspect of His nature that is turned toward the world.

Thus Israel's idea of God is as it were borne upon the polarity of these two extremes: it is the Holy One of Israel who dwells (as a devouring flame) in Israel's midst. And these two extremes come together in the image of Jahweh's Glory, which is manifested in the very fact of its being hidden, and which forms so to speak the point of contact between Jahweh and Israel. It is a kind of manifestation of Jahweh's Holiness which is in itself ineffable and unapproachable, but whose presence in Israel's midst is made tangible by the Glory. But even this Glory may not be seen by any mortal being in its full splendor; it is recognized by the radiance of the light shining out through the cloud which surrounds and hides it. There can be no doubt that Israel was profoundly and tangibly penetrated by the theological truth which later continued to be expressed by the idea of "glory," even when the visible and material appearance of the

75

Glory had disappeared. Its content remains always the same: It is the external manifestation of God's inaccessible Being, which is then recognized as such and glorified by men.

There are a whole series of similar expressions in the Old Testament which together preserve intact for us the different elements of this decisive moment in Israel's experience of God. Among these there is for example the intentionally vague figure of the Angel of Jahweh, who stands in fact, in most of the older texts, for Jahweh Himself in His earthly interventions (e.g., in Ex 3:2). Then we have Jahweh's Face and His Name, both expressions which are exceptionally specific and rich in their theological content, and both of which occur frequently in connection with the ideas of Jahweh's Glory and His Holiness. There is indeed nothing which expresses better all that is most specific and characteristic of a particular person than his "face" and his "name." Thus Jahweh is clearly revealed as an active and personal being, who is, however, in no way bound up with this earth in any crudely material fashion. His transcendence is thus safeguarded, and the expedient of supposing the existence of a whole series of subordinate beings forming a kind of ladder between God and man, which would in reality destroy His transcendence and make Him into a sort of *roi fainéant,* is avoided. He is a God from whom there is no escape, nor can He be got rid of by having resort to formalities. He is the *living* God, who in the fullness of His transcendent majesty is concerned about the details of man's insignificant existence: He searches the heart and the reins, as He does the ocean and the depths of the earth. It is just because He is so transcendent that He is also so inescapably near.

The depth and power of an experience of God which has found its expression in so delicately balanced a pattern of theological reflection is shown by the very variety of these metaphors and categories of revelation, two of which, among those we have not yet mentioned, we shall find in Genesis 1.

76

Another thing that we shall find is that there is evidence for thinking that among the causes of this fruitfulness in the development of doctrinal forms an important factor was the necessity to react against the ever-present popular tendency toward a drift into paganism.

7

Creation

The Dynamism of Faith

JAHWISTIC religion would appear to have been, in its beginnings, a national affair. The creation story in Genesis, however, is far wider in its horizons: By the time it had taken shape, the original Jahwistic view of Israel's past had become extended into a wider vision of the past of the whole created world and of the human race.

Stories about the origin of the world and of humanity are common enough in the various national literatures of Israel's geographical neighbors. They are all, however, impregnated with polytheism, with the result that the universalistic elements which they contain are swamped in their national character.

The only empirical source of information which Israel possessed about the distant past was in the vague memories which continued to be current in the traditions of the Semitic civilization of which it formed part. It is this primitive tradition, handed down with these memories from Israel's own earliest days, that lies behind the biblical creation narrative that we now possess. Hence its fragmentary nature, and other rather strange characteristics. Hence too the fact that these fragments which we now have in Genesis are closer in their content to similar narratives of the ancient Near East than to those of the rest of the ancient world.

78

It is true that the prophetic writings, for example, contain essentially the same Jahwistic conception of the world and its origins that we find in Genesis 1, but in the former case this conception is entirely subordinated to the theme of national redemption which is emphasized above all else. The account of the creation in Genesis, on the other hand, is there because the religion of Jahweh could not but take account of the traditional stories about the origin of the world and of the human race that were already in existence and formulate its attitude to them explicitly. The creation narrative is the result of this process.

We may take what the Jewish scholar Martin Buber has said about the Sabbath as being equally true of the creation narrative as it is of the whole economy of the Mosaic law: "This too [the Sabbath] was clearly not simply created from nothing, although it is not yet clear where its origins are to be sought. What is at all events certain is that an immense dynamism of faith has appropriated to itself whatever material was available, has resmelted it and constructed from it an imperishable monument of the life of faith."[1]

It is the religious element in Israel's vision of things that is so original, and we often find that, as a result, the narrative material is treated in a way that is also quite original, amounting sometimes to the creation of something entirely new. Since the biblical authors are concerned first and foremost with the religious content of their story, they handle what may be called their "available material" with great freedom and independence. For this material is there not for its own sake, but because it has a task to perform, and it is therefore subjected to a process of selection and adaptation in the course of composition. On occasions the author will even create his own material by analogy with (or in reaction against) conceptions with which he is familiar, but if so it is always with his eye on the events them-

[1] Quoted in G. van der Leeuw, *Godsdiensten der Wereld,* I (2 ed., 1948), pp. 197 ff.

selves and on the doctrine of which they must needs serve both as an illustration and as the ordinary means of communication.

"In the Beginning"

Set in such a context, there should be no further need to labor the fact that the otherwise inexplicably profound doctrinal content of Genesis 1 can derive only from Jahwism. Hence our efforts in the foregoing chapter to measure the distance that separates Jahwism from the heathen religions of the same period. And it is just this same distance that we shall find again as we turn to Genesis 1. And nowhere is this more evident than when we compare the Prologue of Genesis 1 with that of the principal "cosmogonies" which have come down to us from the literature of ancient Mesopotamia.

There is for example the epic, *Enuma elish,* so called from its opening words, which dates from about the year 2000. It may certainly be taken as representative, since it was very widely used and rewritten in various ways, copied and commented on until shortly before the beginning of the Christian era. With the help of numerous fragments which have been discovered since 1875, we now have about 900 verses of this work, amounting to about four fifths of the whole poem. The Prologue reads as follows:

When that which is above the heavens had as yet received no name [= did not yet exist], when that which is beneath the earth had as yet no name, when Apsu the original, the father of the Gods, and Mumu-Tiamat, the mother of them all, had not yet mingled their waters [i.e. the fresh and the salt waters respectively], when there were neither bushes nor reeds, when none of the gods yet existed, when neither the name nor the destiny of any was yet decreed, then was it that the gods were formed in their midst [i.e., of Apsu and Tiamat].

The starting point here, as in both the Genesis narratives, is a "description of chaos" (cp. Gn 2:5 ff. and 1:2). The difference between them is that whereas the cosmogony of Genesis is authentic, here, on the other hand, in a manner altogether true to the type of polytheistic religion, cosmogony and theogony have become confused. In Genesis 1:2 *tehôm* (= the primeval sea) is a masculine generic noun, even though there is an undeniable etymological connection between it and Tiamat, which here in our text is a feminine proper name for the mother of the gods, and is thus manifestly a mythologization of the forces of nature.

If we look at the principal clause of this text, it states that "then were the gods created," and the word "then" is further explained in the secondary clause: when all was still in a state of chaos. The creation of the world is only mentioned much later on in the course of the epic, after (among other things) the appearance of Marduk (= *Bêl*) and his elevation to the status of creator god has been recounted. According to this text, then, the chaos—in modern language we should say "matter"—is clearly prior both to the process of creation and even to the gods themselves. In fact Apsu and Tiamat are identified with the chaos, since it is out of their bodies that the world is to be constructed. In Genesis too we find mention of a "then," i.e., in the beginning. In Scripture, the whole of God's activity outside of Himself (*ad extra*) is contained between a beginning (*reshit*) and an end (*acharit*), both of which "moments" are entirely unique and *sui generis*. For this end is in reality the absolute end, i.e., the definitive establishment and fulfillment of the Kingdom of God in a new heaven and a new earth: An end which in the nature of things can be followed by no afterward. In the same way, there is also a beginning of which it cannot be said that there was anything before it, for it is the beginning precisely of the very first existence of all things. In Genesis it is God who creates "in the beginning." Just as St. John says: "in the beginning was the Word," so too in Genesis it is taken for granted that "in the beginning was God," since it was "then" that He created: Before anything began to be, God was.

81

Thus there is no place in Israel's concept of God for a theogony, or beginning of God. God is, and by His act of creation He gave existence to all things, and this act was their beginning, the beginning, for it is only in terms of this beginning that we can speak about a beginning at all. However far back we may try to imagine it, we are always obliged to say first of all that "in the beginning God created."

Thus God is simply *there,* before anything else at all, and with the very first, simple words of the Genesis narrative the usual dualistic starting point is set aside. The heathen gods, by contrast, come into existence at the same time as the created universe, in which precisely those spheres of influence are allotted to them with which they have, literally, grown up and with which they thus also remain confused. And conversely, it is likewise consistent that the one God who exists and has existed independently and in Himself before all else remains also inviolably exalted above everything of which it can be said that it has begun to exist, and that not independently of Him but precisely through His initiative.

In this way every part of the narrative contributes to the total impression of a clear and powerful rejection of every form of dualism: the almighty will of God is the *sole* ground of the existence of all things.

Chaos and Nothingness

The time has come to elucidate further what has been said in Chapter 4 about chaos and matter. If we could have asked the sacred writer where this world-in-a-state-of-chaos, or, in other words, matter, came from to begin with, he would have given us a perfectly clear answer. There was in his own mind no question either of matter having existed eternally, or of it having come into existence independently of God the Creator. Indeed the whole purpose of his argument is to emphasize that there is nothing whatever that is outside the sphere of God's almighty power. He only actually mentions by name things which can be concretely perceived, and even here his enumeration of them is not meant to be complete. The point of it is to convey the conviction that God is in principle the ultimate source of the intelligibility of everything that exists, whether it is mentioned or not, and indeed whether its existence is even known or not. He quite explicitly declares this principle in the very first verse, where the expression "heaven and earth" is to be understood (in our opinion) as broadly as possible.

Such a question was however never put to our author. And it is therefore just as mistaken to suppose that the creation of matter is the chief doctrinal content of verse 1, as it is to maintain that according to him matter existed before the moment of the creation. Verse 2 must then be understood in terms of the writer's technique, as an essential component of the way in which the narrative is presented. It comes naturally to him to embroider his story upon the existing canvas of the generally accepted cosmogony of the ancient East, in which the chaos is assumed to be already there at the time of the creation, conceived of in terms of a terrible struggle between the creator and the powers of chaos. In Genesis 1, however, this chaos has been reduced to the status of a merely conventional narrative element, and it must be understood according to the general conception which is quite obviously that of the story as a whole, and not in terms of the function that this same chaos may appear to have in other narratives.

It would not be difficult to find other examples of the way in which a particular way of representing or of saying something can be a survival of some out-of-date conception which has in reality long since been abandoned. An example which lies at hand would be that of several poetic passages in the Bible, in which Jahweh the creator is represented as in combat with the primeval sea (Ps 89:11; Jb 26:12; Is 51:9 ff. and elsewhere).

In the same way the "works of separation" in Genesis 1 are a relic of a more ancient world of ideas; but there is no doubt in the mind of the author that they are true acts of creation.

The most that one can say of such cases is that the sacred writer has not in every case found the terminology which is from every point of view appropriate to express his own particular vision, and that as a result he sometimes uses expressions which as such really belong to a completely different world of ideas. It is clear enough that in such cases these elements are to be interpreted not from the point of view of their original meaning, but rather from that of the new vision into which they have been taken up. This is all the more true in cases when the part which they are called upon to play is only secondary and conventional, and they have simply been used because no better expression lay at hand. And in this particular case of the biblical and nonbiblical cosmogonies, which differ so completely and fundamentally from each other, it is more than ever unjustified to turn for the meaning of a particular biblical detail to that of its nonbiblical "parallel," in view of the fact that in the Bible as elsewhere the meaning of detailed expressions is dependent upon the general mentality of the whole passage.

And anyone who is prepared to give careful and patient attention to the text of Genesis 1 will certainly come to the conclusion that this *tohu-wa-bohu* is in reality nothing more or less than a very concrete way of saying: "absolutely nothing whatever." This is confirmed by the way in which the word *tohu* is used elsewhere in the Bible (*bohu* occurs rarely and then only as an emphatic correlative of *tohu*). In 1 Samuel 12:21, for example, it is used in order to emphasize that the idols are of absolutely no value whatever: "Serve the Lord with all your heart; and do not turn aside after vain things [*tohu*] which cannot profit or save, for they are vain [*tohu*]."

This text can help us to clarify the question with which we are concerned. The point is that Israel was not interested in the concept of "being" as such, considered in itself, in the way that we think of it. The biblical concept of being is of something dynamic and efficacious, of which the presence makes itself felt (cp. the primary meaning of the name Jahweh: He is, which is as much as to say: One can be certain of Him). In the same way, the biblical concept of "nothingness," or "vanity," is the precise negation of the biblical concept of being: In the text quoted above, to say that the idols "cannot profit or save" is simply a concrete way of saying that they do not exist. They are absurd, and therefore they are "nothing."

Similarly, it must be remembered that our generally accepted definition of creation as "to bring forth something out of nothing" (*productio rei ex nihilo*) presupposes a concept of being and of nonbeing which is simply not that of the Bible, or at any rate is there only as part of a much broader and more concrete way of looking at things. Thus if we must go in search of a biblical foundation for our concept of creation, then (insofar as nothingness enters into it at all) we shall have found everything that we need or can expect to find once we have understood that the chaos of Genesis 1 is as much nothingness as anything can be in the Bible. This general conclusion is confirmed not only by the text quoted above, but also by most of the other texts in which *tohu* occurs, especially those in Isaias: "All the nations are as nothing before him, they are accounted by him as less than nothing and emptiness [*tohu*]" (40:17). "Who brings princes to nought, and makes the rulers of the earth as nothing [*tohu*]" (40:23). "Behold, they are all a delusion; their works are nothing; their images are but wind and emptiness [*tohu*]" (41:29).

Isaias is much nearer to Genesis 1 than to *Enuma elish*. And we may confidently conclude, in the spirit of Isaias, that the meaning of chaos in the Bible is not merely *tohu,* but *tohu* and *bohu,* i.e., nothing at all whatever!

85

Creation

It follows from the above that there is absolutely no reason whatever, on grounds of possible scruples about strict scientific exactitude, for hesitating to say that the traditional doctrine of creation is explicitly stated in Genesis 1. In addition to what has been said about the clear tendency of the whole narrative, there are three other definite pieces of evidence to be considered, each of which tells the same story. In addition to these, there is yet a fourth fact which comes, as it were, to crown them, and is perhaps the most consoling of all—that the sacred author does indeed employ the term, "to create." But even if this were not the case, and he had used "to make" instead, we should still have had no alternative but to conclude that his meaning was "to make out of nothing."

Our evidence is as follows:

1) The expression "in the beginning" presupposes that there was as yet nothing in existence before the act of creation; *2*) the terms "heaven" and "earth" are to be understood in the broadest possible sense (cf. p. 45), and thus in themselves already constitute a complete résumé, if in a highly abbreviated form, of all that exists. Moreover if they are indeed to be understood as expressing the two outer limits of a totality (cf. p. 275), then the intention to make it clear that everything without exception is dependent upon God's creative power becomes even more obvious; *3*) chaos is a biblical equivalent for nothingness; *4*) the content of the biblical word used for "to create" (*bara*).

No doubt the later scholastics were a trifle premature in being so content with the word *creavit* which they found in the Vulgate text. Modern theologians, however, have tended to be rather overscrupulous, perhaps by way of reaction. And we must remember that in scholastic theology quotation from Scripture was done for purposes of illustration and edification as well as of demonstration in relation to the strictly speculative argument;

and it must at all events be admitted that it was with a true instinct that they attributed such importance to the word *creavit*, even if their reasons for doing so were somewhat inadequate.

Further investigation of the use of *bara* in this text shows conclusively that the writer chose this expression deliberately, and that he did so in order to express quite specifically the incomparably great and unique character of God's act of creation. In making this choice of words he is simply seeking to employ yet another means of putting into words the self-same idea that lies behind each of the other expressions that we have already examined. There are forty-four places in the Bible in which it is critically certain that the word *bara* occurs, and the following conclusions are to be drawn from an investigation of them:

1) The active subject of the verb is in every case the God of Israel, i.e., Jahweh. He is referred to as Elohim only in Genesis, where the sacred writer, even though he is not as yet writing the history of his own people, has Exodus 6:3 in mind.

2) Even though *bara* unquestionably signifies a kind of making (i.e., God's way of making, cp. Gn 1:26–7), no mention ever occurs of the material out of which (accusative *materiae*) this making is done. This may be contrasted, for example, with Genesis 2:7: Then the Lord God *formed* man out of the earth of the ground.

3) This creative activity of God is sovereign and almighty; it knows no obstacle, no laborious struggle with a recalcitrant matter. The Creator does His work with the greatest of ease, almost playfully, and the result of it needs no time in which to grow—it is just there, all of a sudden, and time does not enter into it. This last point is powerfully suggested in Genesis 1 by the fact that even the most tremendous acts of creation are achieved in a single day. For each of them, a single command is enough, and there is a perfect correlation between the word that is spoken and its effect: "Let there be light. And there was light [*jehi ôr wa-jehi-ôr*]."

87

4) The result of *bara* is always something which exceeds the potentialities of the preceding situation, and is thus also above the capacity of anything that man is able to do (cp. no. 1 above). Hence it is described as being wonderful (Ex 34:10), and above all as new, something wholly and entirely original and unprecedented. It is no accident that *bara* occurs five times in connection with the idea of *newness* (Jer 31:22; Is 48:7; 65:17; Ps 51:12: *crea/innova;* 104:30: *creabuntur/renovabis*).

5) Not everything, however, that is new can be said to have been created, but only that which is completely and utterly new, i.e., that which constitutes the very first beginning of a whole series, of an all-embracing order of being. It is only when there is such a beginning that we are in the special and exclusive domain of *bara*. And the characteristic result of this kind of divine intervention is creation and re-creation, and, more particularly, the setting in motion of either of these processes, which are such that before them nothing of the kind could have existed or indeed have been thought of as existing. It is as a consequence of *bara* that the whole order of the cosmos comes into being (this use is peculiar to Gn 1–6, occurring eleven times); and it is by an analogous sort of divine intervention that the soteriological order is called into existence (this use is peculiar to Is 40–66, occurring twenty times). The use of *bara* in all of the remaining thirteen cases where it occurs can be reduced to one or other of these two types; they are all either an echo or an anticipation of either Genesis or Isaias. This fifth characteristic of *bara* is present wherever the word occurs. In reality, it includes the other four. Still more than our word "to create," the Hebrew *bara* implies that the totality of the effect mentioned is to be ascribed to the activity for which it stands. For it is not sufficient that a thing should entirely and *totum quantum* owe its origin to God; the species to which it belongs and the very order of being itself must be original.

Our Definition

Anyone who has got to the point of being prepared to take all the above evidence as it stands, and who, by means of it, has penetrated to the heart of the inner faith of a believer in Jahweh, will probably not be overconcerned about the terms which are in fact commonly used in our own day to define the notion of creation. In this he will be right, for abstract concepts can never provide the means of contact between ourselves and the author of Genesis. Only an actual and living affirmation of belief, which has the whole of oneself behind it, can suffice.

The affirmation contained in Genesis 1 and that of our dogma of the creation are undoubtedly identical, but the fact remains that the conceptual terms in which each is made carry indelibly the marks of two entirely different ways of thinking, belonging to two quite different worlds, and that these cannot be simply identified without doing violence to the texts. Insofar as our modern formulation really contains anything positive in the way of truth, it is to be found whole and entire in what the author of Genesis is saying in his own Hebrew way of expressing himself. We may indeed go further, and say that if only we are prepared to go and seek to learn from him in all humility, we shall find the wherewithal to fill our own definitions (with all their greater clarity) with a living content that in Genesis is so much fuller in spiritual richness and primary authority. To bring forth out of nothing is a respectable definition which may perhaps find some support in 2 Maccabees 7:28 ($οὐκ\ ἐξ\ ὄντων$), but it is and remains a relatively negative fruit of Western logic, and is therefore not particularly well suited as a criterion by which to judge the doctrinal content of the Genesis narrative, which is so pregnant with a living and positive awareness of truth. It would perhaps be more fruitful (and certainly more correct theologically) to begin the other way round, and judge our more recent definitions in the light of Genesis 1. And if we do this we shall find that we arrive quite naturally at a more positive definition which we also, incidentally, inherit from the scholastics: "productio rei secundum totam suam substantiam." This latter definition is much more suitable as a basis for an exposition of the doctrine of Genesis, and if we turn back again from it to the biblical text we shall not have the slightest difficulty in discovering there the roots of our own belief about the creation—in other words we shall find the same thing in a more concentrated, total and primary form: God created all things, which means that He made every single thing in the totality of its being, for He is the ground and source of the totality of *all* being. The hesitations of modern authors here derive from their one-sided preoccupation with the idea of *ex nihilo* (from nothing), a concept (?) in regard to which we have but small grounds for self-congratulation vis-à-vis the sacred writer. The old (Dutch) Catechism stated (no. 37) that "We call God the Creator of heaven and earth, because He has brought forth everything that is visible and invisible out of nothing." The new Catechism on the other hand says (no. 23) that "We call God the Creator because He has made all things by His almighty will alone." The change thus made is a great improvement, for the new text directs the attention immediately to a positive concept of creation, i.e., that which we find in the Bible. Now indeed the Catechism and Genesis 1 are saying the same thing. This need not however mean that we may not still use the negative definition as a kind of secondary approach. The very structure of the human mind is such that, in our thinking about God, we cannot dispense with the *via negationis*. We do need negative formulations as an aid to our reflection, but these can only be meaningful in function of what is positive. The sacred writer, too, found himself obliged to construct a negative *ens rationis,* the chaos, but he keeps it well in the background. He could not, however, do without it altogether, for he was

90

reflecting just as we are, though in a very different way from ours, and his reflection led him in the same general direction as our reflection leads us. This is indeed but another indication that his affirmation is no less weighty in its import than our own.

8

The Nearness of God

THE faith in the creation which we find expressed in the first
story of Genesis provides abundant proof that Israel's experience
of God was at the same time the source of a profoundly authentic
awareness of His transcendence. What is even more remarkable
is the fact that the same narrative contains such a strong implication of the *closeness* of the divine presence. As a result, we are
forced to the conclusion that the Creator God of Genesis bears
to a striking degree the same characteristic traits as Jahweh, as
He has made Himself known to His people since the Exodus.
The Holy One of Israel is a living God, whose hand is everywhere, and whose nearness Israel experiences in all the occur-
rences of nature and of everyday life, just as much as in the unfolding of its own destiny as a people. Every aspect of an
Israelite's life was soaked in the presence of God, and this
presence was a fact for him more than for any other of his
Oriental neighbors, precisely because it was accompanied by
such a profound awareness of God's transcendence. It was a
tremendous reality for him, a source of holy seriousness in everything that he did. It was precisely because Jahweh could never
be localized in any particular earthly phenomenon, or embraced
within the limitations of any earthly category, that this reality
of His presence was so all-embracing and all-pervading a thing.

Anthropomorphism

Israel's constant awareness of the nearness of God is expressed
most vividly by means of the anthropomorphisms which occur
repeatedly in the Bible. Grate as some of these may on Puritan-
ical ears, there is in reality nothing in any of them which need
shock us, and indeed if we will but pay attention to what they
have to say to us, we shall find that we are richly rewarded.

There is a certain kind of mentality, which belongs really to
a past age when Reason was enthroned as goddess, which would
consider these anthropomorphisms simply as a sign of primitive-
ness. According to this conception, Israel's religion was the
product of an evolution from a lower stage to something higher,
and it is considered that the priestly Jahwism of the postexilic
period (during which the last recension of the nation's sacred
literature is deemed to have taken place) did not succeed in
purifying it of all traces of animism, polytheism and suchlike
conceptions.

The supporters of this preconceived evolutionary idea consider
that it is possible to reconstitute, from the text which we now
possess, the different stages of Israel's progress toward the final
state of orthodox Jahwism. And for them, these anthropomorphisms are among the traces which remain, despite this evolution,
of a primitive conception of God which thus (needless to say)
derives not from an original historical revelation but simply
from the general religious inheritance of Oriental heathendom.

Nowadays, however, it is generally recognized that the anthropomorphisms which we find in the Bible are in fact of very
considerable spiritual content, and that they possess a highly
authentic religious value. To divorce them from the organic
whole of biblical revelation, with the idea of analyzing their
material content and of arriving as a result at a conclusion about
the concept of God which they imply, is simply not possible, for

93

they form a vital part of that revelation and are intimately bound up with it at every point. We should rather admit that to speak anthropomorphically about God is a normal and universal human necessity—a necessity which the Israelite, with his intensely concrete way of thinking, was least of anyone in a position to set aside. For him, these anthropomorphisms were a realistic and indispensable form of expression, which he used thankfully as the vehicle of the Jahwistic faith to which he was so deeply committed. We must seek to understand the anthropomorphisms from the point of view of Israel's faith in God, and not the other way round. It remains true, of course, that in the earlier stages all kinds of anthropomorphisms were employed with a good deal less restraint than was later the case, when a more reflective state of mind led to a tendency to avoid them, either because of the danger of misunderstandings, or because of the need to disassociate as completely as possible from certain heathen ideas and concepts.

It must therefore be admitted without hesitation that the author of Genesis 1 was a learned man, a theologian who consciously chose his words and expressions for his purpose of putting his knowledge of God into words as adequately and as surely as he was able. There are many passages in the Old Testament (the story of Paradise to begin with) which can rival Genesis 1 in religious depth, but there is nothing that can approach it as an example of theological reflection and carefulness of expression.

It is true that there is a difference between the expressions used in the earlier and in the later of the two narratives, but if they are taken together as a whole and then compared, it becomes quite clear that it is a single theological conviction which dominates both. Nor is it accurate to say that the highly anthropomorphic narrative of Genesis 2 stands on a lower plane than Genesis 1. If anything, the reverse is the case. It is indeed, on the contrary, not for nothing that Holy Scripture is full of anthropomorphisms from end to end. They are, in fact, a positive guarantee of the purity of the conception of God which they serve to express, in that they provide a constant reminder of the immediacy and the reality of God's intervention, of how personal it is, and of how *close* and *living* a God is the Holy One of Israel.

Not only do we find this essential characteristic of Israel's idea of God fully present in Genesis 1, but it is, again, the anthropomorphisms that express it, and they do so with the particular note of theological circumspection that comes out in the whole of the narrative. These anthropomorphisms are of the kind that we might expect from a biblical writer for whom the ancient, concrete, and experiential knowledge of Jahweh's supramundane nature had developed into a conscious awareness of the truth that He is pure spirit, and has sought to make this truth understood by his own people as well as he might, without encouraging the growth of popular misconceptions.

There are in particular three notable anthropomorphisms which he employs: 1) the creation comes into existence through the agency of God's spirit and of God's word; 2) the creation is fully achieved within a week, according to Israel's reckoning; 3) man is created in God's image.

The first two of these dominate the entire narrative, and it is with them that we shall be concerned for the rest of this chapter. The third, even though it dominates a single passage only, is no less important and indeed illustrates the title of the chapter no less well than the others. We must, however, put off any consideration of it until the next chapter.

Spirit and Word

It should now be easier, in the light of the above introduction, to understand the real significance of the teaching of Genesis 1 that all things have come into being by the spirit-laden word of the Creator. The idea has become extremely familiar to us through the many later texts which derive in one way or another from Genesis. But we should not allow this familiarity to prevent us from noticing how characteristic it is of the author of Genesis that he takes these expressions from that part of the national literature which relates the story of God's redemptive activity, and applies them so explicitly (and for the first time) to God's work of *creation*. One can hardly imagine a more immaterial and "spiritual" (and yet also how immediate and personal!) way of describing God's relationship with the object of His concern.

"Spirit" and "word" are both anthropomorphisms, and both serve strongly to emphasize the immanence of the transcendent God. To illustrate this point, we must content ourselves with a brief reference to the world of ideas to which these expressions belong.

Our word "spirit" provides, unfortunately, only a one-sided translation of the Hebrew *ruah,* lacking as it does the two-dimensional meaning present both in the Greek *pneuma* and the Latin *spiritus*. In the physical sense, *ruah* means "wind" or "breath." A man's breath is life itself to him, and the wind, too, symbolizes life; hence *ruah* also means the "life force." Then, a man's breath comes from his inward being and manifests the variations in his feelings and emotions; hence the psychological meaning of *ruah*: "anger," "emotion," "spirits," and, lastly, "spirit" in the sense of a dynamic principle. Wherever *ruah* occurs in the Bible, it is seldom detached from the whole of this rich body of meaning, and even in very late texts the basic physical and material background of it all can still be felt (Ez 37:9; Jn 3:8; 20:22 ff.; Acts 2:2; cp. the rite of baptism and the ritual for the blessing of a baptismal font). This is certainly true of Genesis 1:2: The modern French translation which gives "le souffle d'Elohim" brings it out well. Spirit and word are as it were an extension of the person, and function like nonmaterial limbs by means of which, while remaining himself, he is able to enter into relation with other people and things, to influence them effectually and bring them within the sphere of his own life and power.

The ancient East thought in a realistic way about these things. Once a word had been well and truly spoken (especially in the case of a curse or a blessing), it became a sort of independent, form-giving power, laden in some way with all the energy of the speaker's inner being and personality. For the Oriental of those days, the spheres of the spirit and of the word were much closer to the facts of everyday life than they are for us. With his extremely concrete and therefore totalizing cast of mind, he thought of them together, as a vital unity, and he would, indeed, have scarcely been able to think of one of the two without the other. The saying, "l'idée passe à l'acte," which for our rational way of thinking is already quite a discovery, would for him be inadequate and weak. It is no accident that in Hebrew, concepts which for us are as far apart as "word" and "thing," or "lie" and "crime," are expressed by the same word. And so for him, too, words such as "know," "think," "truth" and so on were far fuller of meaning than they are for us. Speculation as such meant nothing to him; his problems were not in the realm of abstract ideas, but were the practical problems of life.

Even these few indications should make it possible to feel how realistic an impression of the divine activity Israel must have received from a story which is dominated to such an extent by God's efficacious "speaking." Later Jewish exegesis saw in these "words" an analogy with the Decalogue, and in accordance reckoned ten words of creation. "Spirit" and "word" are thus characteristic categories of the theology of the Bible, and they are used by the author of Genesis to describe God's direct and personal intervention in such a way that there is not the slightest danger of His being dragged down to earth, either in a literal or in a figurative sense (cp. Gn 11:5).[1]

The Week

The impression of God's closeness is further and above all due to the way in which the author has arranged the story of the mystery of creation over the days of a week. The anthropomorphism here is a bold one: for men work, and they can make things, but only God can create. The point is that creation is presented as being God's way of making, as a truly "Godlike" sort of work. So truly, in fact, is it work, that it can be set down in order according to the succession of the days of the week: six days of work, followed by one of rest.

This arrangement does not spring spontaneously out of the material of the narrative, as if it were in some way implied in it. There are on the contrary *eight* distinct "works," and in deciding to concentrate them into six days the sacred writer undoubtedly had a purpose in view—a purpose which is, indeed, transparent

[1] Considerations of a Trinitarian nature are perhaps more to the point here than they would be in connection with the plural verb of Genesis 1:26. It is of course in the New Testament that the Holy Trinity is directly revealed, but in a terminology that in many different ways had grown out of the Old Testament. It is therefore something more than a mere accident that in the Old Testament, next to Jahweh Himself, His Word and His Spirit play such an important part. Genesis 1 cannot be understood apart from this preparatory terminology, and even comes back again in the allusions which are present in the Prologue of St. John. It would therefore be a one-sided attitude to take it for granted that there can be absolutely no meaningful connection made between Genesis 1 and the revelation of the Holy Trinity. The link between the New Testament and Genesis 1:2 which is made in the Preface for the blessing of a font does not rest on a merely literary comparison but on an objective relationship between the different stages of revelation which has only recently been recognized as being stated in the New Testament itself. And if in the Vulgate *Spiritus* is here already written with a capital letter, this is a result, not merely of an uncritical piety, but rather of the sensing of the mysterious analogy that exists between God's different works. This is, incidentally, a point that is not all that easy to situate in the classical treatise on the meaning of Scripture. And it is now recognized that the fault concerning this could well lie with the aforementioned treatise!

enough. Behind it all there lies the need of the ancient Israelite to be able to see a relationship between his own work and that which has been done by God, and to be able to recognize the one in the other. And so in Genesis we find that God works in the same way that a man does, so that His work may serve as the norm and prototype of human work. The crucial point which this principle brings with it is that the sabbath day of rest is a sacred law, which is grounded upon the eternal will of God as well as on the nature of things here on earth. The character of the narrative, descriptive and at the same time hinting at things it does not actually say, is maintained in this respect also: for the actual term *sabbath* is avoided, but God's exemplary repose is described with deliberate care. There is emphatic repetition of words such as "the seventh day" and *sabat* ("cease"), and in addition other terms, such as "sanctify" and "work," are introduced, which recall the legislation about the sabbath in a way that cannot be an accident.

As we have already said, the structure of Genesis 1 is not to be explained by supposing that in some way or another the writer was in possession of information concerning the actual manner of the creation, but rather that if he was to present his teaching in a way that was both didactically clear and appropriately striking, he needed to arrange his description of the work of the creation in stages. We have already seen in Chapter 4 how the actual structure of the world as he found it provided him with these stages already at hand. But we can now also, for the first time, understand why he chose to divide his story into six stages precisely, no more and no less. His motive was a religious one: the sabbath. It was necessary for God's work to have been done in such a manner, that it justified and supported the laws concerning the sabbath. Thus it is that we must seek for the roots of the arrangement of Genesis 1 according to the days of the week in the institution of the sabbath, which already existed when the author wrote. This is the reverse of what was previously thought to be the case: that the sabbath derived from Genesis.

Sabbath

The assumption was that the law of the sabbath had already been imposed by God on the first men, and that Moses had later been responsible for restoring this primitive legislation to a position of honor. Support was found for this in the words of the great lawgiver, where he says: "Remember the sabbath, that you keep it holy . . . for in six days God created the heavens, the earth and the sea with all that is in them; but on the seventh day he rested" (Ex 20:8, 11). And yet there is no text which says explicitly that man was from the beginning under an obligation to observe a day of rest. According to the texts, it was God who did this, not man! Genesis says that the Creator rested on the seventh day, and blessed and sanctified it. It was perfectly natural that, as a result, this day should once and for all have acquired a special character, which men were duly obliged to take account of. And it was equally natural that they should have done this by following God's example and likewise abstaining from work. But in Genesis these conclusions are left to the reader; it was for the Law to draw them explicitly.

The opinion that the sabbath derived from Genesis, instead of the reverse, was in reality based not upon the texts, but upon the mistaken belief that the content of Genesis 1, complete with all its imagery, was known to primitive humanity. In fact, Genesis 1 is addressed to Israel, and derives most probably from the same source as the texts about the sabbath which invoke its authority, since both are closely related in form and content. In any case there is little doubt that someone (i.e., the author), for whom the law of the sabbath was a matter of the greatest concern, has taken advantage of the doctrine which he possessed about the creation to express it in such a way that it redounded to the

100

greater honor and glory of the sabbath. In this way his narrative provided a foundation not only for the existence of the world, but also for that of the sabbath. And in both cases the essential purpose is theological rather than historical in the scientific sense.

We, of course, would tackle the whole thing differently, and would do our best to produce an attractive theory, which might read as follows: "The sabbath is a positive law of God which is a more precise determination of the natural law, according to which man is obliged to devote a part of his time to the worship of God." The Oriental, however, prefers to say the same thing in the form of an attractive story, in which the same theory is contained, without logical distinctions, but with at least as much profundity and presented in a much more striking way. The consequence is that the Bible's way of teaching something may often be so clear and striking in its manner, that we tend spontaneously to assume that it is intended to be accurate history. It is not true that the Creator worked for six days; and yet the lawgiver appears to appeal to this as if it were indeed a fact. To us, such a procedure seems to leave a choice between two possible alternatives only: error or deception. But the biblical writers saw it quite otherwise:

1) The Oriental is extremely sensitive to the suprahistorical dimensions of meaning which even pure fiction may possess. The real foundation for the sabbath is not the outward form of the story in Genesis, based on the days of the week, but the relationship of Creator to creature which the story is simply a striking way of putting over; thus the appeal of the law is made via the outward form of the story to its essential meaning.

2) The Oriental has a great feeling for the piquancy of the various possible kinds of play upon words, and for the whole range of verbal artifice. When he uses a story to illustrate a point, he is concerned that it should be well received as a story; and if he has succeeded in making the application in a sufficiently

101

striking way, the necessary rhetorical effect will have been achieved. The general principle may be stated that whether or not a particular ancient text is to be interpreted historically cannot be decided from the use made of it in later texts alone, whatever may appear to be implied, even quite categorically, in the said later text. In fact, the way in which ancient texts are used in the Bible to prove some particular point forms in itself quite a distinct literary genre, of a highly diverse and at times disconcerting kind, so that there is not a great deal that can be safely concluded from such cases until the text which is quoted has itself been examined and considered in the light of its original context.

The question of the historical origin of the number seven as a sacred number governing the structure of the week and the sabbath is too complicated and obscure to be considered here. What, at least, is certain is that the Hebrew week must have a quite original and independent origin, since there is no relationship between it and the cycle of the four phases of the moon: The weeks are counted through in sequence, without beginning again every time there is a new moon, as with the months. It is not difficult to see from this how easily the sabbath could come to be regarded as a sign of the covenant, that distinguished Israel as a people set aside by Jahweh for Himself (Ex 31:12–17). We may also note that this arrangement is typical of Jahwism's firm rejection of everything that could possibly favor any kind of astrological superstition (cp. Gn 1:14–19). The sun and the moon do possess a certain dominion—but they do so because the Creator has thus ordained. The text is concise and matter of fact: The sun and the moon are mere things, "the greater and the smaller light." Their impersonal character is still further underlined by the deliberate omission of the actual words "sun" and "moon" which, since they had virtually become the proper names of gods (*Shamash* and *Sin*), were full of polytheistic undertones. As far as the sabbath is concerned, we have in Genesis 1 not profane historiography, but pious exposition of the Law. The same teaching is given again in the account of the first shower of manna (Ex 16). There are two other places in the rest of the Pentateuch where the law of the sabbath is given with an invocation of the authority of the Creator's six days of work (Ex 20:8–12; 31:12–17), and two others again where the motive is a social one: hired servants and slaves, draft animals and beasts of burden must be allowed a breathing space (Ex 23:12; Dt 5:12–15). In Deuteronomy 5:15 there is a reference to Egypt, where Israel too once dwelled as a slave: the sabbath rest should therefore be a true celebration of the memory of the redemption—which it is indeed in any case inasmuch as it is a sign of the covenant. It is in this broader context that we can see the natural background of the creation narrative, and can best understand its real significance. God's rest is, in fact, the climax of the story. In the Prologue, God steps out as it were from the stillness of eternity, and at the end of the story, we see him withdrawing once more into His eternal Rest. The creation is a self-revelation; in it, the Holy One of Israel comes near to us. For Israel, the realities of this world constituted a great and rather overwhelming mystery. Genesis 1 does not resolve this mystery; what it does is to bring it into relation with the mystery of God Himself, with the consequence for the believer that he feels able to find his bearings. His life and religion are no longer dominated by obscure and anonymous powers, but by Jahweh. Wherever he goes, he can be aware of the closeness of the presence of the One and Holy God, and of this conviction his weekly repose on the sabbath is a veritable confession of faith.

9

Image of God

IF the seventh day is the climax of the story, the sixth is the climax of the work. The last of God's acts of creation is also the greatest. The king appears as the culminating figure in the procession which he has himself contrived. The king here is man; everything which has been created up to this point is now put under his dominion by the Creator. He comes in onto the scene of a brand-new, virgin world, like a king entering his own domain, where everything exists and functions for his own sake alone.

Context

The general effect of the narrative is thus to envelop man in glory. There are a number of elements which combine together to create this impression of splendor:

1) The account of the creation of the tame and the wild animals appears to be cut suddenly short; the narrator seems to be anxious to press on with his story in order to make a beginning on man, to be saving space as it were, so that as much may be left as possible for what is about to come, given the limitations of the whole composition.

2) The word of command is short—to allow more time for reflection, it would seem. The Creator is going to work according to a deliberately thought-out plan. What He is now going

to make is not something which is to be done simply as a matter of course. A work is being prepared that is going to demand the whole of the divine artistry—it will be a bold stroke, a masterpiece that will give tangible proof of the greatness of the Creator's resources and of His wisdom.

3) All the other things which cover the world's surface, or which inhabit it, have been brought into being by God's creative word either from the waters (fishes and birds) or from the earth (plants and beasts). But the origin of man is the Creator's own secret: none of the earthly elements plays any part in it, even in a secondary manner.

4) It is a notable fact that the sacred writer here repeats the word "create" three times. The only other occasions on which he does this are in 1:1; 1:21; and 2:3—thus when he is summing up the whole of God's work at the beginning and at the end of the narrative, and also where the sea-monsters are mentioned (with fishes and birds). In the latter case, the author's purpose is most probably to emphasize that there is nothing at all of which God's almighty power is incapable. He also, perhaps, wants to mark the transition over to the stage of the living creatures. For these, again, are an entirely new phenomenon (the previous mention of the plants is no objection to this—for true and evident life, movement is necessary); and in the same way man, compared to everything that has gone before, is, in a much higher degree yet, something entirely new.

5) Again, while all the other living things are created each after its kind—in a teeming multitude of countless examples of the same species—man rises high above them in his individual, personal value. He is not made in a general way, a whole species at a time, but individually, one after the other, man and woman, "created after the image of God."

6) Is it mere fancy to feel that there is a certain stirring of emotion in this part of the divine counsel, in addition to wisdom and knowledge? In comparison with the concise and matter-of-

fact tone of the rest of the narrative, there is a personal ring about this passage which sets it apart: "Let *us* make man in *our* image, after *our* likeness, that they may rule . . ." Is this the reason why the Creator has reserved this "work" entirely to Himself? (cp. no. 3 above). In any case, it is undeniable that the writer here abandons for a moment the tone of an outsider who is merely observing what is going on: His prose slips into poetry, and his didactic style becomes lyrical. Poetic form has greater solemnity and sureness, its impressiveness comes to the aid of the memory, so that it is in itself a safeguard against the danger of its content being inaccurately handed down from one generation to another. Thus its use at once betrays that the author is conscious of having arrived at the center and heart of his teaching:

> Then created / Elohim / man / in his image
> in the image / of Elohim / created He him
> male / and female / created He them.

Function

There is material enough in the Bible to allow us to say with some confidence that we know what is the general significance of the expression "image of God." But when it comes to being really precise, one feels a little less confident, in view of the wide variety of different opinions which exists. The best method will thus no doubt be to begin with a general approach to the question from the starting point of the undeniable indications which we have in the narrative, so that when a certain basis has in this way been established we shall be in a better position to attempt a more precise definition in the following chapter. It will be clear enough from what has already been said, that this formula cannot be regarded as having simply been borrowed from somewhere or other and thereafter remained gratuitously lodged in the periphery of our narrative as a relic of some primitive way of thinking. Apart from the fact that no convincing parallel to it has yet been found, the expression undeniably presents itself as a fully deliberate and highly characteristic spiritual asset of the author himself. The emphasis which he gives to it proves that he is completely in earnest. We are in any case beginning to know him now—with his sensitivity of perception, his eyes wide open to all the bright things that are in the world, and with his passion for defining and classifying everything exactly.

Now it is man's turn. The author's reflective mind has already climbed and descended the steps of the ladder of being many times, and everything has been allotted a place. Now he is going to give man his place! What, we may ask, will he say? Will he perhaps make of him a higher kind of animal? Or an inferior sort of god?

To us, once it has been done, it seems fairly obvious to describe man as the image of God. But which of us could have thought this out for himself? The sacred writer, like so many before him, had found himself face to face with the mystery of God. His Jahwistic faith enabled him to achieve an expression of that mystery that was unrivaled in its authenticity and depth. Now, he stands before the mystery of man—that strange mixture of the highest and the lowest, belonging as he does both to this world here below and to the world that is above. And here too his Jahwistic faith showed him the way to the happy mean by which he could avoid the extremes of Oriental heathendom. He did find it, and we can see him seizing hold of it as of a precious and personal discovery.

Content

To start with, it is three times repeated, with emphasis, that man was created by God. However unique man's place in the creation, there remains thus always, between him and God, the gulf of the relationship between the creature and his Creator.

The fundamental division is maintained intact: on the one side, God; on the other, everything else. And it is this very fact that gives its full meaning to the other division, which cuts across the first: that on one side there is God and man, and on the other, everything else. From this point of view, God and man are together on the same side, over against all the rest. The reason for this latter division is that, whatever may be the variety of gradations in the scale of being, "all the rest" belongs wholly and completely to the material world, whereas man belongs, with God, to another and higher world. "The rest" was created out of material elements, whereas man. . . .

The writer does not venture a more precise description of what happened; he simply gives the words of creation in which he specifies more what man is in fact intended to be, and what he truly is, than the manner in which he was created by God. He is created "in the image, in the likeness of Elohim." We have here without question a description of man in terms of the writer's concrete and actual way of thinking, whose purpose is to distinguish carefully man's special and unique place in the world over against everything else that exists. As regards the precise content of this formula, we must say first of all that it appears to describe what man is in two directions at once: 1) man is essentially different from the whole of the rest of the created world; 2) this essential difference lies in the fact of a particular relationship with a higher sphere, that to which God Himself belongs.

We have direct evidence, provided by the author himself, of the correctness of this first conclusion. For he evidently considered the formula to be of such importance that he returns to it on two further occasions.

"On the day that God created man, he made him in the likeness of God. Male and female he created them, and he blessed them and he called them man on the day of their creation. And when Adam was 130 years old, he became the father of a son in his own likeness, and he called him Seth" (Gn 5:1–3).

It is a fact of experience that the later generations of the human race do not come so directly from God's hands as the first man. This passage gives an answer to the question whether this fact is of any consequence in regard to the image of God in man; for Adam's descendants possess the same essential dignity as the first man himself. To be in the image of God is therefore not merely a personal privilege of the first man, but is something which belongs to the human race as such: By the very fact that one is human, one is made in the image of God.

No other conclusion is possible when we consider the deliberate connection which the author makes, here as well as in Genesis 1, between creation in the image of God, and creation as man and woman with the blessing on their fruitfulness. The author means to leave us in no doubt that God, on the day that He created them, called them "man." Here, as always, he first describes what it is that God created, and only then gives it its name. What is first described (as the image of God) is none other than the well-known phenomenon, man. And the explanation for the existence of this phenomenon is that, because of God's blessing, the first human couple were able to bring forth men. For Adam too begot in his own image.

With this we have at once a valuable analogy which can provide us with a better insight into the meaning of the expression, "image of God." Just as there is a specific correspondence between one man and another, and just as (still more to the point) a child is the living image of his father, so too man is the image of God. And it is the *whole* man who is image of God—there is no reason at all for thinking here only of the child's soul, and every kind of reason against doing so.

Since the Flood, man is able to dispose according to his pleasure of the whole animal world in order to supply his own needs, but woe to him who sheds human blood. Man is inviolable, and

109

this because he is holy, "for God made man in his own image."

This is again a clear confirmation of the first impression which we gained from Genesis 1: That "image of God" describes man's place in the creation. There is an unbridgeable gulf which separates man (and a fortiori God Himself, Acts 17:29) from all the other beings that inhabit the earth, and this is because he stands in a unique relationship with the sacred sphere of being which is that of God Himself.

We may now sum up as follows such conclusions as we are able to state with certainty: man is image of God *in the totality of his being,* and this is because he differs in the totality of his being from everything else, i.e., in particular from the animal world (cp. also the summary in Gn 1:26b and 28b). This essential difference lies in the fact that there is about man something that is characteristically divine, as a result of which he participates in the holiness of the divine sphere.

This quite special and particular status of man as image of God is then made clear by the fact of his dominion over all the animals and over the whole of the rest of the world. Just as the child represents his father, so man, as image of God, is the visible representative of the Lord of all, and so is king of the whole creation.

Background

If it is indeed so that this formula is a personal find of the author of Genesis 1, it is not surprising that it seldom occurs in the rest of the Old Testament. For if it had in fact formed part of the teaching of the prophets, he would of course not have had to have discovered it for himself. Psalm 8:6–9 is proof of the impression that it made. And just as it is generally speaking only in the very latest books of the Old Testament that we begin to find allusions to the creation narrative at all, the only other places where we can detect the influence of this formula are in Sirach 17:1 ff. and Wisdom 2:23. Israel needed a very long period of reflection before it was able to achieve an expression of so delicate and so frequently misunderstood an idea as the image of God in man, such as could be wholly and entirely reconciled with the content of its own faith in God. But the result, once achieved, has all the marks of the most mature and authentic Jahwism. Though it occurs so seldom, quantitatively speaking, it is nevertheless one of the most important and typical ideas of the Old Testament. This is shown by the fact that the New Testament seizes on to it gratefully and uses it to express in words what is the specific dignity of a Christian.

At the same time, the formula lies manifestly in the direct line of descent from the more primitive stages of revelation. One needs only to think of the much earlier narrative of Genesis 2–3. Here, although great emphasis is placed on man's mortality (how could it be otherwise in a narrative whose purpose is to give an explanation not of man's greatness but of his tragic destiny, which is shown precisely as the consequence of his desire to be as Elohim!), there is no less emphasis on the total distinction existing between man and the animal world. This suggests that it must indeed be deliberate that "image of God" seems to emphasize this distinction. This becomes clearer in the light of a text such as the following:

> Jahweh spoke to you out of the fire. You heard then the sound of words, but only a voice, you saw no form . . . Since you saw no form when Jahweh spoke to you from the midst of the fire at Horeb, beware lest you act corruptly by making a graven image for yourselves, under the form of whatever figure: in the form of a man or of a woman, in the form of *any beast that is on the earth,* in the form of *any winged bird that is in the air,* in the form of *any animal that creeps on the ground,* in the form of *any fish that lives in the water under the earth.* Beware, lest you lift up your eyes to heaven, and when you see the sun and the moon and the stars, all the host of heaven, you be led astray to worship and to serve them. For Jahweh your God has left them

111

over to all the people under the heaven: but you he has chosen out, and led you forth out of the iron furnace of Egypt to be his own people, as it is now at this day (Dt 4:12, 15–20; cp. Ex 20:4; Rom 1:23).

Such is the Jahwism from which Genesis 1 was born. We can now see the reason for the precision with which Genesis 1 gives everything its proper place, for Israel is surrounded by heathen peoples for whom these things are utterly and completely muddled up. Polytheism and pantheism go together. One has no need to be a specialist in the literature and sculptured art of the ancient East to be aware of the extent to which, in Mesopotamia and in Egypt, gods, humans, and animals were all mixed up together in the greatest confusion. There are literally hundreds of sacred animals (cp. Wis 12:24), and beings that are half-human, half-animal, and half-god.

Genesis, by contrast, assumes and brings together everything that appears to man as mysterious and that might therefore threaten to capture his religious instinct wholly for itself, and leads it all back to the one supreme mystery of Jahweh. Nature is thoroughly undeified, as someone has very aptly expressed it. Jahwism thereby constitutes an enormous liberation from the otherwise universal spell of polytheism. Just as Jahweh redeemed Israel out of Egypt and made of it His own people, so Genesis 1 liberates man from every kind of subjection to the animal world, in order that he may, as the image of God, depend upon God alone. Thus Israel's conception of God determines also its conception of man: by the fact that the animal world is undeified, man is set definitively above it. This is at the same time Israel's reaction over against the perverse practices of the Canaanites (cf. Lv 18:23 ff.), especially when these are understood as a transgression of the first commandment.

10

Image of Elohim

Is there really something hidden away in man that belongs to the sphere of the divine? The feeling that there is is perhaps almost universal in the human race, but so vague is it that such further explanations as have been attempted by so many of the poets and thinkers through the ages who have wrestled with the mystery of man's being have followed extremely diverse directions.

The originality of Genesis 1, which is at once so profound and so discreet in its formulation of the truth which lies behind this universal awareness, is here (and here above all) nothing less than the originality of Jahwism itself.

The Originality of Jahweh

The ancient East in general sought to explain this undeniably unique situation of man in terms of a relationship of some kind or another with the world of the divine. Jahwism made no attempt to reject this approach, and could indeed, without difficulty, have taken over the terminology in current use elsewhere more or less just as it stood. The real differences are not the external ones. For if it is true that what distinguishes man from everything else that is not man is his relationship with divine reality, then it follows that one's concept of man must necessarily depend upon one's concept of God, and that in consequence an

113

identical or analogous terminology could well be totally diverse in content according to whether it occurred within the context of Israel or outside of it.

The formula, image of God, quite clearly raises directly the question of the concept of God which lies behind it. Here more than ever, therefore, objective scholarship demands a careful and thorough attempt to understand the real significance of this Jahwistic formula.

Man's deepest aspirations are everywhere the same; and it may be stated as a general principle that even when he goes astray in the more immediate selection and determination of the real object of these aspirations, the devil (who then enters on the scene) seems to prefer above everything to imitate God. And we do in fact find that, taking the whole range of the terminology of the Old Testament, there is a certain degree of material correspondence between it and the phraseology of the surrounding polytheistic cultural world. We find too, however, that Jahwism is forever pouring entirely new wine into the old bottles, and that sooner or later, in many cases, these do indeed burst.

There is moreover no reason whatever for supposing that the sacred writer borrowed this formula from elsewhere, but, on the contrary, every indication that it has arisen directly out of a strongly Jahwistic background. This does not mean, however, that it is not a typical enough formula of the ancient East: The author's thought has all the concrete plasticity of his own time, and he makes use of its characteristic vehicles of expression. If he is indeed original, it is unquestionably within an ancient Eastern framework. It is therefore possible, as with a good many other biblical expressions, and with a certain degree of verisimilitude, to give a heathen content to this formula, since all the related nonbiblical expressions are in fact found in heathen documents. To say that man is the *image* of God is a strong anthropomorphism, since it presupposes in God a certain similarity with man. Thus far, then, the formula fits well enough into the background of the anthropomorphic theology of the ancient East. The real difference, however, between the authentic Jahwistic faith and Oriental heathendom does not (in the first place) lie in any difference of terminology, for in both cases the terminology has the same anthropomorphic structure. Everything hangs on the mental perspective in which these anthromorphisms are employed.

In the present case, the vital question is that of the side from which the initiative in the comparison is taken—whether it is man who is dragging God down to his earthly level, or God who elevates man into His own holy sphere of being. The question is whether man understands his likeness to God as a gift, a grace, and a calling to let himself be led by his higher aspirations, or whether he uses it as a kind of religious sanction or license to live his life autonomously in any and every direction that his nature leads him. We may summarize the essential difference between the two things by saying that whereas polytheism thinks of the divine in the image of everything that is human and even subhuman, monotheism on the other hand confesses that man, and man alone, is created in the image of God.

Expressions that are outwardly similar can cover realities that are in fact diametrically opposed, and it is no doubt misleading that in either of these two cases it is possible to speak of a *likeness with God*. But in truth, here as ever, monotheism and polytheism stand over against one another, as historical divine intervention and divine truth over against human fiction and caricature.

A Testimony above Suspicion

To say that there is in man something divine is to say very little indeed if it is said by someone whose whole mentality is polytheistic. It does not even imply that man is in any sense above the lower world of animals and things, for the consequence of polytheism is to reduce the divine to a commonplace, and, in effect, to undeify it. But the same statement, made from a Jahwistic point of view, signifies a very great deal.

When a convinced Jahwist such as the author of Genesis 1 says that man is the image of God, he is indeed saying something unheard-of. He is attempting to express a truly overwhelming mystery, a mystery which for the Israelite is the source of a holy awe of himself and of his fellow man, and which reveals to him that he owes everything that he is and has more to Jahweh than to himself, and that in this life he has a task to fulfill and a responsibility to bear.

There can be no suspecting the authenticity of our author's witness. The mere fact that he should have employed this formula, and perhaps even composed it, proves abundantly to what an extent the divine nearness formed an essential part of his understanding of God. For the stronger his Jahwistic faith (and thus the more transcendent his idea of Jahweh), so much the more does his use of this formula imply the existence of a close and personal bond between God and man. With it, the author is making an irresistible challenge, no longer now to the people in general, but to each Israelite personally, to come as it were in a flash face to face with the holy God of the covenant.

"Covenant" and "image of God" are parallel realities, for both express God's nearness. Just as Jahweh commits Himself to His people Israel, so the Creator commits Himself to the human race. The general principles which we have expounded in Chapter 5 are applicable here: the historical relationship between Jahweh and Israel brought in its wake a full and authentic realization of the nature of the relationship between God and man.

We may now return to the question of how it was possible for the writer, in the very same narrative in which he has so imperishably established the differences of degree in the order of creation, to describe man as the image of God. After making so many careful distinctions, he now seems after all to reintroduce a principle of confusion. And how, above all, is such a description to be reconciled with the famous ban on images? When Jahweh spoke out of the midst of the fire, there was no face or form for Israel to see; every image, of whatever shape or form, is therefore forbidden: In the form of a man or of a woman—so begins the pointedly exhaustive list (Dt 4:15 ff.).

We can see here once again how concerned the sacred writer was to establish the fact of man's special relationship with God. If he had wanted to emphasize one-sidedly the divine transcendence, he would have done better to have said nothing at all about the likeness of man to God. But instead he turns at once to bring out in full measure this other side of the truth. He does it, however, with all due prudence, remaining true, here more than ever, to his character as a cautious theologian.

The formula is indeed a delicate one. The careful studies of Paul Humbert and T. C. Vriezen have, however, contributed much to our understanding of its dimensions and shades. Some of their points may be judged to be less than certainly proved, or even incorrect; but if it may be taken for granted that the only acceptable interpretation of the formula is one which is to be reconciled with Jahwism, then they have at all events quite certainly shown that there are a number of different ways in which it is possible to arrive at such a reconciliation.

Only an Image?

In the epic *Enuma elish,* as soon as Marduk has returned from the chaotic struggle of the gods as the victor and the recognized chief among them all, he begins with the work of creation: First the heavenly ocean, with the blue dome of the firmament beneath it, and then afterward the heavenly spheres. After this there follows a gap of 125 lines, and when our text begins again, he has just come to the creation of man. He is determined on a masterpiece, and he says how he is going to do it: "Blood will I mix and thicken, and bones shall I bring into being; I shall create man, and his task shall be the service of the gods." To this end, one of the gods must die, and who else should this be than the instigator of the rebellious tumult called chaos? So he dies, by having his veins cut open, and from his blood man is created. According to another text, the goddess of birth mingles the flesh and blood of the god who has just been killed with clay; and the result is man.

We give this as a specimen of the way in which these things were understood in the ancient East: The likeness of God in man is based upon a physical blood relationship with the divine sphere. So much so, that sometimes the national god is considered to be the physical ancestor of the whole people, and very frequently he is the ancestor at least of the dynasty through which the divine life-giving power is held to be communicated to the nation.

This background is possibly the explanation why the sacred writer does not call man either a "child of God" or a "son of God," as he very well might have done without departing in the least from the general tendency of his thought (cf. Gn 5:1-3). Such a formula was undoubtedly in existence, ready at hand—but it was colored polytheistically. "Child" definitely signifies an identity of nature as well as participation in the same nature, whereas "image" can also refer to something that is essentially lower in the scale of being. "Image of God" leaves a place for the necessary distinction to be made, while it is at the same time a most effective indication of a particular and unique relationship with God.[1]

---

[1] In the rest of the Old Testament, the idea that the individual man as such is a child of God seems also to be avoided. The relatively few texts which refer to this idea are concerned mostly either with Israel's sonship as the chosen people, with the king as being the anointed one of Jahweh,

The Image of the Likeness

"Image of God" is nevertheless a strong expression—too strong, as we shall see. "Image" (*sèlèm*) is a sculptured or cast (in one case, painted) representation—thus a plastic, visible image. Now for the Oriental, the image and its original are very much more closely bound up together than they are for us; there are many texts in the Bible which go to show that the image of a god was habitually more or less identified with the god himself. Hence Jahwism's fierce reaction in the face of every kind of image-worship, even when directed to the honor of Jahweh. For Jahweh is not made by the hands of men, as are the gods, of wood and of stone, which can neither see nor hear, eat nor smell (Dt 4:28; Is 40:18). It cannot be the meaning of Genesis 1 to say without qualification that man is an image of God.

And indeed the sacred writer does not in fact say that man *is* an image of God. He says: after God's image, which at once diminishes the directness of the affirmation. Some scholars would however support a direct interpretation, i.e., He made man *as* (= in the capacity of) image of God. This is indeed grammatically possible, but it is tempting rather than convincing.

In any case the writer does not just say "after our image," but "after our image, after our likeness." This can be understood either as emphasizing or as diminishing the force of the expression, but it is in any case some kind of qualification.

The Septuagint (LXX), followed by the Vulgate, connects "likeness" with "image" by means of a conjunctive particle

---

and later also with the devout man as being the son or child of God. In other words, the sonship which is attributed in each instance presupposes a previous and special divine election. The New Testament takes up the latter idea and continues to build with it, bringing the image of God terminology together into relation with it, so that the Christian's divine sonship becomes practically indistinguishable from his status as image of God (1 Jn 3:2; Rom 8:29; cp. 1 Cor 15:47–8).

(*kai, et*), thus indicating that each is to be interpreted separately. "Image" (*sèlèm*) and "likeness" (*demuth*) certainly each possess a particular shade of meaning, but since in the original they occur in one case separately, and then again both together (but in the opposite order), the distinction does not here appear to have a great deal of significance.

In the whole group of texts, the LXX employs three different terms (*eikōn, homoiōsis, idea*), and of these only *homoiōsis* is to be found in 1:26. It is no doubt a pure accident that this is so, but the fact has been interpreted as meaning that after man's sin the *eikōn* remained intact but the *homoiōsis* was lost; hence the well-known exegesis according to which the "image" was taken to mean the natural image of God in man, and "likeness" the supernatural image. In the original, however, it is clear that man has remained both *sèlèm* and *demuth* of God even after sin.

When two terms occur together asyndetically (i.e., without a conjunctive particle), it can normally be assumed that the second stands as a further determination of the first. Thus here, the author is speaking not of an image without qualification, but of a particular kind of image, a likeness. *Sèlèm* by itself would be too strong an expression, so that further definition is required, and the particular shade of meaning indicated by *demuth* provides well against any overrealistic (i.e., unduly external and material) interpretation of "image."

Sèlèm elohim was indeed too familiar as an expression for an idol, to be used purely and simply. Some scholars, for this very reason, see this passage as a later stage of some mythological narrative. For them, the author is referring to man's outward form only, and is saying that it was made after the likeness of a graven image. It should be clear enough from the earlier part of this chapter that such a view is untenable, but it is perfectly true that *sèlèm elohim* calls spontaneously to mind the thought of a graven image.

There are, however, two texts in the Psalms (39:7 and 73:20) which show that *sèlèm* by itself can have a different and less dense shade of meaning, with the sense of "*only* an image," i.e., an appearance or a delusion. If this may be taken to indicate that there is already a certain degree of fluidity in the meaning of *sèlèm*, any further mitigating addition to it becomes all the more effective.

Demuth has also sometimes the meaning of a tangible representation, but it is generally agreed that the word is a much vaguer and more general one than *sèlèm*. Its particular shade of meaning is well illustrated in the following passage: "And above the firmament that rested upon their heads, there was something that appeared as a sapphire-stone; it had the likeness [*demuth*] of a throne. And seated above the likeness [*demuth*] of a throne, there was a likeness [*demuth*] as it were of a man. And above what appeared to be his loins I saw as it were gleaming bronze . . . so saw I the likeness [*demuth*] of Jahweh's glory" (Ez 1:26–28).

The sphere of meaning to which *demuth* belongs, and the kind of expressions with which it is synonymous, can be seen even from such a short quotation. The choice of words throughout this passage is dominated by the concern to avoid any inadequate expression of Jahweh's transcendence; and for this purpose *demuth* would appear to be very well suited. It is true that Genesis does not always employ *demuth* with emphasis on this particular aspect of it; but when it is used together with *sèlèm* to form a single expression, the effect of the contrast thus provided is to bring this aspect quite clearly to the fore. Thus in 1:26 the sacred writer states his understanding of the question quite precisely: man is an image of God because of a certain resemblance, he is in this world *as it were* as a representation of God Himself. Later, in referring again to this doctrine, he uses *sèlèm elohim* or *demuth elohim* indifferently, meaning to convey the same idea with either formula.

121

Our Image

In the expression "image of God" there is one shade of meaning—and it is perhaps the most important one—that is lost in the process of translation: for "image of *God*" is a much stronger expression than "image of *Elohim*." "Elohim" and "god" are nouns in Hebrew, which when they are used to refer to the one, true God often take on the significance of proper names (cp. the difference between *god* and *God*). As proper names they are identical, but as a noun *elohim* is broader in meaning than "god." Not only can it mean either "god" or "gods," but it can also have the still more general sense of one or more beings who are not of this world, and especially of beings who belong to the *sphere* of God (angels) or who represent God in some other way (cp. Ps 82:1, 6 about the judges).

The question now, therefore, is that of the content of the word *elohim* in the expression "image of *elohim*" . . . does *elohim* indeed refer here without qualification to God Himself?

The answer would at first sight appear to be in the affirmative, for the word "elohim" occurs about thirty times in Genesis 1, and always as a proper name for the one Creator God. Unless therefore there is some compelling reason to the contrary, we cannot in verse 27b suddenly make an exception in favor of the broader meaning.

Moreover, verse 27a says that "Elohim (proper name) created man after *his* image." The possessive pronoun "his" here refers back to the subject, i.e., God Himself, so that "after his image" must mean "after the image of God." The only weak point about this undeniably "strong" expression is that it stands entirely alone, and it may even be doubted whether it is authentic. It is omitted altogether in the LXX, and in the Hebrew original it breaks up the rhythm of the text and creates an unnecessary doublet. Without it, what we have is a poetical aphorism whose subject is man, and which consists of three lines, each of which has three accents (cp. p. 106). If however we accept "after his image," the first line then has four accents, and the text reads repetitively "after his image, after the image," which could well be due to dittography (double copying). This argument is not absolutely conclusive, for it could also be the case that the shorter text is the result of the reverse copyist's error of haplography (single copying). Thus it is not certain whether it is the Hebrew text that is too long, or the Greek text that is too short. It is also not impossible that the LXX should have omitted such a "strong" expression for theological reasons. This would be in accord with the tendencies of the period from which the LXX dates, and also coincides with its constant usage elsewhere, which is always to interpret *elohim* strictly as a proper name (*ho theos*), except precisely in this formula, which it translates *eikōn theou* (instead of *eikōn tou theou*), i.e., "image of something divine" rather than "image of God."

All things considered, it is safer in this case to preserve the Hebrew text unaltered. But this still does not provide an answer to the real question, that of the meaning of *elohim*. For the expression "after his [i.e., God's] image" is also capable of having an acceptable meaning even when *elohim* is understood in the broader sense. I can describe man as an image of God because of a likeness to some property that belongs strictly to God alone, but I can also call him an image of God because of some more general characteristic, for example, his nature as a spiritual being. Man's likeness, as a being who is composed both of matter and spirit, to purely spiritual beings who belong not to this earth but to the world of divine things, would then be considered a sufficient basis for describing him as an "image of God." In other words, the "strong" expression in v. 27a, which does not occur anywhere else, leaves our real question open. The normal form of the expression elsewhere is: "He [God] created him [man] after the image of *elohim*" (1:27b; 5:1; 9:6). One might think that the obvious way of reading this would be: "He

123

created him after *his* image." This "after his image" would then refer back to the strictly individual "He" (i.e., God). In fact, "after the image of *elohim*" spontaneously suggests that God did not make man after his own image, but after the image of something else, i.e., *elohim*. This is however not conclusive as regards these three passages in Genesis, since each of them also has Elohim to express the active subject (God). Fortunately we also have one text in which Jahweh occurs as the subject.

The literary connection between Genesis 1 and Psalm 8 is certain. And here in the Psalm we find not "Thou hast set him a little below Thyself," but below *elohim*. The Psalmist is addressing not Elohim but Jahweh, so that the meaning is quite definitely: "Jahweh has set man only a little below *elohim*." The meaning of the words Jahweh and *elohim* cannot be identical in this case, for since Jahweh is never anything but a proper name, *elohim* cannot be a proper name in this same text. And in fact the significance of this distinction becomes apparent in the LXX, which gives *below angels* (cp. Heb 1:7). Psalm 8 is thus good evidence that we should understand the same distinction in the text of Genesis.

In short, it is impossible that Israel would ever have dared to speak of man as the image of Jahweh, not only because of the ban on images, but also and above all because Jahweh can never be anything but a proper name, and thus immediately calls to mind the incommunicably transcendent deity, the Holy One of Israel. For the same reason, man could only have been described as image of *elohim* if *elohim* is understood in the broader of its two possible meanings.

Genesis 1, however, invariably uses *elohim* in the strict sense, synonymous with Jahweh; so that in this one case the sacred writer was obliged to find some way or other of indicating that he is going over to the broader meaning of the word. And so we have the much-debated plural form: "let us make man after our image." The "majestic" first person plural does not occur in Hebrew, so we are forced to conclude that God is here represented as taking counsel. To say that He is taking counsel with Himself is not a genuine solution. The truth is that He is taking counsel with the council of the heavenly court (Ps 82:1; 1 K 22:19 ff.; Jb 1). Thus what we are given here is a picture of the Creator turning toward the court of heaven (as in Gn 3:22; 11:7 and in Is 6:8). For an audience of exclusively monotheistic faith a sudden plural occurring in such a manner could only have one possible meaning: the actualization of the broader sense of *elohim,* so that, in our formula, the proper name which would otherwise have been understood becomes dissolved in the generic noun.

Jahwism could never have tolerated an expression such as: "I shall make man after my own image." The expression in the text of the Bible (let *us* make man after *our* image) cannot therefore be simply equivalent in meaning. On the contrary, the effect of the plural is precisely to exclude such a "strict" interpretation. The first person plural "we" works, as it were, infectiously on the latent plural in *elohim,* and turns it, too, even of necessity, into a plural, if indeed man wishes himself to be considered as the image of a "we." For God the Creator is one and unique, but the divine world, the world of the *elohim,* is wide and great. The writer's meaning is that man, in contrast to everything else that God has created, stands in a relationship with this world. Man possesses distinctive *elohim*like characteristics, and hence he also possesses a certain likeness to God Himself, who is Elohim par excellence. Because he is image of *elohim,* he is image of God.

In this way our traditional speculative theology about the *imago Dei* becomes all the easier to situate as a continuation of Genesis. We can see that it does no more than provide a clear and distinct formulation of what for the sacred author is a concrete intuition: that man is image of God in virtue of that which makes him to be a man, i.e., his spiritual nature.[2]

For it is by his spiritual powers that man is mysteriously related to the world whose inhabitants are not bound by the limitations of this material and earthly existence, because they possess a nature that is wholly spiritual. And so man himself manifests, in every aspect of his concrete existence, the primacy of the spirit over matter, and ultimately the primacy of the Creator, who is *the* Spirit, the Great Spirit, over all things.

The desire to formulate biblical teaching with precision can easily lead to one-sidedness. Such is the case with those for whom man's dominion over the animals is not simply a consequence, but is rather the essence of the divine image in man. The same is true of those who would maintain that the sacred writer is referring only to the human body in speaking of the image of God, and, correlatively, of those who would exclude the body. The same must lastly be said of those who seek to limit the meaning of the formula in such a way as to apply it either to a natural or to a supernatural image.

For it is clear that, on the one hand, sin does *not* wipe out the divine image, and on the other hand that grace elevates man's nature also and specifically inasmuch as he is image of God. Genesis 1 is based upon a perception of man as he is (and thus, fallen). But from this starting point it reconstructs a picture of man as he corresponds to the supremely good plan of the Creator.

It is for this reason that the full significance of the formula,

[2] ". . . Homo ad imaginem Dei factus [dicitur], secundum interiorem hominem, . . . ubi est ratio et intellectus: unde etiam habet potestatem piscium maris et volatilium caeli; . . . omnia enim animalia cetera subiecta sunt homini, non propter corpus, sed propter intellectum, quem nos habemus et illa non habent; quamvis etiam corpus nostrum sic fabricatum est, ut indicet nos meliores esse quam bestias, et propterea Deo similes. . . . Ita intelligitur per animum maxime, attestante etiam erecta corporis forma, homo factus ad imaginem et similitudinem Dei" (Augustine, *De Genesi contra Manichaeos* i. 28; P.L. 34, 186f.).

image of God, only becomes apparent in the light of the supernatural sonship of God which was the privilege of the first
man. Here we must also have recourse to the teaching of the
New Testament, and especially that of St. Paul, concerning the
image of God. In such a perspective, Genesis 1 can be seen as
the revelation of the first stage of a mighty plan of salvation,
in which the creation of man, understood as the *incarnatio
imaginis Dei* (Closen) finds its deepest meaning as a prepara-
tion for and prefiguration of the *incarnatio Dei.*

11

Introduction to Genesis 2–3

The Pericope

THE Paradise narrative forms a single and clearly defined pericope, which begins at Gn 2:4b, and continues to include the whole of the second and third chapters. It no doubt constitutes, like the preceding pericope, an independent text. The editor who was responsible for putting the whole of the book Genesis together as a single continuous narrative, has included it in his book just as he found it, with little or no alteration. We may also consider him to be responsible for verse 2:4a, which closes the first pericope with words taken from the pericope itself ("the heavens and the earth," "to create"), and a formula (*èllèh toledôt* = "these are the generations, the destinies") which occurs again nine times in Genesis and which apparently belongs to the structure of the book as such.

The second half of the verse (2:4b) betrays at once the hand of another writer ("earth and heavens," "make," "Jahweh Elohim"). The entire new section of the narrative which begins here continues until the end of Chapter 4, and is then interrupted by Chapter 5, in which we immediately again recognize the style and mentality of Genesis 1, and finally comes back again in a number of further fragments. The author of the book Genesis has thus sought his material from a number of sources, and among these the Paradise narrative belongs to the so-called Jahwistic source (J).

This latter narrative must not only have existed independently of the book Genesis, but it must also have been independent of the Jahwistic narrative itself. Its content alone marks it out as a separate whole, complete in itself, but the main tangible indication is the constant reference to God as Jahweh Elohim. The fact that this striking appellation occurs here so frequently (twenty times) and *only* here (it occurs once in the whole of the rest of the Pentateuch, in Ex 9:30) can only be explained by supposing that the author or editor who shows such a predilection for this name either found the complete narrative as a separate literary entity, or that he himself was responsible for making it so. There is no other possible reason why, in Genesis 4 and the other Jahwistic passages, this name should be so conspicuous by its absence.

Unity of the Pericope

At the time of the first and long-lived enthusiasm in favor of an extremely statically conceived division of the Pentateuch according to the sources (in which, as is well known, the various names used for God played an important part), the name Jahweh Elohim gave rise to the theory that Genesis 2–3 was a compilation, made up of two older narratives, a Jahweh narrative and an Elohim narrative. Two trees occur in the text as we have it; man is formed out of dust from the earth (2:7) and condemned to return again to dust and to earth (3:19); there is a double planting of the garden (2:8 and 9), a double setting of man in the garden (2:8 and 15); there is a condemnation to a nomadic way of life (3:18, 19c) and also to the tilling of the earth (3:17, 19ab, 23); man is twice driven out of the garden (3:23 and 24), and there is a double guard (the cherubs and the flaming sword) placed over it, etc.

It has since been convincingly shown that most of these "doublets" are not doublets at all—that both, in fact, of the

129

two elements of which each is composed is essential. One crucial point that was overlooked in the heat of the chase after double elements is the fact that the Hebrew narrator is extremely given to describing his subject in general to begin with, and then returning to it again in greater detail.

Thus 2:8 should be read as a first and general indication consisting of two distinct points: 1) Jahweh Elohim planted a garden in Eden; 2) there He set man. The sacred writer then proceeds to devote separate consideration to each of these points: 2:19 ff. expands the first of them, and 2:15 ff. the second. There is thus no reason at all for saying (as do the enthusiasts for a double source) that 2:9 and 2:15 are doublets of 2:8, making it necessary in this case to presuppose two authors, or two documents, or a later re-writing of a narrative that in its original form was more compact.

The Lord God

This insistence on a double source was no doubt heavily influenced, consciously or unconsciously, by the composite name, Jahweh Elohim, which was supposed to be an obvious doublet, despite the fact that it then remained unexplained why the name does not occur in this form more often. In any case many pericopes were considered to derive from a combination of a Jahwistic and of an Elohistic source. The correct explanation of this manner of referring to the deity must however be sought in an entirely different direction.

In Genesis 2–3, God is always called Jahweh Elohim (except in the dialogue between the serpent and the woman), twenty times in all. In the rest of the Old Testament this name occurs another twenty-three times, including those cases which are critically doubtful. Of the sixteen cases in which it is certainly authentic, thirteen are in Chronicles and Nehemias, i.e., in the historical chronicles of the Jewish people, and this in passages where there can be no question of a compilation of sources. The conclusion is evident enough: Jahweh Elohim is not a name that has been artificially put together by some author, but one that was actually in use, most probably in certain Jewish circles of the postexilic period. The LXX also provides evidence of this later usage, in that it more than once translates the name of God in the singular by *kurios ho theos*.

Moreover the use of this form of the name of God fits in well with what we know of the Jews' conception of God during the later biblical period. There was a growing tendency among them to emphasize the divine transcendence, and the sacred name of Jahweh came more and more to be thought of as the exclusive expression for this transcendence. This much is clear, for example, from a comparison between the books of Chronicles and Samuel-Kings, in both of which documents the same sources are frequently reproduced literally.

The Chronicler thus habitually alters the name Jahweh in cases where according to his sensibility the divine transcendence is not sufficiently respected, for example where Samuel employs an anthropomorphism, or where Jahweh Himself appears to be too directly involved in earthly affairs. He achieves this by means of a number of devices, of which the following are two of the more important: *1*) He simply replaces Jahweh by Elohim. Elohim lends itself better as an expression of the divine immanence, and at the same time has a more general kind of ring about it. It is a vaguer appellation than Jahweh, and does not recall so strongly His character as the holy God of the covenant, and is thus at the same time more appropriate for use in foreign lands or in a heathen society (the Diaspora).[1] *2*) There are however also some passages in which he appar-

---

[1] The same thing has of course occurred in the course of the history of the text of the Psalms. There are about forty Psalms (42–82) in which the name Jahweh has been changed to Elohim. It is no doubt correct to conclude from this that this Elohistic collection of Psalms must have existed separately from the others.

ently does not wish to allow the traditional Jahweh to disappear. In these he chooses a compromise solution: he leaves Jahweh in the text, but adds Elohim to it, which thus has a neutralizing effect.

We must therefore suppose that the ancient pericope of Genesis 2–3 had a definite (probably cultic) function in the circles out of which the Chronicler's narrative has come. *Jahweh* must originally have stood everywhere in the Paradise-narrative, except of course in 3:5b ("you shall be as elohim"). The holy God of the covenant was thus shown as being intimately involved in human destinies, upon which, moreover, the impure shadows of sin and of the devil were cast. This must have been shocking to the Jewish mentality in this later period, and we can in fact see the self-same method of the Chronicler at work on Gn 2–3: *1*) in the dialogue between the woman and the serpent (3:1b–5) Jahweh is entirely replaced by Elohim; it is more likely that the Chronicler is responsible for this than that the original writer should have had such theological scruples; *2*) in the rest of the narrative, Jahweh has been allowed to stand, but with the addition of the modifying Elohim.

With this explanation, which is by far the most satisfying that has been suggested, and for which in its final form Paul Humbert is responsible, the main "doublet" in Genesis 2–3 disappears for good.

One and Yet Composite

The Paradise narrative forms a clear and indeed powerful unity, and yet from the literary point of view it is by no means smooth, not at all as much of a single piece as Genesis 1, for example. There is a certain unevenness, and there are definite points at which one senses a hiatus, or has the feeling of coming across a seam where the edges of the composition have been drawn together. The sacred writer has in fact not composed his

132

narrative out of nothing. He has, on the contrary, inherited the work of others, and represents in his own person the culmination and the synthesis of a tradition that may well have been a long one. So long as we do not know the history of this tradition—and we shall certainly never know its details—there will always be many points which remain uncertain. But if one starts blind, one is liable to miss even that which *is* clear and certain. This has been the fate of the defenders of the "doublets" theory, of which the chief fault is that it concentrates attention on hypothetical and otherwise unknown older narratives to the virtual exclusion of the actual narrative which lies before us and whose understanding should be our major concern. The point is that the writer whom we have to thank for Genesis 2–3 has indeed got something to say which will reward any attention which we are prepared to give to it. That he went to work with already existing material is most likely, but this is a secondary question, since he most certainly considered this material to be appropriate, or made it to be appropriate, as a means of expressing his own mind. And it is with this that we are concerned in the first place. For this reason the received text of Genesis 2–3 as we have it is the only right starting point for a sound exegesis.

If we then find that the meaning of each detail of our text is not immediately clear, this may well, indeed, be due to the fact that the writer was working with ancient narrative material which was already in existence under one form or another, with the result that he may have considered himself bound to take over certain conceptions or turns of phrase, which he then sought as best he might to incorporate into his new synthesis. From this it follows that some of the details are most likely older than the synthesis itself as we now have it.

If it is indeed the case that each and every part of the narrative did not come into existence at the same time, but has been re-formed and adapted according to his need by the genius of the sacred author, this could well be the reason why no completely

133

conclusive exegesis of Genesis 2–3 has yet been given, and one should therefore not attempt to force one. An all too common mistake is to succumb to the temptation to dispose of inconvenient elements by resorting to correction of the text, etc. Most often, the effect of smoothing away one crease in the narrative is to make a couple more appear somewhere else, but occasionally the result of such efforts is to produce an attractively logical whole; nevertheless, what the Bible itself gives us is always of more value than the best possible modern construction.

It is certainly useful to know that the narrative as we have it has a history behind it. We should need to know the course of this history more exactly than we do in order to be able to give a satisfactory answer to the problems raised by a number of particular material details, but even if we could do this we should most probably not be much wiser as to the real meaning and purport of the narrative. And this is just because it is in its present form far too original in character, too much the obvious product of a single mind, too full of conviction and intellectual power for any such detailed solutions to make any difference. The last word must remain with the sacred author who has given us such a synthesis; it is the completed building that must command our attention, not the individual stones from which it is constructed.

12

The Origin of Genesis 2 ff.

MANY of the books of the Old Testament have come into being as the result of a far more complex process than the average reader of the Bible would dream of suspecting. Many difficulties can arise from the instinctive assumption that each book of the Bible is a single continuous composition—that one or other among the sacred writers simply sat down and began to write, so that in due course, chapter by chapter, a complete book came into being. The reader expects the book as a whole to possess a certain coherence, but instead, all too often, he not only loses the thread of the argument but also comes up against all kinds of apparent contradictions.

The first two chapters of Genesis, when they are compared with each other, provide a classical example of this sort of problem. Attempts at harmonization go back at least as far as the oldest existing translations, but here as so often tinkering about has tended to do more harm than good. The contradictions are there and in fact should far rather be underlined. Only thus will each of the two narratives be able to speak for itself, and (what is even more important) only thus shall we be able to distinguish those elements which are permanent and essential in them from what is more transitory and of merely secondary significance.

Both narratives are deeply rooted in Israel's Jahwistic faith, but beyond this they cannot simply be reduced to a unity—they belong to different periods, they have different authors, and their subjects are likewise not the same. The misunderstanding which can be caused by confusion about this is thus liable to be fundamental. We shall probably find the truth somewhere between the extreme positions of radical source criticism on the one hand, and that which chooses to ignore the existence of this type of problem on the other.

The Documentary Hypothesis

The classical documentary theory, dating from about the year 1900, held in regard to the first six books of the Bible (Hexateuch) that the text which we now possess is the result of a combination or mingling of two or more older documents, which may in turn have been the result of a combination of still older writings. It is now generally recognized that in its original form this theory was the outcome of an approach to the question which was far too academic and theoretical to provide a complete solution, but it has, nevertheless, taught us a great deal. The period of patient and at times penetrating analysis which produced this theory has given us many results that are of permanent value, connected not so much with the many and various theories which were constructed during this time as with the vast amount of literary data which was successfully extracted from the text in its present form.

This evidence brought about a far greater awareness of the stylistic and doctrinal many-sidedness of the Old Testament, as this appears from a more careful and scientific comparison of the different books among themselves. Scholars learned how to determine the literary and religious "type" of a book more accurately, and also how to situate it more accurately in its historical context. But there was also another, and less familiar, fact that began gradually to be apparent at the same time: that not only the Bible as a whole, but also some of the more ancient books considered in themselves bear the traces of many different epochs and generations, in other words that they are the outcome of the literary activity not of any one particular writer or period, but of almost the whole evolution, with its different and variously typical stages, of Israel's spiritual development. And so it gradually became a universally accepted fact that the Pentateuch had undergone a long period of growth in Israel, before it took on the form in which we have it today. One is tempted to ask, how indeed could it have been otherwise? How, for example, could a movement as radical and momentous as that of the prophets have simply left Israel's traditional collections of laws and of narratives untouched? All the more so inasmuch as the deepest inspiration of the great prophets' faith is drawn from beginning to end from the Jahwism of the Mosaic tradition in which it is rooted at every point.

An example of this would be the book of Deuteronomy, which is wholly prophetic in its inspiration, even though it also makes use of ancient material. And we can find these same literary and religious characteristics of Deuteronomy occurring again and again elsewhere in the Bible. The same may be said of the style of Esdras-Nehemias-Chronicles, which is again quite different but equally characteristic. There are, moreover, a number of other books in the Bible which would appear to have taken on their definitive form in the same spiritual climate as these latter works of what may be called chronistic historiography (cp. 2 Mac 2:13–15).

It is no doubt true that source criticism became something of a mania, but it did at least make it possible in many cases for the various differences of mentality and of style, which are in fact often present in one and the same book and even in one and the same narrative, to be brought to light. The fault of the method was simply the presupposition that it was possible to unravel a book completely and, by a process of sorting the various re-

137

sulting strands, to reconstitute the literary sources which the sacred author was presumed to have employed. Thus what was in reality the outcome of a living process of development was too often taken to be that of a mechanical process of redaction.

It is, of course, possible that in a particular case the last editor of one or other of the books of the Bible may indeed have gone to work in such a somewhat unoriginal manner, but, if so, he must have employed narratives, laws, collections of sayings, etc., which were already complete, and such clearly recognizable literary entities are quite a different matter from the "documents" of the source critics.

Thus in the case of the book Genesis, either its last author or one of his predecessors must have put together the biblical creation narrative (Gn 1–11) by a process of arrangement and manipulation of already existing narratives, of which the text must to a great extent already have been fixed. The Paradise narrative, for example, gives the impression of being a clearly defined pericope, which is to some extent distinct from the wider context of the book of Genesis.

The precise form in which these texts did in fact lead this kind of independent existence is sometimes difficult to determine with precision. With regard to Genesis 1, it is extremely probable that the original form in which it was handed down was that of some kind of liturgical hymn. Of Genesis 2, all that can be said with certainty is that the pericope has the character at once of a prophetic exhortation and of the instruction given by a teacher of wisdom.

Not from Written "Documents"

The composite character of Genesis 1–11 is there for all to see. The weakness of the source critics is that they are all too inclined to want to apply their dissecting knives to the individual pericopes as well, in an attempt to reconstruct out of them still

more ancient narratives or parts thereof. In this their fundamental mistake is not the conviction that certain narratives cannot be regarded as wholly coherent and homogeneous in character—setting aside all undue exaggeration, this may certainly
be accepted as regards Genesis 2 ff.—but rather their presupposition that this heterogeneity can only have arisen as the result of
a particular kind of literary activity, to wit the artificial putting
together of more ancient independent narratives. Even if this
may have been the case on occasion elsewhere, it is certainly not
true of Genesis 2 ff.

The only part of this text which may indeed well have been
taken over from a more ancient narrative is the passage about the
river of Paradise (2:10–14). This curious piece of description
gives the impression of being a kind of ancient showpiece, in
favor of which the author, as it were, stands aside for a moment,
to take up the thread of his narrative again in 2:15. It is really
a piece of ancient learning that stands out strangely from the
rest of the story which, even, and above all, in its deliberately
imaginative forms of expression, is wholly directed to the purpose of theological instruction. Our author is a thinker, not a
scholar. He is not really interested in information for its own
sake, and yet at the same time he obviously did not want to leave
this particular passage aside, all the more since it. contributes
considerably to the building up of the desired atmosphere.

This is however precisely an exception which underlines the
basic point that the rest of the narrative has *not* come into being
as the result of borrowings of this kind. It is certainly possible
that in this narrative a number of different traditional strands
have been brought together, and there can indeed be no doubt
that the sacred author employed more ancient material and ideas
in the course of its composition. Some of this material he may
have taken over more or less directly, in other cases he may
have been inspired by what he found to create something better
himself, and in other cases again he may have been provoked to

set out a directly opposed conception to that which he inherited, for polemical reasons. In none of these cases, however, can it be accepted that this process of collection and assimilation and reworking of other material took place in the manner suggested by the documentary hypothesis.

But from Living Sources

How then *are* we to think of it? The first and most important point may be stated as follows: That certain very definite convictions had gradually taken shape in Israel as the outcome of a long series of historical experiences of Jahweh as the living God of His people, and that, in due course, at a certain point in this history, our author came along with his own mature and quite definite personal conviction. He thus gives in his own narrative a synthesis—strongly colored by his own originality—of the content of Israel's Jahwistic faith concerning the subject under consideration.

The second point is this. It is clear that a larger number of heterogeneous ancient conceptions and themes had been circulating in Israel for centuries, and it was doubtless only gradually and with difficulty that Jahwism gained control of these, by a process of excluding some of them, transforming others, and itself creating still more. Finally, our author came on the scene, with his own synthetic and didactic genius, and proceeded to select and combine together all this material into a compelling whole that is entirely subservient to his own deep religious conviction, so that it became the deliberate and authentic expression of the teaching and the facts which he was concerned to communicate.

It is obvious enough that if this is indeed the way in which the Paradise narrative has come into being, there can be no question of trying to unravel it, and that any attempt at reconstructing literary documents from it is doomed from the start to be unfruitful. This judgment is confirmed by the evidence of the extremely diverse results obtained in the various attempts of this kind that have been made, even quite recently, and despite the most strictly methodical and prudent techniques. The story is always the same: rightly or wrongly, a certain number of dualities in the narrative are fastened upon, and from this starting point an attempt is made to distinguish a double thread running through the whole narrative. This is a procedure which can inevitably never succeed without having resort to the introduction of subjective elements such as amendments in the text and other presuppositions, which differ radically from one scholar to the next.

It is true that if the level of inspiration in the narrative as a whole is remarkably homogeneous, there is also a certain unevenness in its composition. Source criticism tends to pay attention only to the latter, while those on the other hand who can think only of the part played by the sacred writer are able to account only for the former truth. There is, however, between these two extremes, an approach which can provide for a recognition of both of these undeniable facts: by affirming that the Paradise narrative has come into being as the result of a living process of evolution in the course of which both the ideas which it contains and the form in which these are expressed have undergone a long and slow process of development, at the end of which the crucial part of the work in regard to both still remained to be done by the actual author of our text, so that it can indeed be said that to a large extent his work was original.

A confrontation of these general principles with the actual text with which we are concerned will help to clarify their meaning.

Having agreed that the narrative is not wholly the work of the sacred author himself, we have answered the question of where he obtained the ideas and expressions which he has used by having recourse not to "documents" but rather to a whole body of traditional narrative material. This material is to a greater

141

or lesser extent (though always incompletely) known to us, in the form of various continuations of these traditions both within Israel and outside of it.

It is unnecessary to suppose, and it is also quite improbable, that these other narratives and traces of narratives which we are able to discover were used by the sacred author in the form in which they are known to us. But they do provide us with an historical and very concrete picture of the kind of fund of conceptions (themes or motifs) which must have formed the common ground in which these narratives and the Paradise narrative together must have originated.

In other words, our method will be to try first to gain some impression of the "parallels," both biblical and nonbiblical, to our Paradise narrative, and in doing so we shall attempt to distinguish between the ideas, the convictions, and the teaching which these stories embody on the one hand, and, on the other hand, the forms of expression in which this content is clothed and which constitute, as it were, the material from which they are composed. We shall not need to repeat the expert work of generations of scholars in the way of comparison, appraisal, and assessment. Indeed we may gladly take their fundamental conclusion as our starting point: that the biblical narrative is wholly unique of its kind, and thus has no parallel *as such*. The most that we shall be able to do is to speak of parallel elements.

Nonbiblical Sources

As regards the variegated and fragmentary nonbiblical material, a global conclusion will suffice. Beyond this, if a particular biblical text seems to call at any point for a comparison to be made, we can then take an example, as has already been done in connection with Genesis 1.

As regards content, the correspondences are few and vague,

and may be attributed more to the fact of the unity of human experience in general than to any direct or indirect form of mutual dependence. Among these are certain general motifs, which are to be found also in Greek and Roman literature and elsewhere, such as the fact that the hero of the narrative seeks to escape from the normal destiny of mortals and fails in his attempt; or the idea that there existed once upon a time an ideally happy state of affairs which as the result of some kind of misfortune or intrigue has been lost or become unattainable.

The situation is different when we come to consider the actual materials out of which the narrative is constructed. Although strict parallels are again few, we may say with Lagrange that as regards the symbolic material, one feels that one is moving, in the Bible as outside of it, in the same circle of symbols.[1]

This goes indeed not only for the symbols, but for all the material ingredients of the narrative, although "parallelism" is really hardly an appropriate term, for the relationship depends far more upon the fact that certain more or less conventional forms of expression were habitually in use in a given society or cultural milieu. The Oriental narrative style is highly concrete and imaginative, and this was something to which everyone was accustomed and knew how to understand. Our author belongs completely to this general background, even if he handles his imaginative material in such a way as to express himself with exceptional independence and even creativeness. Nevertheless, as we have remarked already, "when he is original, he is original within the general framework of his own background in the ancient East." This independence, and the resulting almost com-

[1] After making a global inventory of the relevant material, he remarks: "Tout cela n'est pas très frappant. On ne peut conclure à une dépendance littéraire entre le récit de la Genèse et des récits à nous connus. Cependant si nulle part on ne retrouve une trace de ce qui fait l'esprit du récit de la Genèse,—la félicité perdue par la faute de l'homme,—on se meut, dans le monde sémitique, dans le même cercle de symboles . . ." (*Revue biblique*, [1897], 377).

plete lack of true parallels to the biblical narrative, is the consequence of the wholly unique character of the content to which the writer is giving a form.

When therefore we come elsewhere across such things as a description of "chaos" with a formation of man out of clay, or a tree of life (especially if the figure of a serpent plays some part in the story) with perhaps the cherubim as well, it is indeed an occasion for reflection concerning the historical significance of similar elements in the Genesis narrative. In earlier times, when the Bible was virtually the only source of knowledge about the past available to most people, it was inevitably also treated as a source of other kinds of scientific information, and there were many (though some of the Fathers of the Church form an early exception) who took it for granted that Genesis claimed to be a precise historical account of the origin of things. Then there came the discovery, during the nineteenth century, of the literature of the ancient East, and the spontaneous reaction, in the face of the astonishing new dimensions opened up by this discovery, was to think in terms of strict parallels and literary dependence. These new facts were often taken as a proof, by the rationalistic mentality, that the creation narrative was a mere myth. Orthodoxy, on the other hand, considered them to be a confirmation of the historical exactitude of Genesis, holding that a tradition which had been authentically preserved in the Bible had elsewhere become degenerate, but that the data given in the Bible and those occurring elsewhere must derive ultimately from the same objective and detailed historical facts. The falsity of this construction was, however, soon demonstrated by the evidence itself. Only insignificant elements of the biblical Paradise narrative do, in fact, occur elsewhere, and nowhere is there any hint of the real content of the narrative or of the meaning which the Bible gives to these various elements.

If one is to judge from the material that exists for comparison, there was really no such thing as a genuine Paradise tradition in existence in the ancient East. The sacred author of Genesis 1 did of course share in the general Semitic inheritance concerning the nature of the world, and from this he drew his basic raw material, but a conception of Paradise, which he might have taken as a basis of Genesis 2, formed no part of this. The only places where we do find points of comparison—and these are purely material in nature—prove no more than that in the same general cultural world expressions of a similar nature occur quite frequently.

Israel had new ideas, but no other forms in which to express them than those common to the whole of the ancient East. And so there grew up in Israel traditions in which certain figures and motifs, which in their material structure were identical with popular conceptions and ways of thinking in the ancient East, began as it were to live a specific and characteristically Israelitic life. And then, in due course, the sacred author came along and proceeded to adapt and collate this Israelitic material to form a suitable clothing for his message.

It follows that the relationship between this text and any non-biblical narratives can only be an extremely distant one, consisting in a number of purely external analogies. Such, too, is the unavoidable conclusion imposed by such facts as we possess. With this we may be content, and confine ourselves in the next chapter to the comparative material which the Bible itself offers.

145

13

Biblical Parallels of Genesis 2 ff.

An Example

IN Proverbs 3:18 we read as follows: "She [i.e., wisdom] is a tree of life for those who lay hold of her, and those who hold her fast are to be called blessed." The footnote[1] to the first half of the verse explains it as follows: "She gives immortality to those who possess her." The translator is apparently thinking here of the Tree of Life in Genesis 2, which is indeed a *tree of immortality.* We cannot say for certain whether the poet-author of Proverbs also had this in mind, but in any case this proverb provides an example of what may be called a material point of comparison with Genesis 2 ff., and thus some kind of biblical parallel.

Outside of Genesis, this particular element occurs four times in the Old Testament, all of them in Proverbs and in each case (in contrast to Genesis) without the definite article. Genesis speaks of *the* Tree of Life, possibly even of the tree of *the* Life; Proverbs says simply, a tree of life. This apparently small difference goes together with an important difference in meaning: in Proverbs, there is no mention at all of immortality, but rather of a prosperous, happy life on this earth. This appears also from the other three texts:

[1] In the Dutch Canisius translation [*Translator's note*].

The fruit of righteousness is a tree of life,
  but wrongdoing destroys men's lives (11:30).

Long drawn-out waiting enfeebles the heart,
  but a desire fulfilled is a tree of life (13:12).

Peaceful speech is a tree of life,
  but heated words wound the soul (15:4).

There is thus no reason for supposing that the sacred writer is saying anything different in these texts than he does elsewhere:

They [the commandments of the Wise Teacher] will give you length of days, years of life and abundant welfare (3:2)

It [the fear of the Lord] will bring healing to your body, and refreshment to your bones (3:8).

In Proverbs, the tree of life is similar in its significance and effects to the *fountain* of life:

The mouth of the righteous is a fountain of life,
  the mouth of the wicked conceals violence (10:11).

Wisdom is a fountain of life for whoever possesses it,
  the punishment of fools is: foolishness (16:22; cp. 13:14; 14:26).

In the East (as also sometimes in our own way of speaking) "life" meant a life of happiness. There were for example a number of lifegiving, i.e., beneficial or healing, herbs, trees, fountains, etc.; and these provided an obvious image for the figurative expression of something upon which our *happiness* depends. Thus Israel describes the anointed one of Jahweh (= the king) as "the breath of our life" (Lam 4:20), in the same way that Assyrian princes describe their own regime as a "plant of life." Ezechiel, too, speaks of "trees planted along the water that flows out of the sanctuary, whose fruit will be for food, and their leaves for healing" (47:12). He could have called them "trees of life."

There is no question in these passages of an allusion to Genesis 2 ff. Rather, this general Oriental and Israelitic usage provides

147

us with an insight into the kind of literary world in the context of which the sacred author of Genesis 2 could arrive at the idea of *a definite and particular tree that gives immortality*.[2] For the fulfillment of this theme, we have to wait for St. John, in the Apocalypse, to take up the idea of Genesis and combine it, in his accustomed manner, with the vision of Ezechiel, and then to use this new creation to clothe his description of the heavenly reality which is revealed in the New Testament (Ap 22:1–3; cp. 2:7). This is of course but one example among many that could be given, but it provides us with a starting-point for our argument.

We have already considered, in the previous chapter, the non-biblical material; and we must now concern ourselves with the *biblical* points of comparison which relate to Genesis 2 ff. It would not be possible to attempt to compile a complete list—the above single example should have made this evident enough already—but what we can do is to try to gain some impression of the ideas of this kind that were in circulation *within* Israel during the period before our Paradise narrative came into being. This is inevitably one of the first questions that must be gone into if we are to discover what were the intentions of the sacred writer in Genesis 2 ff.

From a literary and historical point of view, Genesis 2 ff. must be considered as a climax—a product of Israel at its very best and most mature. Notwithstanding its originality, the narrative can only be understood if it is seen as a synthesis of ideas that had taken centuries to develop and mature within Israel, and this both in regard to the content and to the form in which it is expressed. A study of the parallel expressions which are to be found within Israel's own tradition should enable us to free this

[2] The existence of this literary world of ideas does *not* explain the origin of the idea of immortality itself; but it does make it easier to understand how the sacred writer came to express his thought in this particular way, and easier to realize that for him the tree was indeed a *mere* form of expression.

Paradise narrative from its isolation in our minds, and perhaps moreover give us a clue to its meaning. Our object now, in other words, is to discover the relationship between Genesis 2 ff. and the rest of the Old Testament. To begin with, we shall limit ourselves to a general summary of the position, which may be formulated around three facts.

Unity of Spirit with the Rest of the Old Testament

There is one immediate and striking point of correspondence. Genesis 2 ff. is wholly the outcome of Israel's Jahwistic faith in God. This first fact strengthens our conviction that we are indeed concerned here with a genuinely Israelitic piece of work. The very same factor that is so notably and completely lacking in the relationship between Genesis 2 ff. and the nonbiblical material, is present in the highest degree when we come to compare it with the biblical material. This is our first and decisive constatation. The biblical narrative is rooted in Jahwism; whatever apparently similar material can be found elsewhere, is rooted in heathen polytheism.

More precisely, what we have here is Jahwism as it was refined and deepened by the prophetic preaching. If we ignore the form of the narrative, and pay attention only to its inner inspiration, to the religious attitudes and convictions which it serves to express, we might think that we were listening to one of the prophets.

Of course, Genesis 2 possesses an inalienable character of its own, deriving both from its narrative form and from its method of interpreting a present and actual situation in the light of past events. But it also expresses precisely the same *practical and pastoral concern* as, for example, the following prophetic passage in Deuteronomy:

See, I have today set before you life and good, death and evil. If you listen to the commandments of Jahweh your God . . . then you shall

149

live and multiply, and Jahweh your God will bless you . . . But if you turn your heart away, and do not listen, and turn away to worship and to serve strange gods, then I declare to you this day that you shall perish utterly: you shall not live long in the land . . . I call heaven and earth to witness against you this day: I have set before you life and death, blessing and cursing. Therefore choose life, that you may live, you and your descendants, by loving Jahweh your God, and listening to his voice and cleaving to him, for he (or that) is life to you and length of days . . . (30:15–20).

The judgment here made upon sin and its consequences is a familiar one—and it is the same dilemma which the Genesis narrative forces irresistibly upon us. It would be easy enough to compile a long anthology from the writings of the prophets around this theme, but we must content ourselves with a single short text taken from Jeremias: "For my people have committed a double evil: they have forsaken me, the fountain of living waters, and hewed out cisterns for themselves, broken cisterns, that can hold no water" (2:13); or, still shorter: "Know and see, how evil and bitter it is, to forsake Jahweh your God" (2:19b).

When Amos says: "Seek good and not evil, that you may live" (5:14), or "Hate evil and love good" (5:15), he is formulating the same practical conclusion that we are meant to draw from Genesis 2 ff., which was thus certainly not born merely out of an interest in the past as such. The sacred author lets the facts speak for themselves, indeed he uses them as a vehicle for *preaching,* and we shall find that there are many things in the narrative which are to be explained in terms of a reaction against certain ideas or practices which were threatening the purity of Jahwism either in Israel or its surroundings. Without actually being cast in the form of a sermon, the narrative constitutes an eloquent appeal addressed to Israel, and it is the same appeal as that which the prophets make. In this sense at least the Paradise narrative is fully homogeneous with the prophetic preaching.

It will be clear from what follows below, that it was not the

150

prophets who took their inspiration from this narrative, but the other way round: our narrative is itself an outcome of the prophetic judgment on sinful Israel. And this again enables us to set Genesis 2 ff. free from its apparent isolation, for we know a good deal about the things which the prophets were inveighing against. We shall thus not go far wrong in expecting to find similar tendencies in Genesis 2 ff. so that our narrative ceases, as it were, to be something hanging in the air, and we are able to situate it and give it some kind of *Sitz im Leben,* or life setting.

It Is Unique in the Old Testament

Our second fact is opposite and correlative to the first. For if it is true that Genesis 2 ff. is unquestionably firmly rooted in the Old Testament as a whole, it is also true, from another point of view, that it is quite unique. What we are given here is a genuine *narrative,* a highly characteristic one moreover, that would be recognizable among thousands of others. As a narrative, it has a number of highly important facts to communicate, each developing out of the one before in such a way that it is precisely *these* facts, taken together as a series in their mutual interdependence, that make the narrative to be what it is.

The strange thing is that the rest of the Old Testament (with the exception of the very late Book of Wisdom) would seem to be unaware of the existence of this narrative ... there is, at all events, no trace of it to be found. The prophets, for example, do not refer at all to the important facts which it records, even though they would have come in extremely appropriately in support of their message (cf. the preceding section). It is not as if the prophets were unaware of the importance of past events, indeed they are meat and drink to them—the content of their preaching reaches back through David to the cycle of the Exodus and even to Jacob and to Abraham. They break, too, through the framework of national history, and see Israel set among the na-

151

tions of the world, with Jahweh as king over them all. Their vision is thus the same as that of the Genesis narratives—and yet they do not refer to them at all. The New Testament, on the other hand, exploits them gratefully.[3]

Elements in the New Testament

The establishment of these first two facts sets the stage for our third fact to appear in an entirely new light. This third fact is that the Old Testament *does* contain a number of material elements which are to be found in Genesis 2 ff., even if they do not always possess exactly the same significance there. There are, for example, a number of allusions throughout the Old Testament to the double composition of man out of *dust* and *the breath of life*.[4]

Thus we find not only a tree of life, but also the name "Eden," "the garden of Eden," "the trees of Eden," "the garden of Jahweh," "the garden of Elohim," and the figures of the cherubs. We also find elements such as the paradisal fruitfulness and abundance of water, and the idea of a state of peace between man and beast and between the animals among themselves. Lastly,

[3] In following the development of revelation, we are obliged, with regard to some important elements, to make a jump from Genesis 2 ff. to . . . Paul. The jump may appear to be a big one, since it is made from the beginning of the Bible to the end. But *is* it in fact so big? The first narratives in the Bible are indeed concerned with the oldest *events* of all, but they are not necessarily therefore the oldest *narratives*. According to the present state of our knowledge, Genesis 2 ff. may well date from the eighth century, but a considerable time may still have elapsed before it gained its privileged place on the first pages of the Bible and so became generally known and acknowledged. It was bound sooner or later to gain recognition, a fact of which the New Testament itself is proof enough. But this makes the silence of the Old Testament about it all the more remarkable.

[4] These texts are not by any means all necessarily to be taken as allusions to Genesis 2:7. It is much more likely that this verse is to be understood against the background of a common Eastern manner of thinking that was also, as a whole series of texts bears witness, very familiar in Israel too.

there are traces of a narrative in a passage, unfortunately imperfectly preserved, in Ezechiel's song on the fall of Tyre (28:12–19; cp. Is 14:12–15) which recalls Genesis spontaneously to mind, even if closer examination makes it impossible to suppose that there is a direct allusion.

We give here the principal parallel elements; they will be considered in greater detail in connection with the relevant passages of Genesis 2 ff. For the moment, it will be enough to be content with a general conclusion, which will receive its detailed corroboration later.

It is notable that it is the prophets in particular who make use of these elements, especially in their poetic passages. Behind these there must no doubt lie a number of popular conceptions and ideas of which we know little or nothing from any other source. A poetic image has to appeal to the imagination, and to this end even elements which are originally mythological in their origin can be of excellent service.

This suggests—something that we might very well have guessed in any case—that in addition to the authentic literature which was approved by official Jahwism and included in Holy Scripture, there was also a large amount of other narrative material in circulation in Israel. Indeed the prophets themselves remind us, by way of a number of allusions, that Israel also possessed a "profane" literature. The poetry of the Bible does thus contain a number of elements which can serve to bring us into a somewhat indefinite but nonetheless real contact with the living historical context in which the narratives with which we are concerned must have taken form.

In this way, we can, by means of the biblical points of comparison with Genesis 2 ff., gain some idea of the living background and therefore of the historical origins of the Paradise narrative, as far as the actual form in which it is composed is concerned. An examination of this biblical material provides no ground for thinking that Genesis 2 ff. derives from it directly,

153

and less still for the opposite theory. Certain elements which we might be tempted to consider as "reminiscences" of Genesis 2 ff. are in reality simply symptoms of the whole world of ideas which created the literary climate in which both Genesis 2 ff. and the rest of the "parallel" biblical material came to take on the form which it now has.

This conclusion becomes even more inescapable when we consider our second and third facts together. For the fact that the main and essential elements of such an original and characteristic narrative as Genesis 2 ff. are nowhere to be found in the whole of the rest of the Old Testament means that such of its secondary elements as do occur elsewhere cannot be explained as borrowings from it, whatever the nature of the analogical relationship, since as far as we can tell it was simply unknown.

The spirit of the whole narrative is prophetic; from which the right conclusion is not that the prophets were influenced by Genesis 2 ff., but rather that the latter narrative is to be regarded as an outcome of their preaching.

While there is no evidence at all that the prophets were familiar with the narrative itself, it is all the more notable that they do make use of certain of the same elements (though often with a considerably different meaning and purpose), and that at the same time they never refer to any of its more important elements, such as for example Adam in the sense of the first man, or Eve, or the serpent, or the crucially significant Tree of Knowledge.

In short, we may sum up by saying that there is an essential difference, but beyond this also a considerable degree of correspondence, between the biblical and the nonbiblical points of comparison with Genesis 2 ff. In terms of the three facts which have been established above, we may now express this conclusion as follows:

The first fact shows that in the same degree that Genesis 2 ff. is completely homogeneous with the rest of the Old Testament,

154

so also it is completely diverse from the various nonbiblical narratives. It is, however, so the second fact tells us, just as unknown within the Old Testament as outside of it. Nevertheless, according to the third fact, the Paradise narrative does employ material ingredients which are entirely such as we should expect to find from what we know of the world of ideas of the ancient East both from the biblical and from the nonbiblical evidence. The only difference being that with the biblical elements we feel much more at home: for they bring us into contact with the Israelitic milieu in which all the other elements which form the general Oriental background of the narrative take on their specifically Israelitic color and thus also the more direct and specific form which they possessed when they were taken over and employed with great spontaneity by the sacred author of Genesis 2 ff.

14

The Garden of Eden

WHY is it that man, according to Genesis 1, is the last of God's works of creation, while according to Genesis 2 he is the first? How are we to reconcile the account given in Genesis 1 with the fact that in Genesis 2 the birds are formed, *together* with the animals, out of *the ground,* after the first man but before the woman, while the fishes are not mentioned at all? From Genesis 1 we get the impression that the man and the woman were created together, while in Genesis 2 there is a certain difference of place and of time between the creation of the one and of the other. And lastly, in Genesis 1 we are given a detailed account of the creation of the heavens and the earth, while Genesis 2 takes it for granted that Jahweh had already created them; and it does the same, without mentioning them, in regard to the heavenly bodies.

There is, nevertheless, not the least contradiction between the two accounts, for the following three conclusive reasons: *1*) It is quite evident from the structure of Genesis 1 that the sacred author is not concerned to give the objective order of the works of creation, but that he is following a didactic and logical sequence. *2*) Genesis 2 is no more preoccupied with the historical sequence of the works than is Genesis 1. The sacred author simply relates them in the order which best serves the purpose of his narrative, which is to compel the reader's attention and to bring out those elements which he considers to be doctrinally important. 3) In general, it may be said that the subject matter of Genesis 2 is not really the same as that of Genesis 1. Genesis 2 is not in fact a second creation narrative at all. Its purpose is not to relate how all that exists came into being, but rather to give an account of the origin of Paradise and of everything that is destined to have a part in it as described in Genesis 3. In other words, it sets the stage on which the drama of Genesis 3 is to be played out: We are introduced to the principal members of the cast and are provided with the necessary information so that we shall be able to follow the presentation without difficulty.

Not a Creation Narrative

While it is true that we do find a certain amount of material in Genesis 2 that appears to be of a kind that would belong naturally in a creation narrative, in fact the subordination of this material to Genesis 3 means that it cannot be considered as being on the same footing as that contained in Genesis 1. In the account of the creation of man given in Genesis 1, for example, man is unmistakably such as the sacred author knows him to be from experience—and the same goes for everything else. The newly created world, with man in its midst, with which we are presented in Genesis 1 is no more and no less than the familiar world which we know from our experience. Genesis 2, on the other hand, describes everything precisely as it is *not* in our experience; in fact the sacred author has taken deliberate pains to present man and his environment in such a way that they stand out in contrast to what they now really are. This difference derives from the difference of purpose between the two narratives, which have been written with a view to providing an answer to two completely different questions.

Genesis 1 gives an answer to the question of how it came about that things exist at all (*explicat res in quantum sunt simpliciter*).

There was a time when they did not exist; that they now do exist is the result of a divine intervention which we call creation (*productio entis in quantum ens*). It is, therefore, in the fullest sense of the word, a *creation* narrative, since its primary object and purpose is to explain the mere fact that things exist at all.

The problem with which Genesis 2 is urgently concerned is not that of why things exist at all, but of why they exist *thus*. How has it come about that man's status, as it would indeed appear, is that of a wretched mortal in a vale of tears? These two chapters are completely dominated by the *problem of evil:* How is the existence of such a miserable world to be reconciled with God's love and his righteousness? How could He have been responsible for creating such a state of affairs? To this question the sacred author gives the following answer: *1*) Man's original condition, i.e., that in which he was created by God, corresponds fully, and more than fully, with the idea which Israel cannot but have of Jahweh, as the Source of all goodnesss and of all life. *2*) If man has indeed fallen from this original state of happinesss into the condition which experience now shows us to be his, it is because he has, disobediently and thus by his own fault, involved himself with a power which is in enmity with God. *3*) But even this present situation contains the evidence of God's goodness, for it is not in fact so entirely hopeless as it ought to have been according to the degree of man's guilt.

Nowadays, the two sacred authors are often compared to one another as optimist over against pessimist, but this is certainly exaggerated if it is to be understood in the sense of any kind of complete opposition. It would be truer to say that it is the subject matter of the two narratives which itself determines the tone of each, so that there is no reason why this relative optimism and pessimism should be considered as involving any kind of contradiction. The author of Genesis 1 quite deliberately gives his whole attention to God's work of creation, so that for him everything, even in the world as it now is, is very good. In accordance

158

with the purpose of his narrative, he sees everything ontologically, in the structure of its being, in the essential goodness of its objective make-up (*esse et bonum convertuntur*). Man, too, he sees *as* man, in his continuity (which he shares with everything else) with God's original act of creation, which is the complete and final explanation of the problems which the phenomenal world creates for him.

The Object of Genesis 2

The problem with which the author of Genesis 2 ff. is concerned is an entirely different one. The world as we know it is not undividedly good. This is a fact of experience, but how is it to be reconciled with the conviction, which he also shares, that God is the origin of everything that exists? The conclusion to which he comes is that the continuity between the world of experience and the original creation is not complete: there is a break somewhere. He cannot, therefore, see things quite as simply as does the author of Genesis 1, and he introduces a distinction, which he expresses in a perfectly concrete manner. He does this by presenting first of all a picture of an ideal world, which is as it were a logical outcome or deduction from his own faith in Jahweh as He has made Himself known throughout Israel's history, a world, in other words, that fully corresponds to Israel's concept of God. This is the point of the "creation narrative" in Genesis 2. He then proceeds to set along side of this the present reality of our actual world, which he represents in a manner that may perhaps be described as "pessimistic," i.e., as being a deviation from the ideal state of things. The responsibility for this lies not with the Creator, but with man who has disobeyed Him. The world was entirely good, as it was created by God, and it is by man that it has been corrupted. The evil which it contains does not therefore ultimately come from God. The picture

159

which the author gives of man is therefore above all that of a *sinner*.

This is a highly imaginative and concrete way of representing religious truth, and is certainly not intended by the author as a piece of theoretical speculation. His purpose is on the contrary to convey an extremely practical lesson, from which Israel is intended to understand not only how misfortune originally came into this world, but also and especially how it still continues to do so. Unfaithfulness to Jahweh is the source of all evil; faithfulness and obedience to Him is the only way to life and happiness. Perfect and undisturbed happiness, however, must no longer be expected; the chance of that has gone forever.

The point of Chapter 2, therefore, considered in itself, is not (as in Genesis 1) to describe the origin of *our* world. It depicts, quite deliberately, a world that is to a certain degree unreal, for it is a world which is entirely devoid of any kind of evil. We must now take a somewhat closer look at this strange world, leaving aside for the time being the question of to what extent the sacred author makes any distinction between what goes on within Paradise and outside of it.

Man is represented as living in a well-watered place of marvelous fruitfulness, in which no kind of struggle, pain, sickness or sorrow has any part. It is a place of abundance, of peace and harmony between all people and things, from the highest to the lowest. Man has no need there to toil in order to provide for his dependants, nor does he tyrannize over his wife, and she on her part is his life's partner, not slavishly subjected to him but equal to him in honor and dignity, and destined to become the mother of his children without pain. Both of them, like all the animals, use only plants for food, for man and beast, and the animals among themselves live together in peace and mutual trust. In such a setting it does not strike one as incongruous that the cleverest among the animals is able to engage in conversation, and indeed the woman does not appear to be in the least surprised that he does so. This animal is of course the serpent, who had not as yet become the despicable, dust-eating creature, condemned forever to wriggle upon its stomach. Everything was so completely different—thistles and thorns, even, were conspicuous by their absence.

By thus sketching in a few very concrete details, the sacred author succeeds in evoking a whole atmosphere and setting. The solidarity which exists between the whole created world on the one hand, and man on the other, is an authentic biblical idea; for so it is now, so it will be at the end of time, and so it was in the beginning.

Those who are inclined to turn to the Bible as a means of satisfying their own curiosity, and study this first description of the state of things in Paradise as if it were meant to be taken as a body of geographical, biological, and physical information, are doomed to disappointment from the start, for they will inevitably become involved in difficulties that are as classical as they are unnecessary. Whether or not we need to believe that the actual material setting of Paradise was in fact thus, is a question which we shall investigate in the following chapter. But in any case, if we wish to understand things in their correct perspective, we must concentrate our attention on the fact of man's innocence: there was as yet no such thing as sin. Once we have done this, we can see at once that the relationships which are described in the sphere of material things are a reflection or extension of spiritual relationships: Man's relationship with God is one of peace and confidence, for no gulf has as yet arisen between them. As yet, man experiences no sensation of fear in the face of any and every manifestation of the divine initiative, as before a terrible and unknown power, but rather dwells happily in the presence of God. The harmony which exists between man and beast, and, further, throughout the whole material and animal world, is simply a consequence of the harmony existing between God and man. It is only after the entry of sin that the rule becomes: "fear and dread shall reign before you with every animal upon earth" (9:2). And the fact that a like fear of God is now ingrained in man himself is also a consequence of sin (3:10; 4:14).

The self-same harmony prevailed within man's own composite being: although man and woman did not as yet wear any clothes (the climate, too, was paradisal!), they had no feeling of shame about this in regard to each other. And lastly, although man's physical constitution is not represented as being in any way different from our own experience of it, he was nevertheless not condemned to die. Whatever our judgment may be concerning this description of Paradise, there can be no doubt that the main point of the story lies in this last-mentioned group of phenomena.

Did the Garden Really Exist?

The prophets, when they are trying to depict the blessedness of the messianic time, have recourse spontaneously to the same constituents of the paradisal setting: For when that time comes, the original peace and fruitfulness of Paradise will once more reign supreme. The theme of fruitfulness occurs repeatedly, and to a large extent derives directly from the already strong expressions of the Pentateuch (Is 30:23–26; 32:15; 35:1 ff.; Jer 31:12; Ez 34:26 ff.; Amos 9:13; Jl 2:24; Za 8:12). Only once in these texts is Paradise actually mentioned: "For Jahweh has pity on Sion, compassion on all her ruins: He will turn her wilderness into an Eden, her desert into Jahweh's garden" (Is 51:3). "When I have cleansed you from all your iniquities . . . then shall they cry out: this desolate land has become a garden of Eden" (Ez 36:33–35; cp. 31:7–9; Jl 2:3; Gn 13:10).

An even more characteristic theme is that of *peace*. The oppositions between North and South, between Israel and the Gentiles, between the Gentiles among themselves, among men in general and between man and beast—these will be no more when sin has disappeared from the face of the earth, and there is only righteousness and the knowledge of Jahweh.

Then shall the wolf dwell with the lamb, and the leopard shall lie down with the kid; the calf and the lion shall graze together, and a child shall lead them. The cow and the she-bear shall live together, their young shall lie down together, and the lion shall eat hay like the ox. The sucking child shall play by the adder's hole, and the weaned child shall put its hand in the nest of the snake. Then shall no sin or evil be done any more, on all my holy mountain; for the land shall be full of the knowledge of Jahweh, as the waters cover the bed of the sea (Is 11:6–9).

Instead of thorns, cypresses will grow up, and instead of thistles, the myrtle (Is 55:13). If anyone dies at the age of a hundred, he will be said to have died young, for the length of a man's life will be like that of the trees (Is 65:17–26; cp. 2:4; 19:23–25; Hos 2:20; Za 9:10).

This kind of language is of course poetic and imaginative. The prophets are not concerned to give information concerning the precise biological nature of the animals and plants in the future world. The truth which they have to communicate is on a completely different level, and has to do with man's religious and spiritual renewal. And in order to express this truth in a language that is both comprehensible and compelling, they have recourse to a poetic style of speech which is deliberately evocative rather than precise. In so doing they are, it would seem, dwelling on a theme which was popular and more or less conventional, since it recurs regularly in their writings in a more or less stereotyped fashion.

These texts were at one time considered to be allusions to Genesis, in the sense that what had once been an actual, physical reality in the state of Paradise is transformed into a symbol of primarily spiritual realities. We have already indicated in the previous chapter, however, that this view is no longer tenable. These texts are not reminiscences of Genesis, but are much more probably a purely parallel phenomenon: The prophets bear witness to the ideas which were current among the people of their own time. The same popular conceptions, therefore, form the background of Genesis 2 as of the prophetic texts. The conclusion must be that we should not seek to find much more in the story of the garden of Eden than a graphic pictorial representation, which the sacred author uses as a means of saying something that lies beyond the actual literal meaning of the words. His purpose is thus not to offer us a description of the *physical differences* between the material and animal world that we know and the world that preceded it. He is indeed not thinking at all of a chronological succession of one of these worlds after the other. And he does not speak of this ideal world as if it were a fact in the physical and historical order. As Dubarle has put it, his intention with regard to the whole paradisal setting as he describes it is not to make a *jugement de fait,* but rather a *jugement de valeur.*

The difference between the state of sin and the state of innocence is metaphysical, and indeed first and foremost of a spiritual order. The sacred author's purpose is to pronounce a judgment of value concerning these two states, and thus to characterize the revolution which has been brought about by sin in the relationship between God and man. It is this that forms the center point of his inspired and warranted affirmation. He makes this affirmation, however, not in the form of an abstract judgment, but by telling a story, a story which does indeed relate facts, but facts of which the true value and meaning have been transposed into a chronological and material dimension.

False Problem

The world of Paradise as it is described in Genesis, if it is taken literally and then analyzed in the light of modern secular scientific knowledge, poses an insoluble problem. And it is a

164

false problem, for this world neither has ever existed, or could ever have existed. Physical evil is a constitutive element of the material world, based essentially as it is on the *struggle for life;* in other words on the tension and balance between opposed and mutually devouring forces.

If we look at it carefully, the world of Paradise is nothing more or less than the actual world of the sacred author's experience, from which he has by a mental process simply removed all the unpleasant elements. Evil may logically, but not really, be dissociated from the universe that we know. Such a thing would be possible only in a heaven and an earth which were indeed new, in which everything material had been transformed and spiritualized.

Paradise, as it is materially described in the Bible, has therefore never actually existed as an historical reality. In presenting his account of it, the sacred author's purpose is not to teach us about what the world was physically like before the Fall, nor is it to present us with a slice of the history of the material world which chronologically preceded the world which we now know.

The idea that the physical evil which we encounter everywhere in the material world ought to be seen as the consequence of moral evil is a profound one, and of great and permanent value. And there was a time when there was no such thing as moral evil. This is the point which the sacred author is concerned above all to make clear. But the question then arises whether there was indeed ever a time when physical evil did not exist. . . .

The answer lies in the unity of God's plan of creation and redemption. The world which God created was one in which His whole plan of salvation was already as it were called in question; we must therefore say that *He conceived the whole in such a way that the sin of His free creation was already taken account of.*

But the sacred author, whose concern is to express the spiritual revolution brought about by sin in such a way that it can be un-

165

derstood, surrounds man in his sinless state with a material environment that corresponds to the divine plan such as it might have been if sin had never broken into it. In reality, however, it would never be possible to construct a description of such a sinless world on the basis of the categories which we possess by our own powers of observation. And indeed the sacred author has not really attempted any such thing. What he has done is to apply our existing categories in a wholly artificial manner, by as it were sifting out the evil elements from the world which we know, so that what remains is something which could never have existed, i.e., Paradise if we understand it literally. But behind this procedure there lies a vision and an affirmation about a spiritual situation, and about events which have indeed taken place in the sphere of the relationship between man and God.

We have shown in Chapter 4 that chaos precedes the work of creation not chronologically but logically—the author begins with chaos which is *the counterpart of the completed and co-ordinated world of experience,* a logical starting point of which the effect is to make the implications of God's creative activity more apparent.

Here we have a similar kind of device. In order that the narrative may more clearly demonstrate the effects of sin, we are given a description of paradise which is a *counterpart of the actual world,* the solidarity of which with man in his own state of moral corruption the sacred author saw so clearly. This is the sense in which he is "pessimistic." By starting with a Paradise which is plainly artificially constructed out of the good elements of our own world, the narrative brings it home how the present corruption of everything is due to sin, which is thus the ultimate explanation of all that is wrong with the actual state of things. The clear implication is that it is to sin that we must attribute the presence of those elements which, in the narrative, have been artificially abstracted from the world that we know.

The story is one which has always stimulated people's curiosity. But to approach it in this frame of mind is to start off on completely the wrong foot, for the sacred author has more important things to tell us. He is above all making an appeal to our conscience. Man must become aware of the things that make for his peace. The point of the narrative about Paradise is simply to illustrate what has happened in the relationship between man and God, and what, as a consequence of this, is still happening today.

It must be emphasized once more that the interpretation of Paradise which we have given up to now is concerned with the setting of the narrative only, and not with its essential content. But it may be noted here already that, in contrast to what we have said about the setting, man himself, in the narrative, has on the contrary nothing unreal about him at all, indeed he stands out from his paradisal setting on that account.[1] For the sacred author, man, as he is in Paradise, is true to life, composed out of the joint principles of spirit and of matter, and therefore of necessity mortal. But he is, spiritually, in a state of innocence, and this is projected on to his material surroundings, and also appears in a number of secondary elements of the description of man himself, such as his food and his lack of clothing. It would seem likely that this manner of describing man belongs to the heart of what the sacred author wishes to say, for with it we come immediately on to the ground of religion. We need therefore to give particular attention to his teaching about man.

[1] The tendency to make Adam into a kind of superman, according to which man in Paradise possessed a physical and psychological constitution which corresponded to his paradisal environment (understood in a material and realistic sense) belongs entirely to postbiblical fantasy. Certain theological speculations, too, have perhaps not been entirely free from this tendency.

15

The Garden of Eden Once More

The Garden and the Rest of the Earth

THE Prologue of the Paradise narrative states that *on earth* nothing grew as yet, for Jahweh Elohim had not as yet caused it to rain, and there were as yet no men to till the cultivable part of the earth (*adamàh*). This does indeed seem to be a preamble to a genuine creation narrative: What as yet does not exist, it seems to say, is now about to be brought into being. The fact that it is with the earth as a whole that the passage is concerned would seem to fit in with this supposition. The writer, however, does not continue by relating how the earth became covered with plants and inhabited by animals of various kinds. It is in the garden (*gan*) that he puts both the vegetation and (with even more emphasis) the creation of the animals and birds, so that it is well furnished in contrast to the emptiness of the rest of the earth.

This exceptional fruitfulness of the garden is due to the Tigris and the Euphrates and to the two other great rivers, all of which are rivers of Paradise but at the same time are identical with the four great rivers which were known to the ancient world. The teaching about the difference between man and the animals (2:19 ff.), and about the relationship between man and woman (2:18–24) also really belongs more to the general creation theme than to the special theme of Paradise, since it is

168

concerned with fundamental and permanent relationships which are independent of the particular situation of Paradise.

There is thus undeniably a certain ambiguity about the way in which the narrative develops. It is possible that the sacred author has not fully succeeded in adapting the already existing material which he employed to the exigencies of his own particular purpose. The nature of the Prologue, in any case, strongly suggests some kind of dependence of this kind on a well-known motif.

We may also perhaps be tempted to find traces of a similar uncertainty in the way in which the conclusion of the narrative is presented. According to 3:23 ff., man's punishment consists in his being driven back to the *adamàh* from which he had been taken by God to be placed in the garden (2:15). Henceforth he is condemned to till the *adamàh* which lies outside Paradise. This *adamàh* had never possessed paradisal characteristics, and had therefore always been difficult to cultivate. And yet we read in the judgment of 3:17–19 that a curse has henceforth been laid upon the *adamàh*, in consequence of which it will begin to bring forth thistles and thorns. If we are meant to conclude from this that before the appearance of sin *all the adamàh* was paradisal in nature, this would really render the whole image of the garden superfluous.

We have said in Chapter 12 that it is possible that in this narrative a number of different strands of tradition have been brought together. Any reconstruction of literary origins would seem to be impossible here, and in any case would be outside the scope of this book; but the above-mentioned evidence should be sufficient to suggest how it was that *a single doctrinal theme* could have been living and present in Israel in a number of different narrative forms. It is clear at all events that this doctrinal theme included the same three points which still form the heart of the story as we now have it: *1)* Man is created in a state of *privilege*, but *2)* he *sinned*, and *3)* as a penalty for this sin he has lost his privileged situation and come to be in that in which he now finds himself, as we know it by experience.

The unevenness of our present text may be explained by supposing that this basic theme, during the process by which it was handed down in Israel, tended to find concrete form in two different directions:

A. 1) The original *adamàh* was in a state of blessed fruitfulness; from it God formed man, the plants and the animals; 2) man sinned, for example, by eating the forbidden fruit; 3) his punishment: from then on the *adamàh* was under a curse (3:17–21).

B. 1) Man was created upon and from the ordinary *adamàh;* his privileged state consisted in that he was *afterwards*[1] transferred into the garden of Eden (2:7, 15); 2) but when he is there, he sins, e.g., by eating the forbidden fruit; 3) he is punished by being obliged to return to the ordinary *adamàh* (2:22–24).

This suggestion is simply meant to serve as a reference point, and is offered by way of clarification of our three introductory chapters on Genesis 2–3 (pp. 128 ff.). But perhaps it may also serve to throw a certain amount of light on the relative character of the material "framework" of the narrative. It brings home, surely, that the sacred author was not particularly preoccupied with the objective details of the story, but adapts them to serve the demands of the particular doctrinal point that he is trying to bring out. If it is indeed the case that he has combined two different narrative traditions, then we must say that he has taken the image of the garden and has made this the basis of

[1] This is a good example of what we have called "projection on to the chronological dimension." For it is generally accepted that man was created in a state of original righteousness, and yet the sacred author *first* describes him as he is constituted *naturally,* and only then, with the transference into the garden, does he go on to give symbolic expression to his supernatural state of privilege. By means of this procedure he is, in his own way, distinguishing in man between nature and grace; and he explains the relationship between them by describing what is in reality *natura prius* as if it were *tempore prius.*

170

his own narrative, but that he has worked this out in so independent a fashion that he saw no problem in making use of such elements of the other tradition as he found useful.

The image of the garden enabled him to give to his teaching about man's original state of privilege the desired degree of emphasis, but he was also concerned to show that *the whole created world* is in a position of solidarity with man. Thus on the one hand he avoids saying that the earth was given a special blessing, as this would have taken away the doctrinal point of the transference of man into the garden; and yet on the other hand he does say that after man's sin the curse of God did indeed come down upon the whole earth. This material may, if desired, be reconciled by saying that the curse consisted precisely in the fact of the naturally unprivileged state of the ordinary *adamàh,* which is obliged from now on to remember painfully all that it has lost since the days of Paradise. But the letter of the narrative would rather seem to suggest a positive deterioration of the ordinary *adamàh* as a result of sin.

Was the Material World Ever Any Different?

The narrative, at all events, puts the first man down in surroundings in which nature behaves quite otherwise than it does at present. Is there, we may be inclined to ask, any objective foundation for all this? Is it or is it not in this passage the purpose of Scripture to give teaching about particular stages of the history of the material world?

The earth existed, of course, for a very long time before any kind of life was possible on it, and for a still longer time before man appeared on the scene. The earth is several billion years old, whereas man dates from around the last million. Translated into terms of a smaller scale of reckoning, if we suppose that the earth has now existed for a whole year, then man does not appear before New Year's Eve! And it is scarcely credible that at this

171

moment, that of man's appearance, a whole new set of natural laws began to operate. We know, largely as the result of the study of the earth's crust, what the main outlines of the evolution of the material world have been; and it is a fact that even the most sophisticated techniques of astronomy, geology, biology, and chemistry have been unable to reveal the slightest trace of a divine curse thus affecting the earth at the very end of its evolution.

Whatever the earth was like before the Fall, it lies completely outside the domain of Revelation to provide us with information concerning its material structure such as we should not otherwise have possessed. We are therefore not justified in attempting to draw any conclusion whatever of this kind from the texts, for their teaching is on an entirely different plane, even if it is formulated in terms of the conceptions of that time concerning the material world.

It is likewise out of the question that the sacred author was drawing on human recollections of Paradise, derived in some way from information originally handed down by the first human couple themselves. One is free to think as one likes about these things, provided that it is firmly accepted from the start that no sane principle for the interpretation of the texts is to be sought in this direction. We cannot therefore assume that the sacred author had more to go on, as regards the material aspect of his story, than the current ideas of the time, worked on by his own obviously fertile (but at the same time thoroughly controlled) imagination. This is, moreover, clear enough from the narrative itself: the garden of Eden is nothing more or less than an artificial adaptation of the world as we know it to the requirements of the innocent and privileged condition of the first man, and it is indeed an extremely appropriate way of illustrating this condition and of making it real for simple people.

It is also clear, from a number of prophetic texts, that such a way of presenting things was deliberately chosen, as a more or less traditional and conventional method. Even Genesis 1 provides us with a discreet hint that this is the case (29 ff.; cp. 9:3). This interpretation is not therefore something that we have simply invented as a means of getting out of a particular difficulty.

This denial that the narrative means to provide us with concrete particulars concerning the nature of the material world before man first sinned does not however mean that, according to the Bible, the state of the world then was exactly the same as it is now. If it is true that the garden of Eden is really a description of a state of *man's* existence, the question remains open whether or not there was also a corresponding state of affairs in *man's surroundings,* even if this was, at all events, different from that which is literally described in the narrative. To put it in another way, we may still ask whether the garden of Eden, in addition to being a symbol of man's privileged condition, may not also be understood as a symbol of a corresponding state of man's material surroundings.

Faced with this question, the most justifiable attitude would seem to be one of *docta ignorantia.* But if our agnosticism in this matter is indeed to be learned, we can hardly leave the question without some short consideration of the arguments for and against accepting this additional symbolism.

For: Solidarity

The explanation which would understand Paradise as a symbol only of a real condition of man himself (whether spiritual only, or both spiritual and bodily) is no doubt attractive because of its clear-cut simplicity, but it may be asked whether it holds sufficient account of the extent to which Holy Scripture considers, and constantly depicts, human and earthly realities—and the spiritual and material dimensions of existence in general—as a concrete whole. It is precisely those prophetic texts which indi-

173

cate a symbolic understanding of Paradise which calls for a certain reserve in this respect.

There are of course those who would support a *purely spiritual* interpretation. But anyone who is really familiar with the texts which describe the blessings of the future messianic time can scarcely avoid the impression that there is nevertheless a material and earthly aspect which has its own part to play. It is true that a number of these texts refer also to Israel's return from exile, and to a still more complete earthly restoration of the community's fortunes after this return has been accomplished; and there are some who consider that the earthly elements in the prophetic vision of the future are sufficiently explained in the light of this. In and through the first and most immediate object of his prophecy, the prophet is thus understood to be referring to a second, and wholly spiritual, redemption which is to be fulfilled in the period of the New Testament. Such a solution is not, however, particularly convincing, since, normally speaking, these texts should not be applied partly to Israel's earthly restoration and partly to the New Testament, but rather are concerned wholly and entirely with both together.

Others again are prepared to agree that the prophets are indeed referring to good things in the material order, but say that these are only promised conditionally: on condition, that is, that the present (or some future) generation of Israel remains obedient to the laws of God. One thinks immediately in this connection of the earthly well-being that was promised, also conditionally, to Israel in the Covenant on Sinaï. This explanation is however also not a satisfactory one, since the prophets' promises of well-being occur most often together with their prediction that the messianic people *will* remain faithful to Jahweh's law, and that they will be pure of sin and will practice righteousness. In a word, Scripture does take into account the possibility that the Covenant of Sinaï will miscarry, but it does not in any way provide for a miscarriage of the New Covenant.

174

There would seem to be a tendency here to want to prove from the prophecies something which, as we can see from their fulfillment, is by no means entirely true, i.e., that the redemption which the New Testament brings is purely spiritual in nature. For redemption, in the Bible, does not consist merely in the purification and the salvation of souls. The prophetic vision embraces the whole of the work of redemption up to and including its consummation: *it is the whole man who will be redeemed from sin and from its consequences, and the world around him, that was cursed because of his sin, will also in its own way share in the total and final redemption and renewal of man.* It would certainly be strange, if the prophetic vision of the Kingdom of God were to be more spiritual than that of the New Testament itself. The earthly, bodily, and material aspect of things has a real part to play in the Kingdom of God, so that when we find the prophets putting a certain relative degree of emphasis on the earthly blessings of the messianic time, there is no cause for making a special problem of the fact.

To suggest that what the prophets have in mind is a well-being only in the national, political, and economic sphere would be to react far too radically over against the previous, excessively literal, interpretation of these texts. For their terminology is taken from the Sinaitic promises of well-being, from Israel's golden age in the time of the monarchy, and from a body of popular conceptions concerning a hoped-for future paradisal epoch—all of which is so stereotyped and conventional in form that it cannot possibly be meant to be taken literally. There is a patent and conscious impotence about this language, a groping effort to approach and to describe a new reality that is beyond all proportion to anything that could previously have been envisaged, and which can, therefore, only be hinted at by employing these ancient and familiar descriptive categories.

The prophetic theme of earthly well-being is thus a symbol of

175

the future good things, not only as regards their spiritual content but also of this content in its repercussions on the earthly and material sphere.

This kind of interpretation is entirely in accord with the particular genius of Semitic thought, which is *total* in its approach and possesses little power of abstraction: Things are seen in their unity and in their mutual dependence upon each other; and, in consequence, it is always difficult to distinguish one particular element in something that is experienced as a dynamic and living whole, and consider it in isolation, on its own. The Hebrew Old Testament has, for example, no single word that exactly corresponds with our Western concept of the soul; and there is therefore no point in asking whether or not the Old Testament teaches that the soul survives death. For the Old Testament, it is the whole man who dies, and who then continues to exist in a sort of shadow world below. When, later on, clearer ideas about the hereafter begin to break through, it is on the idea of the resurrection of the whole man that attention is centered first of all.

In the same way, Israel instinctively sees man in his solidarity with the earth from which he has been taken, and with the whole material world to which he is so obviously closely related. But this material world lies under the curse of man's sin; and the redemption of man brings with it, in addition to spiritual purification, not only the resurrection of the body but ultimately also a re-creation of the whole cosmos.

It is therefore difficult to believe that our author, in taking for granted the solidarity of sinless man with the world which he inhabited, should have thus pictured it so very differently from its present state simply and solely with the purpose of underlining man's own privileged condition. He must certainly have believed that man's material surroundings must in some way have been in harmony with his own state of innocence, even if he knew nothing at all about the manner of it, so that in his

176

own description he has recourse, of necessity, to purely conventional imagery.

Against: Semitic Thought-Forms

The question with which we are concerned is still that of whether or not the Garden of Eden is a symbol of a different kind of material world, which corresponded in some way to man's state of primeval innocence. In our attempt to elucidate the arguments in favor of a positive answer to this question, we concluded that the sacred author most probably did have such a different material world in mind. It may however be objected quite legitimately that the crucial question is not what the sacred author himself had precisely in mind (he had many ideas in mind which we are certainly not obliged on this account to take over ourselves); but rather whether or not what the sacred author did in fact have in mind forms part of the essential message of the Bible. We are not proposing here simply to cast aside the general biblical idea that the lower creation stands in a relationship of solidarity with man. But the crucial question is whether this concept of solidarity, insofar as it includes an element of positive teaching, refers essentially and necessarily to the physical aspect of things, or whether it should not rather be regarded as forming part and parcel of a whole mass of conceptions which, together, constitute what may be called the Semitic background of the Bible, and which, in the last resort, must be regarded as the vehicle and not the content of the Bible's unique witness. . . . We are undoubtedly safe enough in presupposing such a Semitic element in the question under discussion. It may be recalled, for example, that Israel has a tendency to lay the emphasis one-sidedly on the group at the expense of the idea of personal responsibility. Or we may think of the complex system of laws concerning ritual cleanliness, in which there is unquestionably (especially at the beginning) a considerable

177

element of adaptation to popular ideas, according to which sin causes a defilement that is virtually physical. We feel no kind of obligation to kill a horse which has accidentally trampled a child to death—but for Genesis, God says, "For I will surely avenge your lifeblood, of every *beast* will I require it, as well as of men" (9:5); and the Law even goes into the details of how this is to be applied (Ex 21:28 ff.; Lv 20:15 ff.). To our sensibility, such a conception of solidarity is definitely peculiar—there is something of value in it, but also something that is undeniably primitive. We find the same thing recurring throughout the whole narrative of the Flood (6:7,12,17; 7:21–23; 9:10 etc.). If we succumb to the temptation to take all this too literally, we shall very soon find ourselves in questionable company, such as that of apocryphal exegesis for example: "And violence increased on the earth, and the walk of all flesh was corrupted, from man to the cattle and the animals and the birds and everything that moves upon earth. They all corrupted their walk and their manners and began to devour each other, and violence increased upon the earth" (Book of Jubilees, 5:2).

The above is only a hasty summary, based upon general data only. But such indications as we have all tend in the same direction: to bring home that it is a peculiar characteristic of the Semitic way of thinking to extend the implications of human and religious relationships into the subhuman and material sphere. The wisest line to take will thus perhaps be to leave the general question, with which this chapter has been concerned, open, and to take the biblical material for what it is in any case: *a religious doctrine.* When man himself changes, and by sin or by grace comes to stand in a different relationship to the material world, this may be expressed by saying that the material world itself begins to behave differently toward man. For since man, inasmuch as he comes to be in a different kind of relationship with God, comes to see material things also with different eyes, the Semitic narrator expresses this by representing the things themselves as being different, and thus depicts an essentially religious situation in an imaginative and concrete way.

The exegete cannot give a final yes or no to the question whether or not the world *was* really different. Nor can the specialist in natural science offer any data to go on here. The most that the exegete can say is that the texts do not oblige us to accept it as a fact that the world was different.

In regard to the question of cosmic redemption, it would seem for the moment not to be overbold to draw certain conclusions as to Paradise from what we are told about the fulfillment at the end of time. But it will be better to consider this when we have investigated the question of the teaching of the Bible about what will in fact happen to the cosmos at the end of time.

16

"As Clay in My Hand"

The "Chaos" of Genesis 2

IN Egypt and Mesopotamia, the place of the line of division between the fertile land and the desert depends on the extension of the flood banks of the great rivers. From very ancient times there existed in these regions an extensive system of canals, which made it possible, by means of artificial irrigation, for as great an area as possible to benefit from the annual overflow. In Canaan, however, it was different. The level of the Jordan was a matter of small interest to the Palestinian peasant-farmer, and he was constantly aware of his direct and absolute dependence on the rain. It is for this reason that we may legitimately speak of the *typically Palestinian* color of the Prologue to the Paradise narrative, even if there is also a clearly recognizable and authentic ancient Eastern cosmogony motif behind it as well.

The conception which lies behind this "description of chaos" is notably different from the *tóhu-wa-bóhu* of Genesis 1. Fr. Lambert, S.J., in an important article written a few years ago,[1] has contrasted these two cosmogonies as "wet" and "dry." He describes Genesis 1 as a *cosmogonie aquatique*: in the beginning the earth is submerged in the primeval sea, and the water appears as a great, primeval, hostile force which the Creator subdues and bends to His will. In the *cosmogonie sèche* of Genesis 2, on the

[1] *Nouvelle revue théologique* (1951), 225–243.

other hand, water comes in as something that is lacking, and is therefore considered as a friendly element. The background of this cosmogony, however, is not desert or steppe, but rather the dried-up and parched Palestinian earth, as it is at the end of the hot season, before the rains come.

There were still no wild plants growing (literally: "bushes of the field")—this may mean that all spontaneous vegetation was lacking—nor any green herb, which most probably refers to plants suitable for consumption, such as the earth can bring forth when it is cultivated. There were two reasons behind this state of affairs: "The Lord God had not yet caused it to rain on the earth, and there was no man (*adam*) to till the ground (*adamàh*)"[2] The listing of everything that was not yet there serves to underline the effectiveness of God's intervention; for the sacred author then goes on to relate how everything which was thus lacking was provided for. Such a beginning corresponds perfectly with the natural structure of human thought and imagination, and there is no need to seek behind it for some other kind of objectivity.

If the earth was unproductive, it was for the simple reason that the normal conditions of its productivity (the rain and the farmer) were lacking. These are provided for, in the first instance, in an abnormal and miraculous fashion—at the time of the creation, the mechanics of the natural world are set going by factors that are unique and *sui generis*. Thereafter, the normal factors which function according to the ordinary laws of nature, which have now been established once and for all, can take over.

Thus in the absence of the heavenly waters, their task is taken over by the waters beneath: "a flood [?] came up out of the

[2] The typically Hebrew play-on-words, which may be compared to the Latin *homo-humus,* is maintained throughout the whole of the narrative, which it thus clearly marks as the independent work of a thoroughly Israelite mind. *There was no man, there was no-one or there were no men!* From the very start we can feel that the narrative is really only concerned with man.

earth, and watered the whole face of the ground (*adamàh*)" (2:6). The precise meaning of the word *êd,* by which this primeval phenomenon is designated, is uncertain ("flood," "mist," "spring"), but the nature of the phenomenon itself is fairly well determined by its place of origin and by its effect, which exceeds by far that of the rain. Not only did the ground have to be made suitable for the ordinary vegetation to be able to grow, but it had also to be such that Jahweh Elohim could manipulate it to form the first man, and thereafter the animals (2:19). Moreover, it might very reasonably be thought that the miraculous growth of plants in Paradise would have needed land that had been thoroughly soaked in this way.

It was commonly concluded in the ancient world that the existence of rivers and springs was to be attributed to the presence of a great subterranean river, which was either linked with the world ocean in some way or another, or was simply identical with it. It is possible that the word *êd* is an ancient name for this river (Lambert). If so, this verse describes the origin of the springs, in the primeval breakthrough of the waters beneath to the upper surface of the earth. It certainly sounds like an element of a genuine cosmogony.

Man

The benefit of water being thus taken care of, the Creator now proceeds, in an intervention that is most carefully recounted, to provide for the presence of man on the earth: "Then the Lord God formed man out of the earth of the ground, and blew the breath of life into his nostrils, and so [= so that] man became a living being" (2:7). The Old Testament always represents man as composed of two elements—a lower principle that belongs to the material world, and a higher principle that comes from God. Thus, following the most usual terminology, it is the already existing man who is thought of as being composed of flesh and of spirit.

The word "flesh" indicates man's living, and thus animated, "material" organism. We are concerned here, however, not with man as he already exists, but with his origin, from matter which is thus by definition still unformed and lifeless. The special name for this is *afar,* which is elsewhere mostly (but not always accurately) translated "dust," and which we have here called "earth"; in poetic texts we also find "clay" (*chómèr*) for the same thing.

Once this material has been roughly formed into human shape, it becomes flesh, by means of a life-principle that is blown into the earthen nostrils, and so the first man came into being, composed of flesh and of spirit, which together make him a living person.

The word "spirit" is to be understood as a stereotyped expression for an extremely broad and comprehensive biblical idea (*ruach*). Here, however, we have another word, *neshamah,* which has the more exclusive and, as it were, technical meaning of "breath." It is further qualified by the word "life," so that "breath of life" is a quite literal translation.

We have no special reason for supposing that the sacred author had access, by some natural or supernatural means, to special information about how the Creator actually went to work. The details of his description have quite evidently another origin. His starting point is simply the way that was commonly accepted in Israel of thinking about man's constitution, and he makes it clear that in everything that he is, and in all the different constitutive elements of his make-up, man owes his origin to God. And there is also, corresponding with this picture of man as composed out of two distinct elements (dichotomy), a similarly "two-sided" picture given of the rest of the creation.

The sacred author of Genesis 1 teaches in his own reasoned and deeply theological way that man is a creature, and that he

183

occupies a quite special place in the created world. And there can be no doubt that if the details of the narrative in Genesis 2 had really belonged to the substance of Israel's faith, he would have adapted his teaching to harmonize with them. But in fact we must try to habituate ourselves to seeing the relationship between the two narratives the other way round—Genesis 1 gives us the key to the doctrinal significance of Genesis 2, in which we have the same teaching, but given in a very anthropomorphic and popular form. Its meaning is however no less profound: man is the object of God's special concern, and he is a creature from start to finish, both inasmuch as he is a material being, and also inasmuch as he is a living being.

"Spirit"

This is strikingly evident as regards the principle of man's life. It is God who gives life, supports it, and takes it away again; and it is all a great secret to which God alone has the key. He alone lives because of Himself, all other beings live because of Him. These convictions are most often expressed in the Old Testament in a terminology which is based upon the ordinary observable function of breathing. A man who has ceased to breathe is dead; so that it follows that breathing is the criterion of life, and Israel, with its concrete way of thinking and of expressing thought, quite naturally equates life with breath.

Anyone who is tempted, because of this, to accuse the biblical authors of goodness knows what kinds of materialistic or primitive conceptions should reflect for a moment on the nature of human speech (particularly in relation to the subject in question), and he will certainly become aware that we have no other means of speaking about transcendental realities than by using words that are essentially based upon sensory perception.

This sort of terminology, which occurs so often in the Bible, should therefore be understood as a stereotyped and concrete means of description, which is apt to evoke spontaneously the whole *sphere* of experience to which it refers, e.g., that of a man who moves and acts, who speaks and thinks and strives, in a word, who *lives* by the power of a mysterious impulse which has its source somewhere in his inner being.

Whatever the precise nature of this enigmatic principle may be, it is at all events an extremely precarious possession: man has "but a little breath in his nostrils" (Is 2:22), his breath is only on loan (Wis 15:16). God is life, He *is* Spirit; man is "flesh," dust, clay. The parallelism in Isaias 31:3 is worth noting in this connection: "Egypt is man and not God, and his horses are 'flesh' and not 'spirit.' "

Everything that draws breath (Ps 150:5) lives from the breath of God, for God *is the God of the "spirits" of all flesh* (Nm 16:22; 27:16; cp. Ap 22:6).

"When thou takest away their breath [*ruach*]: they die . . . when thou sendest forth Thy Spirit [*ruach*]: they are created" (Ps 104:29 ff.). "If he should turn his thoughts [*lêb* = heart] only toward himself, and should take back to himself his spirit [*ruach*] and his breath [*neshamah*], all flesh would perish immediately and man return to dust" (Jb 34:14 ff.). There is no mortal who knows "how the spirit of life comes to the bones in the womb of a woman with child" (Qoh 11:5), and there is no reason for supposing that the sacred author of Genesis 2 was any better informed concerning the first man of all. His manner of presenting things is based upon Israel's conviction that man and beast alike are dependent upon the Creator for the breath of life. (As regards the beasts, cf. Gn 6:17; 7:15, 22.) "Man and beast have the selfsame fate. The one must die just as the other; for they all have the same breath" (Qoh 3:19). Man's specific dignity as man is thus not dependent upon the mere fact that he owes his life to the breath of God. The crux of the text lies in the personal and immediate way in which God communicates His breath; such a manner of expression could only arise out of an awareness of specifically human life as such: for man stands over against God as a *person*. The expression is no doubt vague, but it is suggestive nevertheless, sufficiently so to be legitimately connected with the later teaching concerning the dignity and the immediate creation of the human soul. The impression we have is that this is an imaginative way of saying what Genesis 1 has said in more theological language by means of the formula *image of God*.

There is however not the slightest allusion here to immortality. On the contrary, the sacred writer deliberately lays emphasis on the fragile nature of the vessel in which man bears the divine breath within himself.

"*Dust*"

Our word "earth" has a number of different meanings, for each of which there exists in Hebrew a different expression: *èrès* (= world, continent), *adamàh* (= land suitable for the growth of vegetation), *afar* (= loose earth, and according to the context, slime, mud, or dust, in the sense of pulverized earth). God formed man out of *afar* from the *adamàh*, after this had been soaked by a flood which came up out of the *èrès*.

We are in favor of adopting a standard translation for *afar*. "Dust," although it does in many ways create a false idea in the mind, should by constant use as a stereotyped expression take on its own color as a specifically biblical expression, like flesh and spirit.

There is in any case one fundamental play upon words which needs to be preserved. Why, it may be asked, does Genesis 2:7 speak of "earth" (or clay), while in 3:19 we have: "you are dust and to dust you shall return," "dust" being equally questionable as a translation here as in 2:7? In 2:7 "dust" gives an entirely false impression—it is too dry, and not pliable. What the sacred author means is "earth," or rather "mud." The classical translation of 3:19 calls to mind above all the fact that the body (the text speaks, as in 2:7, simply of "man") *corrupts into dust,* whereas what the writer has in mind is the burial of the body after death. This is clear both from biblical usage elsewhere and here in particular from the parallelism with "until you return to the ground [*adamàh*] from which you have come."

Just as it is from the earth that man was originally created, he is given back to it again and becomes one with it once more. Man's life is a journey from one womb to another (Jb 1:21; Sir 40:1; Qoh 5:14). Implied in these texts is the idea that man becomes at the end what he was originally, before the Creator breathed into him the breath of life, i.e., earth. There are really two ideas here, both closely connected, and interwoven together in the narrative: *1)* man comes out of the earth and returns to it again (the earth as a *place*); *2)* man is made of earth and falls back into it again (earth as a *substance*). The same Hebrew expression, without any alteration, can express either of these two ideas. One can only judge from the context which of them lies uppermost for the moment. In a text such as the following:

All things finish up in the same place: all have come from the "dust," and all will return again to "dust." Who knows whether the "spirit" of man will go upward and that of the beasts go down into the earth? (Qoh 3:20 ff.)

the representation is spatial, whereas the following text:

When thou takest away their "spirit," they die, and return again to their "dust" (Ps 104:29)

seems to indicate that when a man dies there is nothing left over but a small quantity of earth, the material out of which he was originally created.

The spatial idea is certainly to the forefront when the dead are spoken of as those who *lie* in the "dust" (Jb 7:21; 20:11; 21:26), who *sleep* (Dn 12:2; cp. Ps 22:30), who *dwell* (Is 26:19), or *go down* (Ps 22:30; Jb 17:16). This aspect must therefore not be overlooked in the formula "return to dust" (also in Qoh 12:7; Jb 10:9; 34:15; Sir 17:1; 40:11; cp. also Ps 22:16; 30:10; 103:14; 146:4; Jb 17:13 ff.). The imagery presented by the text of the *Vetus Latina* (and therefore also by the LXX) is worth quoting here: "Et finxit [plasmavit] Deus hominem pulverem de terra. . . . (2:7) . . . donec convertaris [revertaris] in terram ex qua sumptus es: quia terra es et in terram ibis" (3:17).

On 2:7 Augustine notes: "Quod quidam planius interpretandum putantes dixerunt: 'Et finxit Deus hominem de limo terrae'; quoniam superius dictum fuerat: 'Fons autem ascendebat etc.' ut ex hoc limus intelligendus videretur, humore scilicet terraque concretus" (*De civitate Dei* xiii. 24, 1; PL 41, 399). All this only goes to make it all the more clear that the Creator is represented as going to work with loose earth which He just picks up off the ground, as it were. What He then does with it is described by the word *jasar,* which is a technical term taken from the craft of pottery. Jahweh Elohim goes to work just like a potter: He fashions the loose earth and models it until it takes on the shape of a man.

The great variety of figurative uses of this verb does not detract from this basic technical meaning, but rather indeed presupposes it. It is one of Isaias' favorite expressions: for him, Jahweh is Israel's "Fashioner." That he is deliberately using the word in its technical sense is clear from the way in which he continues: "And yet, Jahweh, thou art our Father, we are the clay, and thou art our 'Fashioner,' and we are all the work of thy hands" (64:7). There can be no doubt that we have the same usage in Genesis 2:7, both because the image of the Creator as a *dieu-potier* was generally a familiar one in the ancient East while it is at the same time authentically biblical, and also because the specific mention of the material necessarily gives a concrete significance to the verb. No doubt it is true that a potter does not work with earth (*afar*) but rather with clay (*chômèr*). But it does not follow that the sacred author had therefore abandoned the motif of the potter, but simply that on top of it he wished, by the striking use of *afar,* to bring in another doctrinal point as well. In any case, *afar, chômèr* and *jasar* are all closely related in biblical usage (Ps 103:14; Jb 10:9; 4:19; cp. Jb 30:19; 27:26).

Doctrine

Loose earth is not a very obvious material. It must have been deliberately chosen, and the reason for it is clear. The sacred author wished to establish from the start how poor and unimportant man is in himself, and how mortal (i.e., destined for the grave) he is by nature. This is the foundation for the whole of the rest of the narrative, for it is only in the light of it that it can be seen how unmerited was man's privileged situation in Paradise, how monstrous his desire to be "like *elohim,*" and how righteous, in consequence, was the divine judgment upon him. This example reinforces our previous contention that the imaginative element in the narrative has been carefully chosen, and that the sacred author has used his material with great independence of mind, and molded it in accordance with the doctrine which he was concerned to communicate. We can see how he has not lost the opportunity of introducing this point into his general picture, while he has, at the same time, held on to the motif of the potter, since this, too, had something of importance to convey. Here again there are two thoughts which are both present in the way in which this motif is made use of in the Bible: *1*) man's frailty and transitoriness, which is underlined still more in Genesis by the mention of the material which is employed (*afar*); *2*) man's general dependence: all that he is, he owes to the Creator, who can therefore make or break him according to His pleasure, without being in any way answerable to man for what He may do to him.

189

The second point has found its classic expression in Jeremias 18:1–12: "Can I not do with you as this potter has done, O house of Israel? See, like the clay in the hand of the potter, so are you in my hand" (v. 6). And Isaias: "Woe to him who strives with his maker, the earthen vessel with its fashioner. Does the clay say to him who fashions it, what are you making? Or the object which is being made, are you unhandy? Woe to him who says to his father: why are you begetting me, etc." (45:9). The image is a familiar and stereotyped one (Is 29:16; Qoh 33:13; Rom 9:20 ff.; cp. Jb 4:17–19; 33:4–6; 10:8 ff.).

The main point of many of these texts is to say that man's existence lies wholly in God's hands. Genesis concentrates this idea on to the fact of man's origin, in such a way that this familiar motif takes on a doctrinal content which is expressed, again, by Genesis 1 with the help of the term *bara* (create).

Fr. Lambert relates how he once saw a potter at work in Palestine. The miracle lies in the craftsman's hand, in his grip. The layman receives an immediate impression of *creative work*, from the ease and speed with which shapeless lumps of clay are transformed, as if by magic, into graceful little jars and pots of every possible shape. The real significance of this kind of imagery must have been better understood in Israel than it is by modern men.

The sacred author thus has a great deal to say about the nature of man, and about his fundamental situation and character, and he also has a judgment to deliver concerning his inherent worthiness, and his relationship with God and with the world. Has he also, it may be asked, anything to teach us concerning the way in which man did in fact come into existence? We have seen that the whole framework of the narrative, together with its forms of expression, have been carefully chosen, but not in order to provide a detailed revelation in this latter respect. The details of the story belong essentially to human experience in general, and they are such as can be found all over the place in the literature of the ancient East. The sacred author has taken and used them as a vehicle for the communication of an exceptional wealth of Jahwistic doctrine. Jahweh goes to work in the manner of any Oriental dieu-potier, but in Genesis this image has been transformed into an expression of Jahweh's transcendence and His immanence.

The imagery out of which the whole picture is constructed depends upon the ordinary popular perception of man as a being whose make-up is at once material and spiritual. The concrete, material details are given not in order to teach how man was created, but as what kind of a being he was created (Junker). The various elements of the narrative, which are such as could be obtained from an unphilosophical analysis of man as he already existed, provided the raw material for an account of how man originated, when projected, as it were, into a genetic dimension. Such is the secret of this author: he gives his teaching in the form of a narrative, which is precisely what he needed to do in the context of his own time and people.

Thus Genesis 2 provides neither support nor refutation in respect of modern theories concerning the origins of the human race. The sacred author is no more in favor of evolution than he is against it, for he knew nothing at all about the whole question. His method is simply to show every species of which he had any knowledge as owing its beginning and origin to God's act of creation. *It is God who has made the different species to be what they now are.* He made some of the animals tame, and others wild (2:20), and likewise He made man (before the animals!), who remains something quite separate and distinct from the whole of the rest of the created world.

Expressions such as "fashioning" and "breathing" are imagery —but are they indeed no more than this? A potter cannot go to work without using some kind of material, so that one may reasonably say that the material in question forms an indispensable part of the image, once the latter has been chosen. The question then arises whether or not one is obliged to hold that man was created out of some already existing material? Or may one equally well hold that he was created out of nothing?

There is a group of scholars who are not keen on the idea of evolution, and who would prefer to see in Genesis 2:7 a revelation to the effect that God in fact employed *lifeless* material. Another group, which accepts the principle of evolution, interprets Genesis 2:7 as referring to *already living* (i.e., animal) material. Others again would say that there was at all events some kind of material, whether living or not....

These views are all, however, in their different ways a kind of aftermath of the old attempts at concordism, which rested on the supposition that God who inspired the Bible was obliged for the sake of His infallibility to take into account all the later discoveries of science; that when God speaks, His word must in some way or another express the scientific truth.

If we want to understand Genesis 2:7 we must ask not what our time is thinking about the origins of man, but what was thought about the question in the time of the sacred author. It has not been our way of looking at things, but that of the sacred author which has been the vehicle of revelation, which is not addressed to our own particular brand of scientific curiosity, but to men of all ages for their salvation. Each age has its own understanding of scientific matters, but the Word of God remains eternally.

17

The Image of the Garden

THERE is no mention, in the description of man's creation in Genesis 2:7, of his being immortal. It is, on the contrary, his mortality that is emphasized, and the condemnation to death of 3:19 may perhaps be taken as referring back to this. No doubt it is by the divine breath of life (*nishmat chajjim*) that man has become a living being (*nepesh chajjah*), but this can also be said about the animals (Gn 1:21,24; 9:10,12,15), who are also endowed with a spirit of life (*ruah hayyim*) (6:17; 7:15) and even a *breath of the spirit of life* which likewise comes from God.

It cannot therefore be legitimate to interpret such expressions, which when applied to the animals refer to a transitory form of life, as implying man's immortality when they occur in a series of contexts which is closely related to the former texts about the animals. The whole picture with which we are presented in Genesis 2:7 is moreover in perfect agreement with a whole series of biblical texts which teach how frail and transitory a creature man is in his fundamental make-up.

The sacred author's description of man is therefore based upon his own ordinary experience. As a result of God's act of creation he is now complete, in the sense that he is now endowed with everything that makes him to be a man, no more and no less.

Function of the Garden

Only then did "the Lord God plant a garden in Eden, in the East, and put there the man whom he had formed" (2:8).

The sacred author does not actually say that the Creator later changed anything in man, but he does, in fact, seem now to have become quite different from what we were shown of him at his creation. We no longer, so to speak, recognize ourselves in him; indeed he is a complete contrast to all that we know about ourselves. Only when he has been banished from the garden after his sin do we recognize ourselves in him again, only then do we feel that he has again become what he originally was. This is not some far-fetched interpretation of our own invention. It is on the contrary the crux of the whole narrative.

God's judgment on man, when he has sinned, might be summed up as follows: "I am now making you to be what you really are. You don't yet know what this means, but I am now telling you, so that you need have no more illusions about yourself. You are *adam of the adamàh,* and this in more senses than one: I *took you away* from the ordinary *adamàh* and *put you in the garden,* and now you shall return again to your own adamàh. From now on you shall *live,* not in the garden but on the adamàh, you shall be obliged to *cultivate* (2:15 and 3:23) the adamàh instead of caring for the garden, and you shall obtain your food not from the trees of the garden but from the adamàh (2:16 and 3:17). But above all, you *are adam of the adamàh, because I have formed you out of adamàh.* Now that I am driving you back to the adamàh, it is the beginning of the end for you, for there it is that you belong in the depths of your being, because you are made of adamàh, and will return to it once again, and become yourself adamàh (3:19). And thus your irrevocable return to the adamàh will be finally and completely consummated."

Thus according to the sacred author's express teaching, this

194

return of man to the *adamàh* is in the direct line of human nature as it really is. And yet at the same time he teaches no less explicitly (first in God's warning to man, and then in the condemnation, and lastly by the execution of the latter) that it is all a penalty for sin. *Because you have done this and have eaten of the tree of which I said to you: you shall not eat of it, therefore* . . . It is thus at once a consequence of nature and of sin, at once a natural necessity and yet a penalty.

In this dilemma there is only one middle term possible: the divine grace. God loved man more than He had strictly obliged Himself to love him in virtue of the creation alone, and He therefore wished him to be free of the painful consequences of his involvement with the *adamàh,* and to be endowed with supernatural privileges. But man lost this special love of God by his sin, which brought with itself, as a penalty, that nature now runs her normal course.

Does the sacred author teach anything in particular concerning this supernaturally privileged state to which man was once elevated? The whole structure of the narrative is, in fact, constructed with this in view—this is precisely the whole point of the garden.

Strictly speaking, the sacred author did not need a garden in order to tell the story of the first sin. But he did need it if he was to show that there was a time when man had more than was his due, and that it was by his sin that he lost this. It enabled him to make a distinction between the creation of man, and his being taken and placed in the garden; and thereafter, after the sinful act, to let him return again to the status of a mere creature through being driven out of the garden by God.

This is the sacred author's way of giving his answer to the problem of evil. Jahweh did not originally intend that man should be in his present plight: a primal sin has intervened, and it is this that has caused the situation that we know.

Conversation with a Theologian

Man was created outside the garden. There have been quite a few who would appear to have overlooked this point, even among the theologians, who seem to know a good deal about the first man. The detail has in fact a crucial part to play in the structure of the whole narrative, and one could hardly expect the overlooking of it to be without its consequences. These theologians are thus able to come to the conclusion that there is little or no mention in Genesis of a *supernaturally* privileged state. Indeed, when this point is left aside, there *is* no other evidence of any significance.

It is nowadays a familiar enough idea that in the writings of the Fathers, as also in those of the medieval theologians, we can find passages of exegesis which, while we are obliged, strictly speaking, to consider them to be mistaken, nevertheless sometimes contain thoughts of great value. It may well be perfectly legitimate to hold on to our conviction that man was created in a state of grace, and yet at the same time to be aware that neither Genesis 1:26 nor 2:7 can strictly speaking be appealed to in support of this point, since both texts are in fact concerned with man *as such.* The theologians know this too, but what they forget is that man was at this moment in his purely natural state, *outside* the garden.

The importance of this point was realized in the Middle Ages, so that it could be disputed at which particular moment of his existence Adam received his supernatural privileges. St. Thomas, after a certain amount of hesitation, came to the conclusion that this must have been at the very first moment. For him, the garden simply adds yet one more privilege, that of a miraculous state of material felicity, which appropriately corresponded to his more spiritual privileges. From a speculative point of view, it is more appropriate that man should have been created in a state of privilege, and it also comes closer to the common opinion of the Fathers. But the distinction between nature and grace is of course absent in Genesis, for which sin destroys man's original "human" nature. Origen would seem to have been right: the skins of the animals, in which fallen man is clothed by God, stand for his mortal body. Theology would seem to have no other course open to it than to fly from the arms of Genesis into those of St. Paul.

The only possibility of progress here is to attempt a somewhat less slavishly literal exegesis. This will make it possible to suggest, in the first place, that the narrative is not concerned to provide us with a chronological succession of facts. It is true that the tableau of the Creation does quite clearly describe two distinct stages in God's work: first the creation of the man's body, and then the breathing in of the breath of life. But we are not thereby obliged to think in terms of a *succession* of divine acts. The purpose of the sacred author is simply to make a distinction between the different elements which he, in fact, finds in human nature as it actually is; in other words he is trying to convey a doctrine about man in narrative form. And in the same way, further on, he distinguishes between man's creation and his transference into the garden, and relates the one as taking place after the other. But it is not the chronology that is important. The point is that in the first man, as God intended him to be, there is a distinction between a natural and a supernatural element in his make-up. It is for this reason, and for this reason alone, that the sacred author needs the garden.

In the second place, the exegete may well find it better to leave over to the theologians (with a sigh of relief) the question of whether or to what extent the latter's traditional considerations concerning the first man's state of material blessedness may not perhaps derive from a very ancient exegetical misunderstanding. At all events, the garden is there for a more important reason. The question remains whether or not, even so, anything at all is affirmed in Genesis concerning the first man's material surroundings. The best way of attempting an answer to this may perhaps be to put the question in a more general form.

Throughout the course of the centuries, beginning with the New Testament itself, the exegetical presuppositions which have governed the Church's reflection about the Paradise narrative have remained fairly constantly the same. And it is out of this centuries-long process of reflection that the theological treatise concerning the first man has been constructed, by bringing together into a coherent structure the various elements which were considered to be given by Scripture from the start. Indeed the theologian feels himself most at home if he is able to deduce, say, his whole picture of the first man, complete with Paradise and all, from a single original and fundamental fact. Such a procedure provides him with abundant material for debate, so that it is perfectly understandable that he feels in consequence no particular need to take even a step outside the circle of ideas which he has himself thus created.

No sensible exegete goes to work with a theological deduction lying ready to hand, as it were. But if it should so happen that, out of pure curiosity, he should have occasion to stick his nose somewhere into the workshop of the theologians he will, we would suggest, almost unavoidably begin to ask himself whether this *scholion* or that *corollarium* or even a *status quaestionis* here and there may not have to be radically re-thought, in this field, if they are to achieve the dimensions which are undoubtedly required now that the exegetical starting point has altered.

The Layout of the Garden

Having emphasized the importance of the doctrinal meaning of the garden, we have still said very little about what this actually is. It is a point which we cannot afford simply to touch

198

on in passing; an attempt must be made to determine more precisely the exact meaning and function of the garden in the structure of the narrative. But first there is some preparatory work to be done.

In the text which we have taken as our starting point, two things are mentioned: the planting of the garden, and the transference of man into it (2:8). Both of these points are then elaborated further: we are first told something about the layout and situation of the garden (2:9–14), and then it is again stated—but with a bit more detail this time—that "Jahweh Elohim took man and set him down in the garden of Eden that he might cultivate it and watch over it" (2:15).

The word *eden* is here, as in 2:8, employed as a geographical proper noun (cp. 2:10 and 4:16). It does not follow from this that there was in fact a particular place or region which went by this name and to which the sacred author is referring. To the Hebrew ear, *eden* would at once have called to mind the likesounding generic noun which means "enjoyment" or "pleasure." It would seem likely that *eden* is a proper noun which has its origin in popular fancy—something like our "cloud-cuckooland"—and that it is not a personal invention of the sacred author's, since it occurs another eight times in the writings of the prophets, in Isaias' parallel passage about the garden of Jahweh (cp. Gn 13:10) and in Ezechiel's garden of (*or* of the) elohim. The geographical fiction is made more realistic and takes on more atmosphere by the addition of "in the east" (cp. 3:24 and 4:16), i.e., in relation to Canaan, as the mention of the Tigris and the Euphrates bears witness.

The word "garden" (*gan*) in the original implies an enclosed, circumscribed area of a more or less artificial nature. The Vulgate, with its translation, "Paradisus voluptatis," follows the LXX in understanding the word *eden* as a generic noun and takes garden in the sense of the parklike gardens of the Persian kings. In later biblical Hebrew the word *pardês,* Paradise, which is borrowed from the Persian, occurs three times (Ct 4:13; Neh 2:8; Qoh 2:5). The Preacher makes King Solomon say: "I laid out gardens [plural of *gan*] and parks [plural of *pardês*] for myself and planted in them all kinds of fruit trees. I had ponds made, so that a wood of young trees might be watered from them." "Gardens" is parallel here with "parks." The abundance of water and of trees are not the only things which make the garden of Genesis resemble one of these Persian royal parks; there is also the fact that in both cases admission was only given to the king's own family and to the members of his court. For even if the garden of Paradise was only planted after the creation of man and specifically with his enjoyment of it in view, everything goes to show that it is in fact God's own personal garden. It is not because he has a right to it from birth, but by a pure act of grace that man is allowed to be in it and to cultivate and watch over it. In Nehemias 2:8, Asaf, we are told, is "the royal forester," literally "the caretaker (*shômêr*) of the royal park (*pardês*)." The garden is not handed over to man as his own personal possession, for it remains God's garden; what man is given is the use and fruition of it (2:16), and the responsibility for it as *shômêr* (2:15), that is as its keeper, in order that he may both watch over it and take care of it (cp. Prv 27:18).

And so Jahweh Elohim planted a garden. "And he caused all kinds of trees to grow up out of the ground [*adamàh*] [of Paradise that were] a pleasure to see and good to eat; and the tree of life [stood] in the midst of the garden, and the tree of the knowledge of good and evil" (2:9).

Perhaps we are meant to think of these trees as appearing out of the ground as if by magic. They were at all events no ordinary trees, but rather were like those in the visions of Ezechiel or of John: trees whose leaves do not wither, which possess healing medicinal powers and of which the fruit is never exhausted because they bear it every month (cp. Ez 47:12; Ap 22:2). If it be asked whether these are ornamental or fruit trees, the answer is, both—they are ornamental trees which at the same time bear fruit. There is no mention of any other kind of plant or of vegetable food. It might be supposed that this is because in Paradise man is able simply to pick his food off the trees as it ripens, and is exempted from laboring to produce a harvest, but the real reason is even simpler: it is trees alone which have any part to play in the further development of the narrative.

In this, the two trees which have both already been specifically mentioned have each an indispensable function. The sacred author makes Eve say that the forbidden tree, which according to 2:17 and 3:5 is the tree of knowledge, stands in the midst of the garden (3:3). The well-known difficulty which arises in this connection is resolved in the translation which we have given, without any alteration being made in the text, simply by understanding the last phrase as an independent clause which further specifies the phrase which precedes it; so that both trees are understood as being situated in the middle (not, of course, the mathematical middle) of the garden: *and in the midst of the garden [stood] the tree of life and the tree of knowledge.*

It is in any case not absolutely necessary to achieve a perfect reconciliation of every small detail in the story with all the others. Indeed, the most obvious interpretation of 3:3 would be that there was only one tree in the midst of the garden.

Situation of the Garden

The miraculous fertility of the garden is connected with the abundance of water with which it is provided (cp. Gn 13:10): four rivers rise within its boundaries (2:10–14). Verse 10 is usually translated in such a way as to suggest that there was a single great river which had its source in the garden, and which only divided into four when it was *outside* the garden. A translation according to which the river divides *in the garden itself* is however perfectly possible, and can even be said to be required

201

by the original text, since the latter states that the whole of the garden was watered, a result which could scarcely have been produced by the river dividing only once it was outside the garden.

The last-named river, the Euphrates, is also that which runs closest to Canaan, where it is known simply as *the* River, so that further description of it is unnecessary. Next, there is the Tigris, "which flows to the east of Asshur." This is an especially accurate indication, since "Asshur" refers to the city of that name and quite possibly also to the whole region. The remaining two rivers, Gichôn and Pishôn, would seem to be the least well-known, since they receive a more extensive description. This description gets us (and most probably also the average Palestinian peasant) nowhere at all, but it greatly strengthens the general impression that the garden is situated in a miraculous region of some kind. Attempts have been made to identify these two rivers with various known rivers in North Mesopotamia or Armenia, or with some of the many canals in South Mesopotamia, according to the preference for a northerly or a southerly situation of Paradise. But in fact the problem of where Paradise actually was is a meaningless one. The only valid question is that of where it is represented as being situated in terms of the convention of the narrative itself. And in this case there is a very ancient explanation which seems indeed to be extremely likely: that we must not look for any kind of objectively accurate geography, but rather for a picture that reflects the map of the world as it was envisaged according to the popular scientific ideas of the ancient world.

It would then seem to be clear enough that these two mysterious rivers stand also for great world rivers, since they are mentioned in the same breath as the Tigris and the Euphrates. It is also most probable that they are given from east to west, since the most westerly, i.e., the Euphrates, is mentioned last, preceded by the Tigris. According to this reckoning, the two first-named rivers would be situated further still toward the east; the Ganges and the Indus come immediately to mind. According to the ancient conception of the map of the world, the Ganges constituted the asiatic upper section of the *Nile,* a river whose upper reaches remained a mystery for so long. And the fact that some Greek sources do sometimes use the name Gichôn for the Nile would seem to suggest a confirmation of the idea that it is indeed the Ganges with which we are concerned.

The Euphrates, the Tigris, the Ganges-Nile and the Indus are the four great and famous rivers to which the world of the ancient East owed its fertile regions. And so the best way of conveying an impression of exceptional fertility and fruitfulness was to localize the garden in the unattainable and mysterious region where these great world rivers had their common origin. Hence our acceptance of this ancient view, which incidentally also finds an expression in the liturgy for the consecration of a font. The priest divides the water with his hand, and sprinkles it out toward the four points of the compass, saying at the same time: [God] "who caused you to flow up out of the spring in Paradise and commanded you to water the whole earth in four streams." The only difference is that whereas the ancients believed that this symbolism was based upon an objective geographical situation, we now know that it is based upon a narrative, in which the rivers have a qualitative rather than a geographical function, since they are introduced with the purpose of expressing a judgment of value about the garden. It is with a similar kind of purpose that they are mentioned in Qoheleth 24:25–27, where they are brought in to the greater glory of the Law. All of which may serve to help us to gain a more precise understanding of what the sacred author intended by the garden.

18

The "Earthly Paradise"

MAN'S sin in Paradise is of the kind that Scripture always brands as *the* sin par excellence. In every key—in proverb and in parable, in narrative and in prophecy—it teaches that pride is its own undoing. The king of Tyre was among these proud men, and the prophet sees him as embodying all the pride of the city over which he ruled. It should be remembered, in the following quotation, that in the Bible it is the heart and not the head that is the seat of a man's thoughts.

Son of man, say to the king of Tyre, Thus says the Lord God: because you have lifted up your heart, and have said: I am a god, I sit on the throne of a god, in the midst of the sea; yet you are a man, and no god, though you consider yourself to have a heart like the heart of a god . . . therefore, thus says the oracle of Jahweh, because you have given yourself a heart like the heart of a god, therefore will I let strangers loose upon you, the most barbarian among the nations; they will defile your splendor, and cast you down into the pit, and you shall die a terrible death. . . . Will you then still say: I am a god, under the eyes and in the hands of those who slay you, you who are a man and no god? You shall die the death of the uncircumcised by the hand of strangers (Ez 28:2–10).

It is the same sort of presumption that is condemned here as in the Paradise narrative. In fact, beginning with the episode of the Tower of Babel, we could easily fill many pages with quotations with the same kind of inspiration behind them. This particular passage recalls Genesis even in its phraseology, but we chose it above all, because of the way in which it continues. For the prophet goes on to say the same thing in another way by making the king of Tyre the central figure in a story that was most likely well known to his audience.

The Garden of God and the Mountain of God

"You were full of wisdom and beauty . . . you were in Eden, the garden of God . . . adorned with precious stones, carnelian, topaz and jasper, chrysolite, onyx, sapphire and carbuncle, all set in gold . . . on the day that you were created. I gave you a cherub to protect you [or: I set you as a cherub to protect the garden]; you were on the holy mountain of God, walking in the midst of glowing coals. You were blameless in your ways, from the day that you were created, until unrighteousness was found in you . . . Because you have sinned I have taken away your glory and have cast you down from the mountain of God, and caused the guardian cherub to drive you out [or: I have caused you, the guardian cherub, to be driven out] from the midst of the glowing coals. Your heart was lifted up because of your beauty, you have corrupted your wisdom, and therefore have I cast you down to the ground" (Ez 28:13–17).

We have abbreviated the passage, and left aside a few uncertain elements. On what sort of a narrative has Ezechiel based himself here? *Eden* refers without question to the garden of (*or* of the) elohim, made not for men but for God Himself and His heavenly court to dwell in. The word *kerub* is an indication of this, and *mount of (the) elohim* clinches the matter without any possible doubt. According to Ezechiel 10:2, the glowing coals occupied the space beneath God's throne between the cherubim who carried the throne (cp. 1:13). It is not clear whether or not the tragic hero of the original narrative, with whom Tyre is compared, is intended to be the first man. There is an undoubted connection with Genesis, but, as anyone can see for himself, this is not in the form of direct literary dependence. In what then does this relationship consist? The first point is that condemnation of man's chronic megalomania is a characteristic prophetic theme (cp. e.g., Is 2:9–22). In the second place, the sacred author of Genesis does embody in his otherwise quite different picture (which is of a human, earthly paradise), a number of elements which really belong in the imagery of a heavenly paradise of the gods, which Ezechiel, far more thoroughly than does the author of Genesis, makes his own. In the whole of this question, compare what has already been said in Chapter 13.

The spirit of the Genesis narrative (which is also that of the passage of Ezechiel) is similar to that of the following satirical passage in Isaias, which concerns the fall of Babylon and is in all probability addressed rhetorically to Nabuchodonosor:

How are you fallen from heaven, O Star of the Morning, Son of the Dawn! How you are dashed down to the ground, O ruler of the nations! You, who have said in your heart: I will climb up to heaven, and set up my throne above God's stars and sit down upon the Mount of Assembly in the farthest [the highest] places of the North; I will climb up over the peaks of the clouds and make myself like the Most High! Truly, you are cast down into the underworld, to the depths of the Pit (Is 14:12–15).

The Mount of Assembly in the farthest North (*latera aquilonis*) is the Babylonian Olympus, the dwelling place of the gods, which was considered to be situated somewhere in the high Asiatic mountain range which forms the boundary of the Plain of Mesopotamia on the northern side, and is also the region of the source of the Euphrates and the Tigris.

There, too, to the north of the Aramaic birthplace of the Patriarchs, is situated Ararat, on which, according to the biblical account, Noah offered up the sacrifice whose pleasing odor appeased Jahweh's anger. And in the same region, to the north of Southern Mesopotamia, lies the mountain Nisir, from which, in the Babylonian legend, Noah (*Oota-napishtim*) was taken up (after having made his sweet-smelling sacrifice) into the land of the immortals, "far away by the mouth [source ?] of the rivers" (Epic of Gilgamesh, XI, 192 ff). And it was likewise from this direction that the whole apparatus of the cherubim and the throne with Jahweh's "glory" appeared (Ez 1:4).

The Psalmist, on the occasion of a victory over the king of Assyria (who calls himself "the great king," Is 36:4) sings as follows:

> Great is Jahweh and most highly to be praised
> in the city of our God.
> His holy mountain, his famous hill,
> is the joy of the whole earth.
> Mount Zion, in the farthest North,
> is the city of the great king (Ps 48:2 ff.).

Just as it is neither Sennacherib nor anyone else, but Jahweh alone who is truly "the great king," so too it is not the legendary mountain of the Assyrians, but Zion, Jahweh's dwelling place, which is the only true holy mountain and is indeed the mountain of God. It is not to be wondered at, therefore, that the Assyrians dashed themselves to pieces against it (701 B.C.).

The meaning of "the holy mountain of God" or the "mountain of the gods" in Ezechiel's picture of Paradise is thus fairly clear. The same presumption of which Isaias accuses Babel is attributed by Ezechiel to Tyre, and by Genesis to the first man. In each case we find the same religious attitude: a judgment on sin as lese majesty, that form of human presumption which the Greeks call *hubris*. This is why the passages which have been quoted are so reminiscent of the Paradise narrative, a fact which must not however tempt us to overlook the very great difference of conception.

Earthly Paradise

This difference lies in the fact that the sacred author of Genesis has put Paradise very firmly on earth, and shows it as having been created by God only in view of its occupation by man. His attitude toward accepted conventional images seems to have been much more critical than Ezechiel's, who in other places, too, makes considerable use of conceptions taken from the Babylonian world of ideas. The passages which we have quoted from his prophetic poetry are indeed on the borderline of myth, as regards their purely material form and content, and this is undoubtedly all to the good as far as the poetry is concerned. As regards the author of Genesis, on the other hand, it has been correctly said of him that he has "demythologized" his material, a fact which provides but one more example of the strength of the Jahwism which lies behind Genesis, with its profound religious conviction of the distance which separates the divine and the human spheres.

The ancient East offers a great variety of conceptions about the dwelling place of the gods and, parallel with these, about the hereafter and the destiny of the departed. Israel's moderation in this respect is striking. To begin with, Jahwism rejected quite irrevocably every form of worship or invocation of the dead (1 S 28; 2 K 23:24; Is 8:19; Dt 18:11). Jahweh dwells far above the heavens which we can see with our eyes, while the dead, on the other hand, have their sojourn far beneath the earth, in the underworld (*sheôl*), where, as is well known, their shadowy existence is such as to give no handle whatever to superstitious fantasy. It is reasonable to suppose that in this Jahwism was taking a line of its own, in direct opposition to the general tendencies of the time, as a very practical and necessary way both of promoting and of safeguarding an authentic faith in God. Here again, we can see how the originality of the Genesis narrative has its source in the originality of Jahwism itself: the

208

garden is deliberately and emphatically situated on earth. Nevertheless, some of the traditional narrative elements which had necessarily to be embodied in this new conception still bear traces of their original source: they really belong more in a garden for *elohim* than in a garden for human beings, more in the heavenly than in the earthly Paradise. The sacred author has quite definitely taken an earthly garden as the basis of his narrative, but he has not worked this out in so thorough a fashion that we fail to be reminded of Ezechiel.

For when all is said and done, his garden remains a divine garden (pp. 198–201), conceived of in the last resort as a garden of the *elohim*. It is not simply an earthly garden, but a slice of the supramundane world brought down to earth, in which everything breathes the atmosphere of the world of divine things. We may not perhaps be justified in concluding from 3:8 that Jahweh Himself took a walk in the garden every noon, but one could certainly expect at any moment to come across one or other of the "sons of God," for the things which flourished there in the ordinary course of nature gave access to privileges which were the exclusive monopoly of the *elohim* (3:22–24). This whole picture is confirmed by the motifs of the cherubim and of fire (the flaming sword). Fire is a well-known accompaniment of theophany, in particular as a barrier surrounding the dwelling place of the gods. A cherub is not an angel who is sent out with some kind of message; where there is a cherub, it is a sign that we are on holy ground, and that we are close to the divinity. A cherub is the guardian of the throne, of the palace and the gate, so that a cherub placed at the entrance to the garden is a sign that the latter is a garden of the divine king. Another relevant point is the name "Eden" which, as we have seen, occurs often as a parallel to "garden of the gods" or "garden of Jahweh." This may perhaps be explained by the fact that the place of the source of the great world rivers suggests the center point of the earth, where the Mount of the Earth, which is also the Mount of the Gods, is situated. . . . Another question is whether we are justified in interpreting 2:10–14 as a survival of some kind of "precious stones motif," such as recurs frequently in descriptions of Jahweh's heavenly throne (Ex 24:10; Ez 1:26; 10:1; Ap 4:3; 21). Adam was taken from the *adamàh,* and will return again, by death, to the *adamàh;* but why is it that we are told in 2:15 that he was "taken up" from the *adamàh,* and likewise in 3:23 that he returns again, on being banished from the garden, to the *adamàh* from which he was "taken up"?

Doubtless there is no need, in the present form of the narrative, to take the verb in the strong and literal sense which it has when applied to Enoch and Elias, and it may perhaps be considered as a pure Hebraism, and as such be left untranslated. There is, nevertheless, an undeniable parallelism between the double return to the *adamàh* on the one hand, and the double being "taken" from it on the other, which seems to be a sign that the narrative as we now have it has more than a single motif behind it.

Heavenly Paradise

Against this background, the Vulgate translation—"Plantaverat autem Dominus Deus paradisum voluptatis *a principio*" —provides material for reflection. As it stands, the translation is incorrect, and betrays the fact that Jerome had studied with the Jews, who held that God had created Paradise in the beginning, i.e., before the creation of the heavens and the earth, somewhere in another world. How, it may be asked, did they come to such a belief?

The dominant conception of the Old Testament concerning the dead is that they all go to *sheól,* where both good and bad together lead a similar shadowy existence. The classical theory of rewards, according to which everyone receives the just recompense for his works already in this life, hangs together with this conception. It was not always easy, of course, to bring the facts into harmony with this theory, and this realization eventually gave rise to a real crisis of belief (Job, Psalms). At last, faith was able to take the indispensable leap into the dark against the theory, and dare to say that the experience of being-with-Jahweh, which is given to the believer in this life, must be essentially permanent in nature, so that it cannot be affected even by death itself. It was upon this foundation, once established, that the later books of the Bible (Daniel, Wisdom, Maccabees) were able to build. This they did along side of, and in contrast to, a wide variety of other, apocryphal, pre-Christian writings, which went in for all kinds of detailed speculations on the subject, incorporating eagerly a considerable number of ancient ideas which Jahwism had up to that time succeeded in holding at bay.

This very confused mass of conceptions may be summarized schematically as follows: A distinction is made between the destiny of the good and that of the bad, so that there are in consequence a number of different dwelling places in the hereafter. *Sheôl* becomes more and more of a "hell," and a Paradise is envisaged as a kind of intermediate resting place for the righteous during the interval between death and the general resurrection. This Paradise was then furnished by having recourse to the data of Genesis, but with the distinction between the heavenly and the earthly Paradise becoming more and more blurred: the Paradise into which Enoch and Elias, and also Abraham (cp. Abraham's bosom, Lk 16:22) were taken up is the same as that from which Adam was once driven out. It is situated, most often, in the third heaven (2 Cor 12:2, 4). The last stage is that conceptions which were originally quite distinct begin to run together, so that Paradise begins to stand also for the definitive abode of the risen (possessing immortal and divine life through the tree of life, Ap 2:7), and to be more and more identified with the picture of the ultimate unfolding of the messianic Kingdom (Lk 23:43) and also with the new, heavenly Jerusalem in a new

211

heaven and a new earth (Ap 21). Thus, having started with Paradise, we have ended up with the Christian conception of heaven.

And if we now take the Jewish conception, and purify it of what in its formulation is excessively material and spatial, we shall find that we are left with something which, although it was doubtless not present in the mind of the author of Genesis, is nevertheless very true: that the heavenly paradise did indeed exist before this world was created, since it consists essentially in being-with-God (cp. Mt 25:34).

The Paradox of Grace

The imaginative picture with which we are presented by the sacred author is not however one of future heavenly bliss, but of the state of privilege which was enjoyed by the first man. This, too, consists essentially in a state of being-with-God, freely conferred on him by grace; the Creator sets man in a sphere which far exceeds the dimensions of his own nature, for it is the sphere of the *elohim*. This privilege finds its concrete expression in two directions: *1)* either in the conception of a *heavenly* paradise, which has existed from all eternity and into which man is taken up after his creation on earth and . . . from which, after he has sinned, he is again cast out to the earth below; or *2)* in the conception of an *earthly* paradise, specially created for man when he already existed, and into which he is transferred and permitted to dwell there; after he has sinned he is driven out of it again and the entrance is closed and a guard set before it.

The conceptions are different, but the teaching is in both cases the same. Man's elevation to a privileged, supernatural state can be expressed either in terms of his being taken up into God's own domain, which is, of course, situated above the earth, or else by God's descent toward man, by means of which He

establishes His domain somewhere on earth, and then takes man
and transfers him into it.

The two conceptions are, of course, related to each other, and
can easily run together, so that in general God's whole redemptive work is represented alternately either as a descent on the part
of God or as an elevation of man into the sphere of God:
descensio Dei est ascensio hominis. This paradox of the In-
carnation can be expressed in an endless variety of different
ways, according to its application to the various phases of God's
concern for man. It also comes back again and again in connection with the theme of paradise. The theme of the Promised
Land, which is progressively developed throughout the course
of the Bible, leads on to the dream of a future paradisal Canaan,
which eventually becomes identified with the heavenly father-
land (Mt 5:5; Heb 4:8; 11:10, 13–16). In the messianic time,
the Temple of Jerusalem will be set upon the highest mountain
(Is 2:2; Ez 40:2), but John saw the new holy city of Jerusalem
coming down from heaven (Ap 21:2; cp. Gal 4:25 ff:).

Our sacred author quite consciously and deliberately situates
the garden on earth. The elements in his narrative which recall
a different conception serve to underline all the more heavily
the teaching of which the garden is itself only meant to be the
expression: that the first man was enabled by God to partake of
a higher kind of life.

19

The Part of the Woman

APART from the actual order in which they were brought into existence, Genesis 1 gives few or no details about the way in which the various things were created by Elohim. He commanded that the water was to swarm with fishes and that all kinds of birds were to fly through the air over the earth; and that He created them (20 ff.). Of the beasts it is said that the earth was to bring them forth, and that Elohim then made them too (24 ff.). As regards the plants, it was for the earth to cause them to sprout up, and, on being so commanded, it brought them to light (11 ff.). And when He comes to His last work of all, Elohim first says what sort of a being He is going to make and then He creates man, both male and female (26 ff.).

In Genesis 2 it is quite different. Jahweh Elohim *forms* the first man, the animals and the birds from the adamàh, and He then *builds* the woman out of the man.

The origin of the woman is in fact set in the garden, but this is in no way meant to form a contrast with the origin of man outside the garden. Still less have the animals any particular advantage over man by the fact that they are formed from the adamàh of the garden. This is all simply a question of arrangement: this is the sequence that just happens to fit in best with the development of the story, which in turn has to follow the course of the doctrinal argument. The place in which a particular action is situated is therefore of no essential significance: the tableau with which we are presented in 2:7 is set outside the garden

and is concerned with man *as such,* while the creation tableau
of the animals and of woman is equally and exclusively concerned with a doctrine about the place which belongs to them
as such in the created world, even though it happens to be set
in the garden. Thus both tableaux can with equal justification
be considered as elements of a creation theme which has been
incorporated into the larger whole of the paradise theme (cp.
pp. 167 ff.). Once the distinction has been made between these
two themes—which there is no reason whatever for attributing to
a conflation of two older, independent narratives—the structure
of Genesis 2 becomes considerably easier to understand.

Structure of the Chapter

After the sacred author has recounted the origin of the first
man (creation theme), he goes over to a doctrinal theme of
another kind, in which he is concerned in the first place to express his doctrine about the spiritual state of the first man. It is
to this end that he needs the garden, which provides him with
a natural opportunity to bring in the creation of the plants
(creation theme again). Strictly speaking, he says no more than
that Jahweh Elohim caused all kinds of trees to grow up out of
the *adamàh* of the garden; he does not deem it necessary to
explain separately how the earth got its great variety of *vegetation,* even though it was the bare earth that formed the starting
point of his narrative (2:5). This is left for his readers to fill
in for themselves. The fact is that the creation theme has been
subordinated and adapted to the exigencies of the Paradise theme.

The description of man's spiritual condition is completed with
the mention of the one thing which, as a kind of test, he is forbidden to do. And this is the first occasion on which we are told
that man's destiny was for *immortality* (2:16 ff.). There is no
thought of excluding the woman from this situation; the ban on

215

eating from the tree applies to her too; in fact the whole business concerns her first and most of all (3:1–6). Nevertheless, when the actual prohibition was made known to the man, she was not there and indeed the idea even of woman was as yet unknown to the man. All this is purely a matter of the author's arrangement of his material. A good narrator always leaves something over to the imagination of his audience.

The sacred author is then free again to take up the creation theme once more. His concern is now with the phenomenon of woman, and he proceeds with great care to construct the tableau of her origin: What she is must be apparent from the manner of her coming into being. The sacred author sets out his doctrine concerning the nature and destiny of woman in the form of a narrative about her origins: He projects her, as it were, into a genetic dimension, just as he had done with the first man (cp. p. 189). In doing so, it is an advantage for him that the action of the narrative has now been transferred to the garden. He has greater freedom in such an atmosphere, since it is a natural enough setting for miracles to take place.

The author has certain doctrinal reasons for wishing to make a connection between the origin of the animals and that of the woman, and this is the only reason why the creation of the animals takes place in the garden. This account is given us as a quite sufficient explanation of why there are all kinds of animals upon the whole earth. The reader must fill in the rest for himself.

Beasts and birds are dealt with in a single breath, and both are formed from the *adamàh*. There is no word about the fishes— they have no part to play in the story, and it is clear that they are not even remotely considered as companions for man in this life. Also, there is no place for them in the tableau which the author has chosen: a traveling aquarium or a scene by the waterside would burden the story unnecessarily. As always, the deciding factor in the choice or arrangement of the material is the re-

216

quirements of the doctrinal point in question. And here again, it is an advantage that the story takes place in the garden, for the author does need the procession of the animals to emphasize his teaching, and outside of the garden this would have been liable to have ended in a blood bath.

The episode closes with a short postscript. The narrator is an impressionist—his method is to use a series of striking factual details to build up the total impression which he wishes to convey by a process of suggestion. By using a few characteristic indications, he is able to conjure up the special atmosphere of a whole situation for us. This he does here now once again, by summing up, in a highly realistic manner, the privileged spiritual state of our first parents: the first man and his wife were both of them naked, but they did not feel that there was anything shameful about this in relation to each other (2:25). And so we find that we are once again fairly and squarely in the Paradise theme; and all is now ready for the second act, which is about the sin in the garden.

Our author never loses an opportunity of letting his knife cut both ways. He is a master in the combining of themes, connecting his main doctrine, as often as he can, with other points while he is about it, more or less by way of aside (*ex obliquo*). The principal way in which he does this should be clear already from the distinction which has been made between the creation theme and the Paradise theme, and we have also come across a number of examples of it in matters of detail (cp. the previous chapter, and pp. 186 ff.). And the pericope about the woman (2:18–24) provides a particularly good example.

It should by now no longer cause surprise that it is no idealized, *paradisal woman* who is depicted by the author in this pericope, and that no effort at all is made to present her as any kind of perfect contrast to woman as she has now become as the result of sin. Some, unconscious of the doctrinal pliancy and manysided-

217

ness of the narrative, have mistakenly tried to find something of this kind in it. In the fallen state, too, woman is meant to be the coequal *companion* of man. That she in fact—and especially in the ancient East—has often become the *slave* of man, is certainly a consequence of sin (3:16), but it does not form any part of the normal law of her being, to which she is subject as much as to the law of mortality, for example. The phenomenon of murder is also a consequence of sin (4:1–16), but it remains nevertheless a violation of the law, even of the law of fallen nature (cp. 9:6). Thus if woman is shown to be the life companion of man, this is not by way of idealization. And still less should her motherhood be considered as essentially a penalty for sin, even if it is in fact only mentioned after the Fall (cp. 1:28 and 9:1). The point of the pericope is to depict the eternal feminine, the *phenomenon of woman,* as the whole of the human experience of all ages has known it. Or more precisely, it is to give an explanation of the universal fact of experience, that a man leaves his father and his mother and cleaves to his wife (2:24). For married love is the strongest earthly love, stronger even than that of the child for its parents.

Thus before turning his attention to the problem of sin and evil, which is the actual subject of the Paradise theme, the sacred author has for a moment become entirely engrossed by the great mystery in human life of the relationship between man and woman. And he depicts this relationship neither as a privilege belonging to the paradisal state, nor as a consequence of sin, but as a permanent law of nature, which has its foundation in the wisdom and the goodness of the Creator. For a moment he stops, and considers the relationships which we experience in this world simply according to the fundamental law of their being, in the same way that Genesis 1 constantly does. A creation theme has thus been introduced into the Paradise narrative here. The conclusion of the pericope allows of no doubt as to this, beginning as it does with a very emphatic "therefore," to wit: because the Creator made the woman in this way, therefore the two sexes are forever impelled toward each other.

Structure of the Pericope

The main teaching of the pericope centers on the relationship between man and woman. But there is also another doctrinal strand, interwoven with the first, which is in itself of considerable importance in such an Oriental context, and of which the object is the relationship between man and the animal world. And the whole thing is achieved with such artistry, that far from distracting one's attention from the main theme, this other point serves precisely to throw it into greater relief. Immediately after the beginning of the pericope, the story suddenly begins to take a wholly unexpected turn, a procedure which not only compels the attention almost irresistibly, but is also very effective didactically.

Jahweh Elohim had said: *"It is not good,"*—i.e., it is not in keeping with the given situation, with the nature of man's essential being—"that man should be alone. I will make him a helper fit for him." Literally, a helper as one right over against him, as a counterpart in other words, a pendant or match (cp. "better half"); thus not so much someone who is like him (Vulgate), as someone who is suitable for him, is proportionate to him, and who can be his partner.

The sacred author's mind has turned at once to woman. For man cannot find this, his greatest need, among the animals (20b), but in woman he finds it literally and completely (23). Every animal has a partner, they are in pairs from the highest to the lowest, and only man stands alone.

"Helper" is a general word, intended by the sacred author to indicate the social fact of the family as a whole; to think only

219

of the sexual act here would be to misunderstand completely the universal significance of the narrative. But it is in no sense excluded. This is indeed clear enough from the pericope itself, so that we do not need Augustine's reminder that if it had only been a question of companionship, God would have done better to have created another man.[1] Then, after these solemn words of introduction, the Creator turns immediately to action, to the making of such a helper. The story, however, takes an unexpected turn: "Then Jahweh Elohim formed out of the *adamàh* all the beasts of the field and all the birds of the air and brought them to the man to see what he would call them." And so it was that the animals got the names which they now still have: every animal received a special name from the first man, whether it was tame or wild, beast of the earth or bird of the air. One after the other they were brought before man, but he did not find among them all what he was looking for—a helpmeet fit for himself, as a human being.

We must remember that according to the manner of thinking of the ancient East, the name and the thing are to a great extent identical, so that the essential nature and destiny of each animal is expressed in the name which it is given by man. This naming episode is thus not just an accidental piece of literary ornamentation or expansion of the story, but is there precisely in order to make the real purpose of the whole thing clear: there is indeed no partner for man to be found among the animals. Such is the final and definitive conclusion. Jahweh Elohim continues His shaping and fashioning, each time making a new and higher kind of animal, and each time He brings His latest creation to man and shows it to him, and asks again, is this it, perhaps? And each time, as the naming itself shows, man is obliged to

[1] "Nondum erat labor ut (vir) adiumento indigeret, et si opus esset, melius adiutorium masculus fieret. Hoc et de solatio dici potest, si solitudinis fortasse taedebat. Quanto enim congruentius ad convivendum et colloquendum duo amici pariter quam vir et mulier habitarent" (*De Genesis ad litteram* ix. 5. 9; PL 34, 396).

confess: no, this is not it. Some have sought to explain this curiously round-about sort of narrative as the remnants of a myth according to which the animals were considered to be women gone wrong, or alternatively according to which man should have been content with the animals and was therefore given a wife as a punishment, to be the cause of all his future misfortune. We have however by now gained too good an insight into the sacred author's personal style and method, and into his deeply convinced Jahwistic faith, for there to be any necessity to consider this kind of blunder any further. In reality, what we have before us is quite clearly a deliberate and well-considered construction by the sacred author himself.

It was evidently extremely important to him that Israel should well and truly understand that the gulf between man and the animal world is an unbridgeable one. The quite exceptional emphasis which is given to this point makes one suspect a polemical motive, and indeed the Oriental heathendom in whose midst Israel dwelt provided more than enough justification for such a concern. No animal, of whatever kind, the writer is saying, is or ever has been the equal of man, let alone his superior, as if it could be treated by man as something holy or divine, to be feared and worshiped.

Thus what is expressed in Genesis 1 by means of a prudently chosen theological formula, is taught in Genesis 2 by means of a tableau of a highly anthropomorphic kind. But in both cases we are able to recognize the liberating clarity of Jahwism, assigning everything to its proper place, and making a sharp distinction between God and man, and between man and the lower world of the animals, so that there is no longer any possibility of any one category being allowed to run over into another. The mystery which is indeed present in every earthly reality is made subordinate to the mystery of Jahweh Himself, so that it is toward Him that the whole of human religiosity is firmly directed. The believer must realize that he is someone who has been lost, and is

221

now redeemed and saved. He knows where he is, for he is with Jahweh Himself, who far from being some fatal, fickle, and obscurely mysterious power, is the Holy One who has made Himself known in no uncertain fashion throughout Israel's history.

With such a foundation for his own conviction, the sacred author is able to inveigh without hesitation against Israel's own tendencies to superstition and at the same time bar the road in the direction of the perversions of the Canaanites.

Here again, the naming scene is of crucial importance. In the ancient East, to know and to be able to speak the name of something or someone meant that one was already in a position to exercise an effectual influence over it or them. To be able to give its name to something thus implies the possession of complete power and dominion over it, so that the scene clearly shows man to be the lord and master of the animal kingdom. But there is more even to it than this. There is also the implication that man's dominion cannot be limited or affected by any kind of magical influence which particular names might possess, for it is absurd to imagine that he could be subject to the power of a name which he has himself given, any more than he could be subject to a being which has depended upon him to be given its name, for the name and the thing are identical.

The knife, indeed, cuts both ways in this story. We can see now how the emphasis which is given to the pericope's secondary teaching only serves in turn to give added emphasis to the main point. For as the status of the man is raised above that of the rest of the creation, so is that of the woman along with him. In the narrative, the dignity of the woman is linked indissolubly with that of the man. The story of their creation is so constructed as to be a contrasting parallel with the story of the creation of the animals. For when the woman, too, is created, Jahweh Elohim first goes and fashions her (but out of what material?), and then brings her to the man, and in her case, too, the man's reaction takes the form of the giving of a name, which expresses her very essence and nature.

This reaction on the part of the man leaves nothing to be desired as far as clarity is concerned. In naming the woman, he becomes conscious of himself *as* a man, and his tremendous affirmative answer seems to sum up, once and for all, the answer which the man of every age gives to the miracle of woman.

20

Man and Woman

IT is entirely in harmony with the strictly monogenistic[1] approach of the Paradise narrative, that the first woman should be formed out of the first man, and is thus herself the second human being. That this is so, and why precisely the two things are connected, may not, perhaps, be immediately obvious, so that we must turn again and ask ourselves once more the most familiar and most relevant of all questions in the study of the Bible: What was the habitual approach of Israel to these questions?

Unity and Diversity

There are many different races and kinds of men, but in all the length and breadth of the creation the human race as such forces itself upon us as a unified and integrated whole: it is a group by itself, entirely distinct and separate. It does not occur to the author of Genesis, when he is faced with the many different groups into which we spontaneously divide the things which we experience, to attempt to reduce them to a kind of unity by making them come into existence out of each other. His point of view is the opposite of evolution: each group has a definite and separate beginning as the result of a special divine act of creation. Including man. Israel was well aware that there were many different kinds of men, many races and peoples with

[1] Monogenism: the view that the whole of the human race is descended from a single original couple.

their own particular physical characteristics, language, personality, and way of life, and that the origin of each of these must have had its own particular cause. The whole of the book of Genesis demonstrates a remarkable interest in these questions, and indeed it seeks to give to each human group a beginning at a particular point of time in the past. But this great diversity does not in the least affect the fact that humanity as such forms a closed and quite unique whole over against everything else. The common point of origin must therefore lie somewhere even further back in the past. Moreover there is one variation, in all this "phenomenon of man," which is far more profound and radical in its nature than all the rest, and which can only have originated in the original act of creation itself. It is the fact that there are male and female human beings.

There must, nevertheless, first of all have been *one* man only. This is obvious, for the source of humanity is "man" (*adam*). From one of his ribs, Jahweh Elohim then fashions a woman, and from this human couple all that is human springs henceforth. There is thus, without any compromise, a single point of departure: all spring from *Adam,* and Adam from God (cp. Lk 3:38). Not from several, not even from two, but "He made from one the whole human race and caused them to dwell over all the face of the earth, having established their allotted times [of their beginning, prosperity, and disappearance], and the boundaries of their habitation" (Acts 17:26). The first beginning of all is thus made not with a primal man and a primal woman, but with a primal human being.

Genesis 1 is concerned only with the species, and speaks collectively. But even here, an explanation of the human phenomenon as such is given before the question of sex comes to be considered at all. The mind and action of the Creator is shown as being centered on the image of God; and the use of the term "man" in the collective sense enables the author to move unnoticed from the singular to the plural, and from what is com-

225

mon to humanity to what is characteristic of each particular sex. In Genesis 2, however, it is a single, concrete individual who is created by Jahweh Elohim, a human being, i.e., a being composed of matter and of spirit. This human being, it afterwards appears, was a man, but then only inasmuch as he bears within himself the fullness of all that is human: the origin of the woman is not from outside, but from man himself. The sacred author has thus given an explanation not only of the unity of the human race, but also of the coming together in one of the two sexes. That man and woman are made for each other is a universal law that is so profoundly anchored in the nature of each, that not only must it derive from God's own act of creation but also must provide us with some kind of indication of how the Creator actually did His work: Man and woman were one in the beginning, and this is why they constantly desire to be one again. If God had instead fashioned the man and the woman out of two lumps of earth, the relationship of both to mother earth would certainly have been explained, but not their mutual relationship to each other; we should be left with two independent pieces of divine handiwork, concerning which it might at first sight appear that one of them was less of a success than the other. But now that it has been shown that the woman was taken out of the man, there is no alternative but that they stand or fall together. The sex which is most aware of its own superior strength can no longer regard the weaker sex as essentially inferior, for "no man ever hates his own flesh" (Eph 5:29). From the fact that woman is different, man can only conclude that she is called to a different task; both vocations are, however, fully and equally human. For if man and woman are indeed equal, this does not mean that they are identical; they are by no means a mere repetition of each other, each a perfect monad in himself. There exists between them a kind of gradation, for each fulfills and completes the other. The perfect expression of human nature is only to be found in man and woman together. And if the woman's weakness

226

indicates not her inferiority but rather her vocation to be a help-meet, then the man's strength is a sign not of his superiority but of his vocation as a leader and a protector. To borrow an elegant expression of St. Augustine's, the woman tempers the strength of the man precisely because her strength has its origin in him.[2]

The Text and Its Doctrinal Content

Man did not find among the animals a helper fit for himself, as a human being:

Then Jahweh Elohim caused a deep sleep to come over the man, and while he slept he took one of his ribs and filled up its place with flesh. And Jahweh Elohim made a woman out of the rib that he had taken from the man, and brought her to the man. Then the man said: "This, at last, is bone of my bones and flesh of my flesh. She shall be called Woman [*isshah*], for she was taken out of man [*ish*]." Therefore a man leaves his father and his mother and cleaves to his wife, and they become one flesh (2:21–24).

This deep sleep into which the first man (who was in any case exempt from pain) was made to fall, was not a kind of heavenly anesthetic, conceded to him in order that he might undergo the operation that was about to be performed without pain. The point of it is that married love is one of the greatest mysteries of this life, and that it is repugnant that man should be the eye-witness of the divine act of creation from which it has sprung. The origin of human life in the womb is itself an unfathomable secret which fills Old Testament man with reverence and awe (Ps 139:13–16; Jb 10:8–12; Qoh 11:5; 2 Mac 7:22 ff.). Here, it is certainly a similar kind of reverence which, in regard to the creation of the woman from the man, has commanded the way in which the story is presented.

The translation "rib" is probable, and certainly comes close to

[2] "Quae [mulier] per ipsum [virum] firma facta est tamquam eius osse firmata, ille autem propter ipsam infirmus, quia in locum costae non costa sed caro suppleta est" (*De Genesi ad litteram* ix. 17. 34; PL 34, 407).

227

expressing the sense of the Hebrew word. But the question of why precisely the sacred author chose a rib is not entirely clear, though there is no problem as to why the woman should have been formed out of some part or other of the man. The manner in which the text itself continues provides the clearest possible answer to this.

Man had rejected every being of whatever kind that had been fashioned out of the earth, but when at last he was presented with a being formed from his own body he recognized it at once as a member of his own species, his own *alter ego.* What he had sought for in vain on the previous occasions, this time he found, and still more than he had sought for: a partner who was like himself in very essence! The words which the sacred author uses to express the first man's breathless discovery of the miracle of woman give an indication of how he came to arrive at such a mode of speech.

The evident relationship existing between man and mother earth naturally gives rise to the image of the Creator taking a piece of earth and fashioning it into a human form. And the material connection between man and the earth is confirmed by the striking correspondence between the words *adam* and *adamàh,* since to the Oriental mind a relationship between the names indicates a relationship between the things themselves.

There is no closer relationship on earth than that between a man and a woman; for marriage is the source and foundation of all blood relationship. In Israel, in order to say that someone was a blood relation, one said: "He is my flesh and my bones" (Gn 29:14; Jg 9:2; cp. Gn 37:27; 2 S 5:1; 19:13 ff.; Is 58:7). This expression must therefore possess its greatest fullness of meaning when it is affirmed of the relationship which binds a man and a woman to each other. No more striking way of expressing the depth and intimacy of the relationship which binds each to the other could have been found than by thus making the Hebrew form of words to be a literal part of the narrative.

228

Hence too the striking correspondence between the word "man" (*ish*) and "woman (*isshah*): again, the relationship between the two names reveals an ontological relationship. In Hebrew, the suffix *-ah* is used to form female words (compare -ess in some English words). The sacred author thus gives to the Hebrew word for woman the meaning of a "female man," a "she-man."

And so it is that the manner in which the woman came into being provides an explanation of the universal fact of experience that a man leaves the house of his parents in order to found his own hearth and home. He cleaves (the Hebrew word indicates the psychological aspect of the marriage bond) to his wife; man and woman thus become one being again. (The Hebrew word "flesh" refers not to one part of the human make-up, but to man as a whole, but then with his visible and tangible aspect more to the forefront. To this extent it may be said that the *physical* side of marriage here comes more into its own.) It is obvious enough that the sacred author could not have spoken as he does in this pericope if he had not been convinced that the Creator had intended marriage to be absolutely monogamous. It is worth underlining what an immense spiritual conquest this represents (cp. Mt 19:4–6).

Elsewhere in the ancient world, there were ideas current about the first man having been bisexual, with the two sexes being supposed to have originated by a process of division in two. One can feel with this conception the existence of the same sort of background of ideas as we have in Genesis. Up to a certain point, one might even speak of the two as being related, provided that it is recognized that the relationship is based simply upon a common experience of mankind (the fact of human love both poses the problem and itself suggests the direction in which the solution is to be sought) rather than in any other kind of mutual dependence. And even if one could suppose the existence of something of the latter kind, this would not mean that the sacred

229

author thought of the first man as being bisexual, but rather that he consciously avoided any such idea by formulating his narrative (by the expedient of the rib) in another direction.

Historical Content

We have up to now found no reason at all in the narrative itself for thinking that the creation of woman actually took place in the manner which is represented in Genesis. The pericope can perfectly easily be explained, without any loose ends being left over at the end, as it were, as a well-thought-out interpretation of a certain number of empirical facts: 1) the absolute unity of the human race; 2) the relationship between man and woman; 3) the Hebrew expression for blood relationship: "to be someone's flesh and bones"; 4) the Hebrew words for man and woman: *ish* and *isshah*.

But there is more to it than this. If we do accept this interpretation, we find that the pericope with which we are concerned is entirely homogeneous with the rest of the narrative. The whole chapter, in fact, is a meticulously constructed imaginative presentation of a doctrine, and there is nothing whatever to suggest that this particular pericope forms any exception. It is, on the contrary, a striking parallel with the account of the creation of the first man, and an antiparallel with the account of the creation of the animals.

If we simply take the story as it stands, we are in fact obliged to admit that it offers us no sort of detailed chronicle of events, and that the author's concern is not to teach us in what manner God created woman, but rather as what kind of a being He created her. Jahweh Elohim fashions a lump of earth and breathes life into it. He takes a rib as the raw material of His work. All this is the language of imagery, a fact which in no way detracts from the genuinely historical character of the narrative, which is and remains an account of an actual past event, a divine act, but which at the same time, in and through the account, gives *an interpretation* of this event. The fact that man is what he is, and that man and wife are what they are in relation to each other, is thanks to the Creator. The richly imaginative form of the story is there for a purpose, which is to explain what the intention of the Creator was in doing this work: He has built a law into nature itself to which man is obliged to submit himself.

If God did in reality fashion the woman out of the first man, we must accept too that He did indeed carry out the kind of manipulation that is described in the pericope and that He subsequently provided an Israelitic author with information on the subject. Thereafter we should be obliged—without any justification provided in the text itself—to use two different standards of judgment, not only throughout the chapter as a whole, but even within the pericope itself. For the latter is constructed in three clear stages: Jahweh's deliberation (18); the procession of the animals (19,20) and the reconstruction of the rib (21,22). And if the first two of these stages are to be taken as dramatizations of an idea, why should the third not be thus taken also?

Any such position—as Hauret has rightly observed—also creates a difficulty in regard to the relationship between the first and the second chapters of Genesis. In the Bible, Genesis 1 is placed before Genesis 2, and books of biblical history often tend to succumb to the temptation to regard Genesis 2 as being a further elaboration of Genesis 1. But in reality the second chapter is older than the first, and adds no further historical details to it, in regard to what took place on the sixth day, for example. The correct relationship is in fact the other way round. Genesis 1 is more recent, it represents a later stage of development and is therefore theologically speaking more prudent: Genesis 1 reduces the anthropomorphic tableaux of Genesis 2 to their essential doctrinal content. So too in regard to the origin of the two sexes and their equality in dignity: "in the image of Elohim created He him, male and female created He them" (1:27; cp. 5:1 ff.).

231

It is not likely that the realistic tableau of our pericope has more in it of authentic Israelitic doctrine than has been found in it by the author of Genesis 1.

In making an exegetical study of Genesis 1, we are not concerned to decide how in fact, in the beginning, the Creation actually happened. Our problem is the more limited one of to what extent the narrative which lies before us obliges us to conclude to certain facts. So that if it should indeed appear, as the result of other considerations, that the formation of woman from the first man is an historical fact, there is no reason at all, on the basis of the exegesis of Genesis, for opposing such a conclusion. It may even be agreed that in such a case the text does in fact refer in some way to this event. The competence of exegesis as such is strictly limited, and the exegete must remain constantly aware of this limitation. Only the Church possesses the instinct which is fully proportionate to the ultimate and adequate meaning of Holy Scripture. The exegete must therefore have the humility to confess that with his specialized technique and his consequently limited field of vision, and obliged as he is to concentrate his attention intensively on one particular passage of Scripture at a time, he cannot from the text itself decide as to the historicity of an event which, when the whole question is considered from a higher and more all-embracing point of view, could nevertheless well have occurred.

But even if it is true that exegesis cannot in the nature of things have the last word, it does all the same have its own special contribution to make. It has undeniably its own proper domain, and, within this, its own autonomy in relation to the whole, somewhat as the different senses of the body each has its own relative, but nonetheless real, autonomy. These latter cannot presume in themselves to make a judgment, since their task is simply to present the data provided by the world of experience without prejudice. And yet the mind is in the last resort dependent upon them, since it possesses no independent means of perception, but has to seek the advice of the eyes and the other organs. In the same way the exegesis of Genesis would be failing in its proper task and would be rendering a false service to the various authorities for whom it has the task of providing the necessary material for a higher kind of synthesis than it is qualified to attempt in isolation, if it were to set aside or keep to itself its own doubts and uncertainties in a misplaced zeal for saying yea and amen.

We shall attempt, in the following chapter, to seek an answer to the great question of whether there may not perhaps be other grounds than those we have hitherto considered for recognizing a somewhat greater degree of literal historical content in the pericope.

21

"This Is a Great Mystery" (Eph 5:32)

IF it is indeed a point of faith that the woman was really formed out of the first man, the question which is thereby decided is not only historical in nature, but is also an exegetical one. We should have the answer not only to the question of how the first woman came into existence, but also to that of what the pericope in Genesis affirms about what really happened. In such a case we could hardly consider it to be a mere accident that Genesis presents the course of events in a way which corresponds to the teaching of the faith, be it in a still more concrete form. The Catholic exegete would then be obliged to admit that the sacred text really does teach the origin of the woman out of the man as an objective fact. This would, however, still not mean that he would not be perfectly justified in confessing his inability, using the technical means available to him as an exegete, to demonstrate that this teaching forms part of the intention of the narrative.

To say this is not to attempt to evade the issue, nor indeed is the case an exceptional one. This is particularly relevant as far as the Old Testament is concerned, since, in so many points, it represents only the first stage of a revelation which has been entrusted to the Church as a whole, as a living possession which is being constantly further unfolded within her bosom. It has usually only been after much reflection and conflict that the essential meaning of a particular doctrine has been strictly determined in a dogmatic formula, which then comes to represent the final stage in a process of growth, of which the most ancient biblical texts sometimes offer only the vaguest beginning. It is for this reason that the exegete cannot do without the guidance of the Church in forming his judgment about these ancient texts. In the last resort the decisive criterion is never that of scientific demonstrability. The first principle of all is that in matters of faith and morals the real meaning of Scripture is that which is and always has been held by Mother Church (Dz. *1507, 3007). For, as Leo XIII says, Scripture sometimes contains more than appears from the letter of the text and than the principles of exegesis (*hermeneuticae leges*) are able in themselves to reveal (*Enchiridion bibl.* 134; cp. 93).

The Biblical Commission

This is also quite clearly the position of the Biblical Commission in its famous decree of June 30, 1909, "concerning the historical character of the first three chapters of Genesis" (Dz. *3512–19). The Commission, after it has first in general rejected those systems which destroy or undermine the historical meaning of these chapters (paragraphs 1 and 2), proposes in paragraph 3 a general normative principle by which it is possible to determine the minimum of historical content which must at all events be maintained. This principle is as follows: that where in these chapters the issue concerns "events which touch the foundations of the Christian religion" it is not permissible to call in question the "literal historical meaning" of the relevant passages. There then follow five further paragraphs which expressly concede a certain freedom of opinion in regard to particular points.

This well-known paragraph 3 makes no appeal whatever to scientific scholarship—if it had done so, the scholarship in question would inevitably have been that of 1909—but rather to the faith, which belongs to all times without distinction. Even in 1948, the Biblical Commission[1] was still of the opinion that scholarship had not by a very long way said the last word about these chapters. It still considered the time for a *positive* solution of all these problems to be not yet ripe, and it offers an extensive summary of all that still needs to be done by way of study toward this end. Only then will it be possible to hope for a clearer insight into the real character of certain of the narratives which are contained in the first chapters of Genesis. In the meantime, there is need for patience, and for attention to be paid to the encouragements given in the biblical encyclical of 1943, *Divino afflante Spiritu,* which enjoins both courage and perseverance; light may still be given, as has so often happened in the past, concerning questions which had before seemed insoluble.

The Commission of 1909 was perhaps rather more optimistic in its view, but in any case, apart from the last paragraph which contains one unfortunate hint, we may be thankful that it was so cautious in formulating its opinion. Whatever the opinion of the Commission may have been on the subject at the time, it was, in fact, far less possible in 1909 even than it is at present to resolve all the problems involved in a positive manner. The Commission itself, of course, in no way pretended or desired to do such a thing; there were far too many new elements being constantly introduced into the debate, all of which called for further investigation. The Church, on the other hand, has her own permanently valid principles, which absolve her from the necessity of waiting for the results of scientific research as far as certain points are concerned, i.e., those which bear upon the actual content of the faith. She may in particular sometimes give an immediate *negative* judgment in order to exclude certain solutions which may be brought forward. Thus it was possible for her,

---

[1] According to the letter of its secretary to Cardinal Suhard.

236

even in the situation of 1909, to intervene in such a way as to direct the discussion into safer paths and so save Catholic exegesis from fruitless adventures of one kind and another. And indeed she did more than this: she laid down a positive and literal exegesis for certain passages, in the light of revealed doctrine.

Now among the events which concern the foundations of the Christian faith the above-mentioned decree mentions also "the formation of the first woman out of the first man." Since then it has generally been assumed, perhaps too readily, that there was nothing more to be said on the subject, in view of the decree. From this it has been unanimously (and gratuitously) concluded, without further investigation or reflection, that the rib must "therefore" be held to be a part of the symbolic clothing of the narrative, but that the physical origination of the woman from the man is taught by Scripture as a fact. Only after the letter to Cardinal Suhard were certain proposals put forward here and there in the direction of some kind of freer interpretation. And indeed the said letter gave every encouragment to such attempts, for it says that the decree of 1909 must be understood and interpreted in the light of the most encouraging passage of the biblical encyclical of 1943, and that it must be allowed that the decree in no way presents an obstacle to further scientific research into the problems in question in the light of such results as have been achieved since 1909. For the same reason there is no call for the old decree to be replaced by a new one.

It is also remarked in the letter that, if the Church since 1909 has not maintained an attitude of complete rejection in regard to the doctrine of evolution insofar as the body of the first man is concerned, it cannot at the same time have wished to exclude the same doctrine entirely in regard to the body of the first woman, since the two are inevitably connected. This again presupposes a freer interpretation of the pericope in Genesis than the decree of 1909 would at first sight appear to allow.

237

Significance of the Decree

But is this impression really only one gained at the first sight? The fact that the decree has never really been submitted to more profound examination is no doubt bound up with the circumstances of the time. It is worth calling attention to the remarks which such an authoritative personage as Father—now Cardinal —Bea (who was Rector of the Pontifical Biblical Institute from 1930 to 1949) has formulated in *Biblica,* since his criticisms are relevant not only to the book of Father Van den Oudenrijn, *O.P., De Zonde in den Tuin* (Roermond, 1939), which he considers in any case to be a book of value, but also to practically the whole of the meager Catholic literature in existence on Genesis. The tendency has been to consider the decree of the Biblical Commission too much as an external norm without ever getting as far as asking the question "why," whereas the decree itself makes a distinction, which is certainly not an arbitrary one, between essential and less essential points.[2]

Specifically, too much attention has been concentrated on the nine points which are listed in paragraph 3 of the decree, and too little on the principle of which they are intended to be an illustration. The paragraph has been used as if the Biblical Com-

---

[2] "Es wäre zweckmässig gewesen, näher auf die Frage einzugehen *warum* in einigen Punkte die wörtliche Deutung festgehalten, in anderen dagegen unbedenklich von ihr abgewichen wird. So hat der Verf. keine Schwierigkeit z. B. das 'Bilden aus Ton' und das 'einhauchen des Lebensodems' als Anthropomorphismen aufzufassen, während er das 'Bauen' der Eva aus einen Bestandteil des Leibes von Adam im eigentlichen (literalen) Sinn auffast. Ein tieferer Grund für dieses verschiedene Vorgehen innerhalb der gleichen Erzählung wird nicht angegeben, wenn man nicht als solchen den Hinweis auf das Dekret der Päpstlichen Bibelkommission auffast. Aber diese hat gewiss nicht willkürlich einige Punkte als wesentlich, andere als weniger wesentlich erklärt. Es wäre daher wünschenswert, dass die Frage der literarischen Art . . . und die Grenzen einer freieren Deutung irgendwo grundsätzlich behandelt würde, damit der Leser nicht den Eindruck gewinnt, als ob es schliesslich Sache des einzelnen Exegeten sei, nach eigenen Gutdünken oder nach rein äusseren Kanones bald die eine bald die andere Erklärung zu wählen" (*Biblica* [1944], 75 ff.).

mission was therein formally enumerating which particular points do in fact concern the foundations of the Christian religion. Theologians would have no difficulty at all in formulating twenty or more theses from the nine points listed in the decree. And if, according to their custom, they were to note by each of these theses the extent to which each of them was connected with the teaching of the faith itself, these "qualifications" would vary considerably not only from thesis to thesis but also from theologian to theologian. It should be obvious that the Biblical Commission cannot thus have intended to lay down in passing (the list of points is introduced with the phrase "among other things") twenty or so dogmatic definitions in the course of an exegetical decree.

The authority of the Biblical Commission is limited to biblical questions insofar as these bear upon faith and morals. This latter limitation (bearing upon faith and morals) derives from the fact that the Church's own doctrinal magisterium does not extend further than this, while the first limitation (biblical questions) follows from the fact that the Church's magisterium uses this Commission as its organ precisely in this particular domain. This is clear from the prehistory of the Commission, from the official documents which have been published at the time of its erection, and also since then, and in addition, not least, from what the Commission has itself done and not done. The latter's decrees—amounting all together to about sixty questions and answers—limit themselves without exception to the sphere of exegesis, and are in the last resort always concerned with the meaning of the biblical text itself—the value, origin, composition and authorship of certain books; certain exegetical systems; the meaning of a particular text or group of texts, and so on.[3]

Paragraph 3, with which we are at present concerned, is no

[3] Point one of the official *règlement* reads: "Proteggere et difendere assolutamente l'integrità della fede cattolica in materia biblica" (*Civiltà cattolica* [1903] II, 221).

239

exception to the above. In it, the Commission formally lays down an *exegetical principle,* which is that the text of Genesis must be understood literally when it speaks about facts which affect the doctrine of the faith. In 1909 very little was as yet known about Genesis. All that is clear in the decree is what certainly cannot be allowed (paragraphs 1 and 2) and what certainly can be (paragraphs 4 to 8). But in regard to the broad area in between, the Commission does not simply abandon the exegetes to their own devices—it refers them to the Church's teaching and all that it implies. And it goes on to give a number of examples by way of assuring the practical application of the principles which have been laid down, not with any idea of giving an entirely superfluous doctrinal admonition and still less in order to tie down these principles to any particular doctrinal point.

The principles are therefore binding for the Catholic exegete, but the question of whether or not the formation of the woman out of the man is a matter which concerns the faith need not be considered as having been finally settled. In 1909 this question had hardly even been formulated, let alone investigated. A theologian as cautious as Fr. Smulders, S.J., to whom I owe the worthwhile suggestion of distinguishing between the exegetical and the dogmatic bearing of the decree, remarks that it is clear from the form in which the decree is cast that the theological aspect of the matter requires further investigation, but that in fact the theologians—the exegetes by contrast have been doing their best—would appear to have completely neglected to investigate the question of the extent to which the formation of Eve from the body of Adam belongs to the foundations of the Christian faith. For himself, he believes that, when the question is considered on its own merits, this can hardly be judged to be the case (*Ned. Kath. Stemmen* [1950], 366).

What paragraph 3 provides in fact is a provisional list of a number of points which either certainly or possibly belong to the

240

substance of the faith or are closely connected therewith. This list is quite expressly ("among other things") not intended to be complete, nor is it intended as a formal declaration, which it would in any case be rather for the Holy Office to make. Its real purpose is to call attention to things which should in any case have been known already in other ways, and also to things which call for further investigation in various directions. As long as this research has not been done, the task of the exegete must be to treat the relevant passages in Genesis with prudence, i.e., to avoid abandoning the literal interpretation.

The Basis of the Decree

It is easy enough to conjecture what "doctrines of faith" the Biblical Commission had in mind when it included the "formation of the first woman out of the first man" in its decree. To begin with, this would appear to be presupposed as a fact, or even formally taught as such, in a number of places in the New Testament (1 Cor 11:7–12; 1 Tim 2:12; Eph 5:28–30). Moreover this event, understood in the literal sense, has a very ancient place in the tradition of the Church, which has been very ready to see it as a prefiguration (*typus*) of the birth of the Church from the side of Christ as He slept in death on the cross.

Even now, forty years later, these things cannot just be lightly brushed aside. The fact is, however, that this is an aspect of the matter which can ultimately only be resolved in a wider context, since it is a particular case of the much greater question of the relationship between the two Testaments, in regard to which research has only fairly recently got under way. We cannot go into this here, but must be content simply to indicate briefly why it is that the above-mentioned points do not provide such a final and complete answer to the question under consideration as was once thought to be the case.

First, the question of the value and significance of typology. It

241

is undeniably the normal law of typology that, as the *sensus rerum,* it sets one reality in relation to another, especially an Old Testament personage, institution or event in relation to something in the New Testament. But the example of the "sign of Jonas" proves with all the clarity that could possibly be desired that we cannot make an absolute and radical law out of this principle. In order to decide whether or not Jonas really was swallowed by a sea monster, the study of the book of Jonas is of more conclusive importance than the apparent evidence of Christ's words, so that in this case the exegesis of the New Testament must defer to that of the Old Testament. We may then understand the New Testament text as follows: "Just as—according to the story which you all know—Jonas spent three days and three nights in the belly of the sea monster, so shall the Son Of Man spend three days and three nights in the bowels of the earth" (Mt 12:40). Thus however important the relevant New Testament fact may be in its relation to that in the Old Testament, and however vital this reference back to the Old Testament may be in the context, it still does not follow that the Old Testament fact in question is necessarily an historical fact: it would seem to be enough that it should be a literary fact.

The above example shows clearly enough that even texts from the New Testament do not always lend themselves to immediate, apodictic conclusions. The way in which the New Testament, and especially Paul, exploits the Old Testament, is far too singular and characteristic, and, to our modern way of thinking, too lacking in system, for any such approach to be justifiable. Further research is indeed urgently needed toward a better understanding of the mentality which lies behind the New Testament writers' use of the Old Testament as a framework for the new message of which they were so full. For them, the Old Testament is an arsenal from which they take anything that in any way suits their purpose—sometimes, it may be, a text which has just come into their mind by chance. And when they thus refer back to the Old

Testament, their primary purpose is certainly not to make a declaration *about* the Old Testament. What they have to say is something entirely new, but they are nevertheless perfectly ready to express this in terms of the formulas and categories of the Old Testament with which they were so familiar.

Consequently, in cases where Scripture, as so often, quotes and commentates and re-interprets itself, we are obliged, in answer to the question as to what actually and objectively happened, to come back to the exegetical principle that the most ancient passage which has been the starting point of a whole series of quotations and allusions retains a certain primacy over the whole of the rest of the tradition which it has brought into being. For it is this text which stands closest to the actual event in question, and which mirrors most faithfully the original intention which lay behind it, whereas in the case of the later texts there are other intentions which also enter in.

Our conclusion must be that the evidence of later texts which refer, in dependence on Genesis, to the origin of the first woman, is such that we may well in the last resort have to return to Genesis itself for a final decision. If this does turn out to be so, it may not be out of place to recall that the Biblical Commission itself has recently expressly given notice that its earlier decrees are to be understood in the context of the time in which they were first made public (cp. *Revue biblique,* 62 [1955], 414–419).

22

Monogenism and Original Sin

THE Paradise narrative is based upon the strictest monogenism. This fact does not, however, by itself constitute a Scriptural proof of the doctrine. The question remains whether this monogenism belongs not only to the structure but also to the doctrinal content of the narrative. This question is not, as Renié and Ceuppens assume, automatically decided by the fact that Genesis is an historical book. The latter author is satisfied simply to recapitulate the contents of Genesis 2, and to declare, having done so: it seems to me that it follows sufficiently clearly from this passage, that in the beginning God created only one man and one woman.[1] It will be useful to take a somewhat closer look at the circular argument upon which this declaration is based:

Genesis, it is argued, is an historical book in two parts; both parts, therefore, give us history. The events concerning the Patriarchs took place relatively shortly before the time of the author of the narrative which relates them, so that he could both obtain and verify his source material fairly easily. He also used ancient documents of the highest value. In the case of the creation narrative, on the other hand, there was a much longer interval involved, so that the problem of obtaining information was more difficult. The author was not a contemporary of the events which he relates, therefore he must have used sources. Were

[1] "Le polygénisme et la Bible," *Angelicum,* 24 (1947), 25.

244

these sources of an historical nature? We must assume that they were, otherwise he would not have incorporated them into an historical book.[2]

A Question of Method

When one comes across an argument of this kind in an article that claims to expound the doctrine of Scripture concerning polygenism, one is forced willy-nilly to reflect upon the strain which must inevitably exist between "Israel's vision" on the one hand, and the exegetical system, in which most of us have grown up, on the other. If we permit ourselves to be led on in this sort of direction, we shall find that we are caught in a cul-de-sac of a kind that we have been constantly seeking to avoid throughout this book. Genesis is an historical book, therefore God created our first parents as a single pair. There are arguments in favor of a symbolic interpretation of the garden and the trees, but we give the preference, Renié says repeatedly, to a realistic exegesis. He does not say why, but he betrays his underlying principle clearly enough when he disposes of an attempt to "interpret" the monogenism of Genesis simply by asking the rhetorical question: "With such an approach how can anything historical at all remain in the first three chapters of Genesis?"[3]

The answer is, of course, that there is history and history, and that Genesis is historical in a sense which it is precisely the task of the exegete to determine more closely. This is above all true of the creation narrative, of which the special historical character is the great point of research. To label it "en bloc" either as historical or as unhistorical leads to misunderstanding, said the Biblical Commission in 1948. The point is that a clearer insight must be sought into the true nature of the various narra-

[2] *Art. cit.,* p. 23 ff.
[3] *Les origines de l'humanité d'après la Bible. Mythe ou Histoire?* (Lyon, 1950), p. 104.

tives out of which it is composed. It is only from the starting point of these separate narratives that we shall be able to arrive at a conclusion as to the nature of the whole, and not the other way round.

Half a century ago, exegesis was riddled with this sort of preconception. There were so many new problems pressing in, and it was no doubt tempting to resolve as many of them as possible in this sort of way, without really investigating them in depth. It is in fact only in recent years that the delicate question of whether Genesis really does teach monogenism as clearly as might at first sight appear has begun to be properly faced. Anyone who thinks that he can dispose of this question by resorting to some kind of preconceived idea is really only creating confusion and losing an opportunity of showing his worth as an exegete. Where and in what way does the Paradise narrative really touch anything concerning monogenism? The question is of the highest interest, and it is one which forces the exegesis of Genesis back to a radical rethinking of first principles.

Is it or is it not the case, that the exegetical argument from Genesis that God created a single human pair depends upon the acceptance of the principle that the author of the Paradise narrative must have employed historical sources? He was, of course, not a contemporary of the events which he recounts, but his sources could nevertheless have contained the facts. But from where did these sources get the information that God created a single pair? The truth is that this procedure provides a solution to our question that is purely apparent, since it is arrived at by reducing the question to another one which is itself, in the nature of things, insoluble.

What Genesis has to tell us is indeed weighty with historical consequences, but the purpose of the sacred author is to give us very much more than mere history. If one is looking for history, the only question which need be put to the texts is that of what really happened. Attacks on the historical value of Scripture

246

obliged the Biblical Commission in 1905 to set its historical character in the foreground (Dz. *3373). But ultimately the affirmation that Genesis is an historical book is a much too narrow basis for exegetical research. Over against the conscious or unconscious system that has tended to underlie the exegesis of Genesis, which may be formulated as "the more historical the better," we might define the system followed in Israel's own vision of things by saying that the doctrinal content of the texts is of greater importance than their historical content, while the latter can in turn only be effectively demonstrated and established in safety in the measure that its relationship with the former has been shown.

The Nature of the Question

That polygenism lies entirely beyond the horizon of Genesis is denied by nobody; but this does not mean that Scripture affords a doctrinal proof for monogenism. However little we may be able to conclude from it definitely, a comparison with the notion of evolution may nevertheless help to clarify this point. Evolution, too, falls entirely outside the Bible's field of vision, not only that of the human body but also every other form of evolution, whether of plants or animals. In Genesis we find the most absolute fixism: the origin of each species—and even wildness or tameness constitutes a difference of species— is explained in terms of a special divine act of creation.

It is beside the point to say that Genesis is therefore against evolution. The fixism of Genesis derives from a quite spontaneous process of perception and classification of the phenomena of the actually existing world in all its fullness and variety, in which we are faced with a whole mass of different created things which impress themselves upon us in groups which are clearly distinct from each other. The sacred author is concerned to bring together as many as possible of these groups in his creation

247

narrative, so that there is a divine creative act at the beginning of each. He is not, by doing this, taking up a position in a disputed question, for the simple reason that for him this question does not exist. He is neither in favor of evolution nor against it.

But although both polygenism and evolution are both equally outside the field of vision of Genesis, the attitude of the Church to the two systems is not the same. This attitude is, therefore, not determined solely by the letter of Genesis, which implies in turn that the exegete must dig more deeply. If he is to use Genesis as an argument in favor of monogenism, he will have to be able to show convincingly that the monogenism of the sacred author has a deeper foundation than his historically conditioned fixism.

From an exegetical point of view, this question is similar in nature to that of the origin of woman (cp. pp. 232 ff.). Our final judgment about monogenism will also have to depend upon the answer to three questions: 1) what is the exegetically demonstrable teaching of the paradise-narrative about the matter? 2) what other evidence do we find in revelation? 3) what is the attitude of the Church's magisterium?

The question whether or not monogenism forms part of the teaching of the faith must be left to the theologians. Here we shall simply recall two relevant points: 1) that a proposed canon, which was to have been laid before the First Vatican Council, anathematized anyone who should deny that the human race descends from a single first parent, Adam. 2) that the decree of the Biblical Commission, which we have already discussed (June 30, 1909), counts "the unity of the human race" as being among the facts related in the first three chapters of Genesis which concern the foundations of the Christian faith and of which the literal and historical meaning may not be called into question. The encyclical *Humani generis* declares that it is in no way clear how polygenism—understood either in the sense that after Adam true human beings have existed who were not descended from the first parent by the ordinary process of generation, or in the sense that Adam is a collective concept for a greater number of original parents—can be reconciled with the dogma of original sin, as it is taught in the sources of revelation and in the acts of the magisterium. A footnote refers to Rom 5:12–19 and to the Council of Trent.

Doctrine of Faith and Scriptural Proof

Whether or not it is a doctrine of faith, it follows from the above that in practice the Catholic is obliged to hold that the human race is descended from a single first parent, and that the Catholic exegete, too, must in practice hold that monogenism is something more than an accidental form of expression in Genesis, and thus that it is in some way or another taught in the narrative. But doctrine of the faith or not, it will always remain the primary task of the exegete to investigate what is to be obtained by the use of the technical methods of his profession from Genesis itself. While recognizing to the full that the ultimate implications of the texts can only be understood in the light of the teaching of the faith as a whole, he must nevertheless in the first place do what he can to make it possible for Genesis simply to speak for itself. His first question must always be: What does the actual narrative that lies before us say? What does it "prove"? Otherwise the whole business of exegesis had better be abolished.

Anyone who is prepared to reflect for a moment and consider the gulf that stretches between the last pages of Denzinger and the first pages of Holy Scripture will become aware that there remains a great deal more to be said even when verbal agreement between the teaching of the faith on the one hand and the text of Scripture on the other has been established.

It is undeniably the case that an ancient inspired text may stand in a definite and positive relation to a particular doctrine which after much struggle and reflection has eventually been defined as to its essential substance in a dogmatic formula. And yet it is one thing to understand this text, in its function as a vague starting point, as an essential part of the whole process of spiritual development which has culminated in the dogmatic formulation, and quite another to want to drag this dogmatic formulation forcibly to light, as it were ready-made, from the ancient text in question.

To attempt the latter is asking too much of the text. But there is also the other, and opposite extreme: one can also ask too little of a text by assuming that there is nothing at all there just because it does not contain the clearly expressed and fully developed formula. With Scripture above all, which offers us the first human expression of the great things which God has done, one must not only pay attention to what is said in completely "thought-out" formulas, but also, and just as much, to those so frequent passages in which one can feel that the process of seeking and striving after such a formula is still going on. There are many ideas in Scripture which are still at the stage of being worked out and gradually developed through a kind of wrestling with some great truth. The approach to such a truth is bound to be a slow one, and it is often to begin with rather experienced and "known" than thought out in conceptual form. Not only must one attend, therefore, dictionary in hand, to what the sacred author actually says, but one must also do one's best to guess at things which he is only suggesting, and which he himself is perhaps no more than groping after. And this can only be done by as far as possible becoming identified with his particular psychology, and by taking his words as a kind of instantaneous photograph taken from the dynamic and ever-moving stream of revelation.

250

Monogenism and Original Sin

It would not appear to be an accident that it is to some extent the same authors who (in our opinion) ask too much of the text when it is a case of establishing a Scriptural proof for monogenism, and too little when they are doing the same thing for original sin. This may perhaps be reassuring to some readers, since original sin quite certainly belongs to the teaching of the faith. The actual historical growth of the doctrine of original sin is unthinkable apart from the teaching of Paul (Rom 5) which in turn depends upon its basis in Genesis. Thus Genesis must inevitably, in some way or another, lie behind the doctrine of original sin. And yet there are exegetes, and even theologians, who are of the opinion that in the whole of the Paradise narrative there is no trace to be found of original sin. And there is no one who objects to their holding this position. It is moreover precisely among these that a number are to be found who affirm without further investigation that the monogenistic structure of the Paradise narrative constitutes in itself a Scriptural proof for monogenism. It is to be feared that the association of these two positions can only be explained as the result of an exegesis that has remained far too much on the surface of things. There is indeed no mention in the Paradise narrative of a transmissible guilt for sin, while it does on the other hand expressly say that God created one man and one woman and that from these two the whole of the human race is descended. The name Eve is even explained as meaning "mother of all living things."

As far as one can see at the present moment—and it would seem that the exegetical aspect of the question of monogenism is still in the very early stages—it is only possible to show effectively that monogenism belongs to the doctrinal content of the Paradise narrative in the measure that it can be shown that the narrative does contain an affirmation of a transmissible burden

251

in the religious sense which bears upon the whole of the human race. Not only in *Humani generis* but already in Genesis itself are original sin and monogenism closely bound up together. In fact monogenism, considered in itself, is a question of natural science concerning which the Church only makes a declaration because of its relationship to the doctrine of original sin. In the same way it is no part of the purpose of Genesis to decide such a question, except precisley insofar as it is concerned to teach us— in its own special way, of course—something about original sin.

It is important to realize that as soon as we are tempted to pose the question of monogenism separately, and see it only as one of the possible answers to the purely scientific question of how the human race did in fact begin, we run a great danger of misunderstanding the Paradise narrative and of looking for arguments in places where we cannot possibly expect to find them. One result of this will be that we shall tend to give too much attention to the creation theme in Genesis 2, and too little to the Paradise theme in Genesis 3, in which the sacred author is seeking to represent and to explain the religious status of the whole human race. It is only when we have become aware of this that we can begin to see the evidently monogenistic structure of Genesis 2 in an entirely new light.

23

The Origin of the Monogenistic Idea

Inspiration and Revelation

IT has only been with considerable difficulty that exegetes, with the concept of inspiration inevitably in mind, have succeeded in arriving at the conclusion that the Bible does not contain formal judgments concerning matters which could not even remotely have been in the minds of the sacred authors. The Bible is not only a divine, but also a divine-human book, and this means, as far as the Old Testament is concerned, that we are never in a position to approach the mind of God unless we are prepared to pass first by way of the mind of Israel. Whether or not the human race is descended from one or from several pairs of first parents is a modern question, which has only come to be posed as the outcome of a whole succession of scientific facts and presuppositions which in earlier times were entirely unknown and unknowable. So that it by no means follows, from the simple fact alone that the Paradise narrative only speaks about one pair of first parents, that the Bible is to be found on one of the two sides in this modern argument.

The appeal to inspiration being thus of no avail, it may be tempting to turn to the concept of revelation. But here also great caution is required. Speculative analysis of the concept of revelation is desirable, but it can be dangerous if it is not accompanied by a prudent awareness of the way in which revelation has in fact been realized and manifested throughout the course of history. We would wish to be second to no one in the conviction that the Paradise narrative could never have come into being without revelation. But when and how precisely did God communicate its essential doctrinal content to Israel? To this question we would answer that the Paradise narrative is an eloquent example of how powerfully God's centuries-long concern for Israel had eventually affected and determined Israel's world of ideas and its whole way of looking at things and of expressing them. This is of course a very different understanding of "revelation" than that which conceives of the communication of isolated truths bit by bit, such as, for example, that the human race is descended from a single pair of first parents. The truth is that Jahweh had set Himself in the midst of His own people, as an inescapable divine *fact,* and Israel experienced Him as such. God revealed Himself to His people and spoke to them above all by what He did, by showing who He is by His actions. And Israel began in turn to try and reflect upon this religious experience and to express it as best it could—to make, in other words, a first attempt at theology, by seeking to find an explanation of human existence and of the realities of this world which corresponded to its awareness of God. The Paradise narrative is thus the outcome of a long tradition of reflection within Israel. The outward form in which this reflection has found its expression is that of the ancient East, but it has been fertilized, directed and formed by "the divine Fact." God's word has taken human form in Israel, the actual substance of God's message has been made visible in the flesh and bones of the world of ideas which Israel possessed in common with the rest of the ancient East; and so it can truly be said that the Paradise narrative is the fruit of revelation.

Anyone who seriously wishes to think historically about the Old Testament revelation—and the same goes for inspiration—must get used to thinking in this kind of way. Far from being disturbing, it will then turn out to be a positive and helpful

254

discovery to find from an examination of Genesis as a whole that the monogenism of the Paradise narrative obviously belongs together with the whole sequence of thought and literary structure of the rest of the book of Genesis. The question remains, however, whether this monogenism is thereby sufficiently accounted for. We do not consider—even from a purely exegetical point of view—that the question can be simply disposed of by saying that this monogenism is just one among the sacred author's typical thought-forms, which need cause us as little concern as, for example, his geocentricity. On the other hand, it is difficult to deny that it does seem to have a natural enough place among a number of other peculiarities which we have certainly no reason for interpreting literally.

The Method of Genesis

Genesis' way of putting things can often be most naturally explained in terms of the ordinary impressions which we obtain from our spontaneous perception of the world around us (cp. p. 222). We experience the human race as a closed and separate group of beings, different and distinct from everything else we meet, and the natural reaction to such an experience is to start looking for some special explanation of the fact that there are such things as human beings. Thus it is a natural enough procedure, in the perspective of Genesis, to reduce this experience of humanity to "man" (*adam*) as its origin and starting point. We are not, it would seem, meant to get more out of Genesis 1 than this. On the basis of our ordinary and immediate perception, and without the slightest scientific pretension, Genesis 1 classifies the phenomena of the created world and then proceeds to make each separate class of beings the object of a separate divine act of creation. God establishes the different species, and then provides them with the means of propagation. And when man's turn comes, the sacred author simply continues in the same way. He is concerned in the first place with the species as such, and he uses the word *man* in a collective sense. But God did not create a whole race of people all at once, any more than He created whole flocks of sheep all together. That the first starting point of the human race should have been as simple as possible, numerically speaking, lies in the structure of the whole chapter, and is also underlined by a definition of man in which emphasis is laid upon the personal dignity of the individual.

If we then want to compare the two following chapters with Genesis 1, we must do so by leaving the theme of Paradise and sin on one side for a moment. What we now have to ask the Paradise narrative is not, why is humanity so sinful and unhappy, but simply, how did it come to exist at all? To this question the answer is quite definite: from a single human couple and in the last resort from a single human being.

But the fact remains that so far no exegete has been able to show convincingly that there is more objective factual material behind this narrative than is the case with Genesis 1. These two chapters both belong to the Jahwistic part of the narrative, from which a number of separate passages in Genesis are derived. This having been established, we can say with confidence that we know something about our narrator's character, and his manner of going to work. And it is therefore no surprise to us to find him expressing what he has to teach concerning man not in a general and abstract way, but very concretely. He tells us about a particular man and a particular woman, and he has all kinds of detailed information to give us about their origin. Here again, we should be wrong to conclude from this that we thereby have the clue to a final decision about the monogenism of Genesis; but the question ought to be considered from this angle as well.

Our Jahwistic narrator also shows a special interest in the origins of all kinds of cultural realities, and for institutions and customs of all kinds, whether religious or secular. In his treatment of these he follows a striking method, which is to relate how

256

and why such and such began as if it were an actual event which occurred at a particular moment in the past. He does this in the familiar anecdotal style to which we are accustomed in folklore. These episodes are of course most often more a kind of dramatic characterization of the thing in question, as it is known by experience, than actual history of the past. In the same way, the numerous explanations of names are also a familiar teaching procedure of the same kind.

This method is used most especially in regard to the origin of peoples and races. The actual history of how a particular people has come into being is in most cases in the nature of things unknown and unknowable, for it is only when a people already exists as such that the question of its origin begins to arise. Genesis, however, is careful to provide each separate people with a distinct starting point in time and a definite individual progenitor. The artificial nature of this procedure is manifest enough. There is no earthly reason for supposing that the population of Egypt did in fact derive from a single ancestor by the name of Egypt. It is likewise obvious that the sacred author, because he knew a particular ethnic group that in his time was known as the Arameans, for this reason allotted them a common ancestor by the name of Aram. And so an exegesis which is to avoid simply having recourse to the policy of the ostrich, must sooner or later face up to the question of whether or not Genesis, when it makes the whole of the human race descend from a single man (*adam*), means more than when it sees all the Canaanites as being the descendants of a certain Canaan. We may note in passing, that the behavior of the latter was also the cause of an inherited curse.

Modern Problems

If we are to arrive at any real understanding of Genesis, we must first of all become fully aware of the extent to which our modern problematic differs from the mentality of ancient Israel. Only then will we begin to realize what individualists and materialists we have become. For us, "the man" of the Paradise narrative is nothing more than the individual, Adam, the primal sinner who has ruined everything for us, while we only vaguely understand what original sin is all about. In thinking about our solidarity with Adam, our attention is most often entirely concentrated on the physical and genealogical aspect. We tend spontaneously to transpose the Paradise narrative into the sphere of the positive sciences, for the simple reason that the question which really interests us is that of how the human race actually came into existence. As a result, the conclusion which we immediately and instinctively draw from the narrative is that it all began with one individual, that he committed a personal mortal sin, and that all human beings, being descended from him, are likewise burdened with the consequences of his action.

The approach of Israel, over against this, is first and foremost social, and also religious through and through. It is not for nothing that the first man is called *adam* (= man), for it is in him that the sacred author makes concrete in one individual all that is most characteristic of the race as a whole. In this man, everything that man has ever been is as it were "concentrated." What has rightly been said with regard to Romans 5,[1] that for Paul Adam is a "corporate personality" just as Christ is, is at least equally true of "the man" of Genesis. Just as the whole of humanity was placed by Adam in a state of sin, so is it placed by Christ in a state of righteousness, or rather those who are "in Christ" by grace just as everyone is "in Adam" by nature. The parallel with Christ is sufficient proof that this "corporate" approach does not necessarily exclude the individual personality of the first man.

Thus where the sacred author sees humanity as if through the eyes of God, brought together in solidarity in the concrete figure

[1] K.C.T. in *Streven* (1952), 221.

of the first man (in whom, as in a "timeless concentration," the whole human race is present in one), we on the other hand—because of our individualism—spontaneously think of humanity as spread out over the long road of time in a whole series of individuals of whom a certain Adam was the first.

We are also materialists. It is perfectly true that the sacred author represents the first man as the ancestor of all other men. But here too, our minds go immediately to the material and physical aspect of this. Now there is nothing to show that the sacred author intended to exclude this aspect, any more than he meant to exclude his individuality, as we have just said, but his real message is nevertheless first and foremost of a religious nature: that by the very fact that we are men, we are involved in the primal sin which is a sin of man as such. The sacred author presents this doctrine very concretely, by speaking of a single physical ancestor, but the blood relationship is in the first place a form of expression for the mutual relationship which we have with each other in the sinful condition which is the inheritance of every human being. This requires some further explanation.

Religious Teaching Expressed in a Material Form

The unbiased reader of the early chapters of Genesis will be obliged to recognize that the narrative which concerns the Flood unquestionably rivals the Paradise narrative in seriousness and universality of purpose. Noah is the beginning of a new humanity. After the Flood, a new situation begins, in which we immediately recognize the common human lot of our own experience. In this narrative, the sacred author presents a kind of concrete picture of this situation by bringing together all the different races of which he has any knowledge in the descendants of Shem, Ham and Japhet. It is quite obvious that this "list of races" is not to be understood in a purely ethnographical sense: it is really a kind of family tree, in which blood relationship plays a quite secondary role. Also, it is generally admitted nowadays that the sacred author's horizon is a limited one, and that it does not necessarily embrace the whole of the human race. The real teaching of the narrative is to be sought not on the level of profane ethnology, but on that of religion. And this religious doctrine does indeed give the impression of universal significance: the sacred author would most definitely seem to be saying something about the religious situation of the *whole of humanity*.

It is precisely for this that he needs his ethnographic framework. As well as he can, he tries to bring together the whole of the human race that was known to him and relate it to a single point of origin, so as to show how all without exception are subject to the consequences of the situation resulting from the Flood. His list of races is a means of expressing this intention, so that it does correspond to a real situation, but a religious and not an ethnic one.

Notwithstanding the heterogeneity of the material in terms of which it is expressed, the whole *structure of ideas* in the primal history which we are given in Genesis is fundamentally homogeneous. For this reason it is not only exegetically justified, but is even positively required by the text that this parallel between the two ancestors Adam and Noah be fairly and squarely faced, if we wish to avoid the accusation of measuring by two different standards.

This parallel may also serve to prepare for our conclusion concerning the monogenism of Genesis, which is that even when it has been duly considered in the light of the theme of Paradise and original sin, it can certainly not be presented as a simple and evident fact. We can, nevertheless, claim to have established the following points:

1) The sacred author's concern is with *a human situation that is common to all men everywhere.* It belongs essentially to the situation of man as he now is, that he stands before God not only as a creature but also as a sinner, a corrupt creature. God is life and holiness. We on the other hand are born in a state of condemnation to sin and to death; we are alienated from the world of divine things and stand in fear and shame before it. Even apart from the fact of personal guilt, we are by nature branded with sin and misfortune.

2) The sacred author does not however limit himself to depicting a real characteristic in a purely "literary" first man. If he had wished only to give a *picture* of man's present religious situation, then Adam would indeed have been no more than a symbol of the whole race. The narrative would have been the history of the race as such rather than of an historical first man, speculation rather than history, and we should have been able without reservation to treat this narrative in exactly the same way as the many other passages in Genesis in which we appear to be given a schematic description which reduces a great variety of facts to a single artificial point of origin.

3) It is most certainly the sacred author's intention—for this touches the heart of his message—to *explain* our present situation. This Adam of whom he speaks is not only a reflection, an image, but also the *real cause* of our predicament. Human sinfulness and human misfortune are intimately bound up together and both derive from the sin of Paradise as a result of which we have become an impure race, hereditarily deprived of the paradisal divine good will (*privatio gratiae hereditaria* = original sin, not simply original penalty).

4) This causality is only clearly evident, if Adam was indeed the real ancestor of all. For it is understandable enough—for Israel far more indeed than for us—that the children must bear the consequences of their father's act. So that if Adam's physical fatherhood be taken away, the argument loses much of its power to convince. For our mentality, it even loses all its meaning. However since it is a fact that Israel's approach to these matters was profoundly different from our own, in particular inasmuch as things which really and ultimately belong to the religious

261

sphere were so readily carried over into the physical and material sphere, and since it is the primary purpose of Scripture to give judgment only concerning the former, it is in our opinion difficult for the exegesis of Genesis to risk an absolute decision on the question.

5) In the interpretation of the remaining biblical texts which are based on Genesis, and of the tradition of the Church in the matter (which is founded upon the whole body of the biblical evidence taken together), this margin of uncertainty left open by Genesis itself must be taken into account.

24

Flesh or Spirit

THE principal object of the Paradise narrative can perfectly well be given its full weight without going into the question of the extent to which the narrative is meant to be taken literally. Whether the interpretation in this respect be strict or rather freer, it must in any case end up at the same doctrinal points. And it is indeed the case that in the past, when the literal interpretation reigned supreme, the deepest substance was often enough well understood, to the extent that there hardly remains anything better to be said about it. And yet a literal interpretation does carry with it the danger that the attention will become fixed upon things that are really secondary, so that the main emphasis gets put in the wrong place. How many are there who have left school with the impression that the fate of the human race was decided by the eating of an apple! The proportion between the sin and the penalty then becomes hopelessly lost, and it cannot be satisfactorily restored by enlarging on the black ingratitude of the first human couple or by reasonings about the clarity of their judgment and the strength of their will power in the unfallen state.

Formal Sin of the Spirit

A literal exegesis can all too easily get bogged down in the material details of the transgression, whereas the narrative itself in fact says very clearly indeed what it is all about. For it sets before our first parents the crucial choice between a total yes and a total no, even if the actual occasion of it may seem to be trifling enough. The narrative gives the sin in Paradise the form of the primal sin of all sins. It is of the kind that is often described and characterized in Scripture as *the* sin par excellence (cp. p. 204): it has the nature of a fundamental choice (*optio fundamentalis*), to be compared with the dilemma which Deuteronomy places before Israel (30:15,19).

The first man was under the obligation to determine his attitude to life just as every one of his descendants has been: Either he had to take account of God as the supreme Reality toward whom all his life and conduct must be directed, or else *self-sufficiently make himself the ultimate measure of all his doing and not doing and thus, though he was no more than human, arrogate to himself the place of God.*

Was he, ultimately, going to be ready to make the self-giving act of faith, and anchor himself in God, or was he on the contrary going to put his trust in human means and capabilities, which according to his own calculations and understanding of things would bring him salvation, in the manner of King Achaz, who invoked the aid of the Assyrians although Isaias had insisted to him that the only thing that could save him was trust in Jahweh (Is 7; 2 K 16:7 ff.)? Was he going to follow his own way, or God's way, the way of believing obedience, the way that every Israelite knew that he must follow after the example of Abraham?

From ancient times the narrative has been understood as teaching that Adam's sin was a sin of pride. *This still remains the most pertinent and succinct expression of the main point of the narrative.* All interpretations of man's primal sin which contradict this fundamental teaching of the biblical text are, by the very fact, not worthy of further consideration.

264

Material Sin of the Flesh?

It follows that the question as to the *nature* of this primal sin can only have any meaning insofar as it concerns the actual concrete act in which this pride was expressed. The narrative itself, indeed, offers us a perfectly concrete act: the eating of the forbidden fruit. If this is to be taken literally, then there is of course no further problem. If however it is to be understood as a literary figure of speech, then further enquiry is necessary. The first step must be to ask whether the sacred author speaks about a forbidden fruit simply because Israel could not do without some kind of concrete picture of how the Fall took place, or whether on the contrary he has a quite particular kind of act in mind, so that the actual form of expression which he has chosen is calculated to suggest a particular sort of offense. This really boils down to the question of whether or not the narrative really implies that the sin was a sexual one, since other possibilities do not usually enter in the picture.

Already in ancient times the sexual interpretation had a number of adherents, but it became less and less common in the measure that the literal interpretation became more generally accepted. In the last century, when the narrative began to be considered as a pure myth, the various possibilities offered by this interpretation were exploited in all directions, and since then there are few indeed who have not come across it in some shape or form. It is a naturally attractive explanation, and to those who find that they are no more than half convinced by the literal interpretation, it can often appear as a heaven-sent solution to a difficulty that has long been felt. We must remember to begin with that the exegetical question does not concern what our first parents actually did, but only what conception Israel—known to history as a people of the ancient East who lived in Canaan from about 1200 to 600 B.C.—had concerning this

265

primal sin. When this question has been answered, we shall not *necessarily* be any nearer to knowing anything about the actual material nature of the historical first sin. We have already established that the sacred author represents the Fall as the archetypal example of pride leading to its own downfall; his story is first and foremost a characterization of the fundamental attitude which belongs to all sin as transgression of God's law and rebellion against God. The question which we now have to consider is whether at the same time he intended to set this primal sin, the source of all human misery, in relation to a particular sinful practice which was prevalent in Israel or which in some other way constituted a particular danger for the Israel of his time. This would then be a definite secondary tendency of the narrative, deducible from various details and more or less vague allusions.

By putting the question in this way, we are giving the "sexual interpretation" its only possible chance. Even then, it must, in our opinion, be quite definitely rejected. It is most likely that the narrative does indeed contain secondary tendencies, and it would be entirely in accord with the character of the sacred author, as he has so far made himself known to us, that he should not have chosen the material which he needed for his narrative in an arbitrary fashion. And we may assume that his choice in this matter will have been determined by some particular doctrinal or pastoral concern. The question remains whether or not this concern was with sexual matters.

One of the Great Difficulties

To start with, it is not easy to imagine, in terms of the conventions of the narrative, what kind of sexual sin this couple, who were so expressly created that they might become one flesh, could have committed, at least as long as we remain within the perspectives of the Bible as opposed to those opened up by our modern powers of imagination. It is beside the point to start thinking of any too refined kind of sin, unless we can find evidence for doing so in the Law or the Prophets, and this is not the case. Adultery—which is the greatest and most usual sin in this domain—is scarcely possible, while the suggestion of extramarital intercourse comes up against Augustine's very reasonable dilemma: that there are only two possible alternatives, either they were able to have intercourse together or they were not. If they could not, then obviously they did not; if they could, then it was also no sin for them to do so, unless one considers that they were bound by our present-day formalities in regard to the solemnization of marriage! [1] This is very much to the point. The purpose of the Paradise narrative is to teach how God established the structure of nature, and what is the essence and meaning of the relationship between man and woman. And it is the essence of all human morality to seek to be and to live in actual fact according to the pattern of things that has been laid down in nature by the divine law. Here we are concerned with the first *parents* of the human race, who as such were called upon to do what all parents after them have lawfully and praiseworthily done for the propagation of the human race. It would constitute a profound internal contradiction if this narrative, of which the purpose is precisely to explain and to justify the universally experienced phenomenon of marriage, were at the same time to make the normal sexual relationship between the first man and the first woman to be their great sin. This would involve admitting that God could have reversed His original intention, so clearly expressed in the act of creation in which the profound relationship between creation and the blessing of marriage is such a central point, by some kind of positive interdiction. God created a *married couple,* and that is all there is to it.

In addition to this and other extremely telling elements in the narrative, there is also the command to "be fruitful and multiply," in which the author of Genesis 1 is no doubt faithfully

[1] *De Genesi ad litteram* xi. 41. 57; PL 34, 452.

reproducing the intention of Genesis 2, which goes together with the well-known biblical attitude which regarded childlessness as a scandal. Israel did not suffer from sexual complexes. In those days the great moral crimes were called frankly by their names, and condemned for what they were: "This kind of thing is not done in Israel." On the other side of the picture, we have the "mothers of Israel," the Sarahs, the Rebeccas, the Rachels, who were set as examples before the women of Israel who awaited from Jahweh's blessing the same fruitfulness that had once made Israel to be as numerous as the sand by the sea. It cannot therefore have been the sacred author's intention to say that the primal sin consisted in the fact that the first man had intercourse with her who was destined to be the mother of all living things. The transgression of the first parents must have been something that was obnoxious for Israel, and worthy of condemnation, and it must also have had the nature of a warning, lest Israel should be tempted to follow their example.

Possible Solutions

In short, if we take the narrative as it stands, the popular sexual interpretation of it gives us nothing to hold on to. Insofar as qualified exegetes (the many amateurs who have busied themselves with the question can appropriately be left on one side) appear to hold something of this kind, they have in general arrived at their position by one or other of the following ways:

1) Many of them resort to radical alteration of the narrative—in effect they make it into a different narrative by taking the actual text and reconstructing from it "the original myth." In this way it becomes possible to hold, for example, that our first parents were given the choice between personal immortality or survival in their posterity. There have been others who have considered—the theory has become almost classical—that the

narrative is through and through a psychological myth which depicts the transition from childhood to maturity, being thus concerned in particular with the awakening of sexual awareness and the first sexual experience. Man is given a prohibition, recognizes the woman as a woman, shows that he has moral and sexual awareness, etc. However since these and similar positions are in clear contradiction with the text as we have it, there is no need to consider them further.

2) Another way of avoiding the above-mentioned contradictions is to presuppose an unnatural sexual act of some kind, with all the abundant possibilities which this offers to the imagination. There are few which have not been duly considered.

3) Lastly one can think of a sexual act which was indeed good in itself, but became bad because of the circumstances. We mention this position for the sake of completeness, so as to have an overall picture in regard to the "sexual interpretation." Anyone who has some experience of the complicated variations which have been elaborated by scholars under this heading is liable to finish with a feeling of general dissatisfaction with them all. There are so many of these marginal discussions in the field of exegesis, beloved of scholars if of no one else, and this particular one is certainly no less arid than most. We give the following example by way of illustration.

Professor J. Coppens, of Louvain, has for a number of years past, and under various kinds of reserve, defended a sexual interpretation. Echoes of this have begun to filter through beyond the frontiers of professional exegesis, with the result that quite a number of people have begun to wonder where things stand, with a vague feeling that all is not as it should be. However anyone who has the opportunity of studying the position of the above-mentioned scholar for himself will discover immediately that he rejects the usual sexual interpretation on the ground of a number of conclusive arguments, only one of which is among those we have mentioned. He considers all of the three above-

269

mentioned interpretations before finally coming to his own position as to why the present narrative is a sexual one.

1) The sexual element is only in the background, on the horizon, so to speak, of the narrative, possibly only in the source which the sacred author has employed. He has not assumed it as a part of his own teaching, he has perhaps even consciously tried to filter it out ("palimpsest"). But there are a number of details and implications which remain and which point in this direction.

2) The sin which is thus suggested in the narrative consisted, according to this theory, in the fact that the woman attempted to back out of her marital duty, both in relation to her husband and in regard to her responsibility to bear children, and that the man thereafter supported her in this act of rebellion. The presence of the serpent would be evidence in favor of this view, for in the ancient East the serpent is a sexual animal, especially connected with the male sex, and was often represented along side of fertility gods who would seem to have been much worshipped in Canaan, appearing most often together with a naked female figure. Thus Eve got involved with the serpent, at the same time appearing to abandon her husband. She is thereupon condemned in the judgment to love the man and to bring forth many children. Then only does Adam greet his now converted spouse as the mother of all living things. The text about the fruit that was "desirable in order to gain understanding" can also be translated, without notable alteration, as "desirable in order to become childless" (Gn 3:6). Moreover, it is a perfectly familiar theme that certain plants are capable either of favoring or of inhibiting conception. In the Flemish edition (1946) of his monograph on this question, Coppens is inclined to regard these and other points as being allusions to an unnatural sexual sin, or at any rate as remnants of a more ancient narrative about such a sin.

3) In the expanded French edition (1948), however, he

shows his readiness to abandon such a definitely sexual interpretation. He still considers that there is an unmistakable sexual element in the narrative, but now says that it is simpler to explain it in the following way: that in order to warn Israel against certain Canaanite religious practices, in which licentious fertility rites played a considerable role, the sacred author makes the sin of Adam and Eve to be that they wished to live and fulfill their married life under the protection and blessing of heathen gods, ignoring the Creator. The figure of the serpent is there to remind Israel of the native religious world in whose midst it lived and from whose temptations it suffered so sorely. The misery that this heathendom brings with it can now be seen from the example of Adam and Eve. Thus according to this interpretation, the sin of our first parents was against the state of marriage and its consecration to Jahweh, and so really—but Coppens does not say this—*not a sin against the sixth commandment but against the first!*

Our present concern is not with the opinion of Coppens as such, otherwise we should have had to give it in much greater detail; we have used it simply as an example by means of which the "sexual interpretation" might be somewhat better situated. There is in any case a good deal of material in his study of the question which can find a place to equally good or to better advantage in other interpretations. We shall make use of it, with gratitude, in the following chapter, in considering various other elements in the narrative to which appeal is often made in this connection.

25

The Sexual Stuff under the Hammer

THE tree of life gives eternal life (Gn 3:22). The tree of knowledge—literally the "tree of knowing good and evil" (2:9,17)—is also named after its effect: whoever eats of it, knows good and evil (3:5,22). The formula "to know good and evil" occurs four times in the narrative, to which it is undoubtedly one of the keys, but unfortunately a mysterious key. It is capable of having more than one meaning, and it is indeed possible that the intention of the sacred author is to play upon these meanings. But the sexual meaning does not begin to have a chance here, although it is then more difficult to make out what the formula does mean. In considering this question we shall try to be as little tied down as possible to any one opinion, and so keep our distance somewhat. Better to be vague and correct than precise and wrong. . . . It seems probable, from all that is said in the narrative about the trees and, among other things, the serpent, that the sacred author is making use of certain popular, quasi-magical conceptions, though he is doing so with the purpose of making them serve the cause of Israel's moral and religious convictions. As a result, the function and the name of the tree of knowledge can be explained in somewhat differing ways according to which text is taken as a starting point, and it is important not to try to force these artificially into a synthesis which is quite probably not achieved in the narrative itself.

272

To Know Good and Evil

The verb "to know" occurs hundreds of times in the Bible with the ordinary biblical meaning attached to it. This, as is well known, adds a strongly affective and practical dimension to the meaning of the word "know" as we normally use it, in the sense of mental and theoretical knowing. There are only a small number of cases in the Bible (and they are clearly recognizable) in which the word is used as a euphemism for knowing someone sexually. Protagonists of the sexual interpretation usually appeal to this use of the word, but to do so in this connection is a serious mistake in method: it could only be legitimate to interpret *know* in this sense once the sexual meaning of the narrative as a whole had clearly been proved. And even then, the difficulty remains that "to know" in this sense requires an object, which is precisely lacking here in the narrative. One cannot "know good and evil" in this sense. The sexual element cannot therefore lie in the word "to know."

The same thing has been attempted with "good and evil," it being said that these very general, and common, expressions have a special content here, referring to the joys and burdens of marriage. The fault, again, is one of method. It is revelant, moreover, that there is not a single text in the Bible where *good* has a sexual meaning.

It is sufficient simply to have touched on this "argument." When there is so much hot air to contend with, it is useful to have something handy by way of a gag! In reality, there is no need to discuss the point further, since the formula, "to know good and evil," occurs in this or in analogous forms fairly frequently in the Old Testament, and always with the indication of an entirely different sort of meaning. In such disputed cases, the obvious and sound exegetical procedure to follow is to investigate first of all the biblical parallels. This research has been carefully done, many times over, and if the result is not always the same as regards the precise shade of meaning to be attached to the formula, its general significance is sufficiently well established, and is entirely appropriate in the Paradise narrative.

This can scarcely be said of the sexual interpretation. To know good and evil is a privilege of the inhabitants of the divine world (*elohim*). By eating the fruit, man sought to acquire this knowledge for himself, and so become like the *elohim*. This is not only the obvious meaning of the serpent's argument in the course of the temptation, but it is also what would appear actually to have happened, since Jahweh Elohim—in the most difficult verse in the whole narrative—avows as follows: "Behold, man has become like one of us as regards the knowledge of good and evil." It is difficult to see what opening this gives for a sexual interpretation. Israel's conception of the supramundane world was impregnated with Jahwism, and there was no place for sex in it. Such ideas belonged to polytheism, where in addition to the supreme god, a mother of the gods with sons and daughters was required. Jahweh is in fact the only national god of the ancient East who has no female partner. It is difficult, in a narrative that is so deeply Jahwistic through and through, to see how sexual experience could be a privilege of the *elohim,* and how man could be presented as becoming like the *elohim* as a result of having it. This is quite apart from the fact that there is no indication whatever in the narrative that sexual experience was, so to speak, jealously withheld from the first man; on the contrary, the capacity for it had been given to him by Jahweh Elohim Himself.

Man is in the highest degree blamed for arrogating to himself the place of the *elohim*. This ambition has so many parallels in the Bible, that its meaning here cannot be seriously in question: What man is formally seeking after is not a fleshly but a spiritual good (cf. the previous chapter). The formula is quite

274

obviously used as a means of expressing this striving after a spiritual good, and it is indeed exceptionally appropriate for such a purpose: To want to know good and evil is practically speaking the same as to want to be *like* the *elohim,* and is moreover equated by the narrative with "wanting to gain understanding" (3:6). Thus whether or not the first man's transgression was in the domain of sex, the formula has in the narrative the function of providing a verbal expression for the formal nature of the primal sin.

The formula "good and evil" can have the meaning of "everything whatever." In Hebrew, two opposite expressions are sometimes used together not so much because of their literal meaning as to express a totality of some kind: "Good and evil" are thus two extremes of which the purpose is to fix attention on the whole area, as it were, lying in between ("from good to evil," Gn 31:24; 2 S 13:22). Laban and Bethuel say to Rebecca: "This thing has come from Jahweh, we can speak to you neither bad nor good," i.e. we can say *nothing* against it whatever (Gn 24:50). With a negative, "good and evil" means "nothing," without a negative, "everything," in the sense of "anything whatever." Compare the two following parallel texts, which are also interesting because of the supernatural character ascribed in them to the kind of knowledge which is in question: "The king is like an angel of God, as regards *the hearing of good and evil*"; and "the king is as wise as an angel of God as regards *the knowing of everything that happens on earth* (2 S 14:17,20).

In some cases, the emphasis may however lie on the two extremes which are mentioned, as in the text which refers to the difficulty of the judge's task of *distinguishing between good and evil* (1 K 3:9). Since the same expression may thus have a different meaning according to the context, it is as well in the Paradise narrative to reckon with both possible meanings, especially since a case can be made out for retaining both together, in the sense that man, by desiring to know good and evil, is aspiring to a suprahuman kind of knowledge.

There are, however, two reasons why it is better not to say that our first parents aspired to "omniscience." For it is by no means clear that the sacred author had this kind of total universal knowledge exclusively in mind in using this formula, even though this would indeed be a divine privilege. In any case, since the narrative so expressly places man before the choice between good and evil, and since the terms "good and evil" are so extremely appropriate in the given situation, it is unquestionable that the kind of knowledge which we call the power of discernment is included in the meaning of the formula.

Again, man's sin cannot be thought of as lying in his boundless curiosity for knowledge, for this would be to understand the Hebrew idea of "knowing" too conceptually. In Hebrew, "knowing" is also practical, in the sense that it is to a greater or lesser extent creative: To think of something, or to pronounce its name, is to exercise a real influence over it, to obtain power over it in some way. It then becomes clearer in what sense the knowledge which consists in the power of discernment of good and evil can also be a suprahuman privilege. The *elohim* "know good and evil" in the sense that they have dominion over it, they have the power and the right to decide what it is. For man, the norm of good and evil is situated in another and a higher world than his own, and it only remains for him to submit himself to it. He may not simply do as he likes, everything that seems good to him (here we have the universal aspect of the formula). He has, notwithstanding, arrogated to himself this right: he desires to know good and evil like the *elohim;* he aspires, in a word, to *moral autonomy*. By every sinful action, man turns upside down the true values which are rooted in a higher order of things. That which is evil, he calls good, and vice versa (cp. Is 5:20; Amos 5:14 ff.), he chooses evil as if it was good, simply because he finds it good to do so (aspect of discernment).

Understood in this way, the formula describes a knowledge which has all the characteristics that are ascribed to it in the narrative. It is the knowledge which is reserved to the world of the *elohim*, that man did not possess in the state of innocence but which he arrogates to himself in and through his sin, and which since then has been the common inheritance of fallen humanity, which grasps ever and again after this forbidden knowledge in its every sinful act. It is a knowledge, moreover, that is always accompanied by the same disillusionment as that which it brought to the first man.

The Nakedness

The serpent argued that by the eating of the fruit "their eyes shall be opened"—which is a biblical way of expressing a new and higher kind of knowledge—so that by obtaining a kind of knowledge that only the *elohim* possess, they will become as they are. The narrative relates, with an obvious allusion to the temptation, that their eyes were indeed opened, and that they knew. The knowledge which they thus gained came as a disillusion: "they knew that they were naked." But it *was* knowledge, all the same; they were the richer by one experience. Up to that time they had of course been aware that they were naked, but they did not yet *know* it; they had not yet experienced it as something to be ashamed of before each other. Now for the first time they experienced their nakedness in the way that is characteristic of man in his present condition.

The narrative provides us with an imperishable delineation of the process of sin, in particular of the fundamental contradiction between the results which man imagines will come from his

277

sinful act and the situation which it does in fact bring about. It is an entirely modern reaction to see a sexual reference in this nakedness. To express the biblical meaning more adequately, it might perhaps be better to translate: they became aware that they had been caught with their trousers down! Nakedness is meant as a sign of shame and dishonor, of weakness and helplessness. Man, who in his pride had attempted to reach out into the sphere of the *elohim,* suddenly finds that he is thrown back on to the resources of his own naked humanity, which is completely powerless in itself. Here we may recall the many prophetic passages in the same sense, from which it is possible only to quote a few verses.

When Jahweh called Moses, he found Israel in a state of nakedness: ". . . I spread the edge of my mantle over you and covered your shame. I clothed you with fine garments . . . I decked you with ornaments . . . And so you were adorned with gold and silver; your raiment was of damask and silk." But Israel became unfaithful, and began to run after other gods. Therefore ". . . I will give you over into their hands, they will strip the clothes from your body, take off your ornaments and leave you lying naked and bare" (Ez 16:8–13,39).

Let Israel be converted, "lest I strip her, completely naked, and leave her, just as she was born" (Hos 2:3).

If we carry the analogy between the first man and Israel through to its logical conclusion, we could say that he was in himself entirely naked, a helpless foundling.[1]

Man owes all his dignity and all his privileges to the Creator, so that we may justifiably speak here of the "garment of grace." By his sin, man has fallen back into a state of nature, but it is now a wounded nature. Sin transforms the nakedness which

---

[1] The first human beings who were created immediately in grace did not know this state. When Genesis 2 calls them naked, the doctrinal emphasis is quite a different one.

belongs to man by nature into a "privation." Israel's original nakedness was not shameful, it was simply a fact which underlined the unmerited quality of its election by Jahweh. But after Israel had sinned, things were otherwise. We may recall the distinction between *nudus* and *spoliatus* which theology employs to express the difference between the two states of *natura pura* and *natura lapsa.*

The narrative itself confirms that we are right to seek in this direction. For this nakedness is something which goes deeper than a mere state of the body, and which neither an apron of fig leaves nor the skins of animals can take away. Notwithstanding the covering up of his bodily nakedness, man has always continued to feel ashamed and afraid in the sight of God ever since this first primal sin. The experience of sexual shame is only one particular expression of this, though it is certainly a very significant one. The sacred author has in fact a predilection for this kind of suggestive detail, and this image is for him simply a concretization of the awakening of man's lower impulses over the whole range of concupiscence. But the idea of nakedness is in itself in no way a proof that the narrative as a whole is concerned with sexuality.

The Serpent

The figure of the serpent was bound up with so many different ideas and images in the ancient East, that it must likewise be judged a methodological error to use it as an argument in favor of the sexual interpretation. It is by no means a proven fact that the serpent *was* above all a sexual symbol, and still less that it functions as such in the Paradise narrative. The words of the serpent in the temptation scene, and the fact that it is described as being "more subtle than all the other wild animals,"

279

tend much rather in a direction which is strikingly parallel with the idea of "knowing good and evil."

The sacred author seems to find it necessary to say that the serpent was an animal created by Jahweh Elohim, and further, to lay great emphasis on the fact that it is an extremely contemptible animal. This emphasis makes us suspect some kind of polemical background. The role which the author gives to the serpent seems to presuppose in his hearers a certain familiarity with the idea that the serpent is in some way a kind of divine or holy animal that is in a position to have contact with the world of the gods. In Canaan, the serpent was not an animal of misfortune, but on the contrary a bringer of life and fertility. One finds it pictured everywhere, often no doubt simply as an ornamental motif, used to fill up a bit of space, but also undoubtedly as the emblem of certain gods, and in particular that of a Canaanite fertility goddess. There is a certain point of contact here for the sexual interpretation, but neither the Canaanite nor the biblical evidence encourage any limitation of the serpent's significance to this particular aspect.

In addition to the magical role of the serpent, it also has the character of a "beast of wisdom," an animal which possesses the secret of a higher and divine knowledge. Wisdom and life are indeed intimately bound up together, and both ideas are present in the image of the serpent; and both are characteristic elements of which we can find recognizable traces in the Paradise narrative. Hence it is not so surprising after all that the serpent is able to speak, that it seems to be initiated into the secret of the tree of knowledge, and that its assurance "you shall surely not die" makes a big impression. The sacred author would seem to have had both conceptions in mind in sketching the figure of the serpent, but at the same time to have then set them both definitely aside: The serpent is not a good but a cursed animal, it brings not life but death.

Rather than engaging in a polemic against any particular sexual practice, the sacred author seems rather to be condemning, though in passing only, the native Canaanite heathendom with all its accompaniments. The new evidence which we now possess about Canaanite religion confirms that the serpent would have been a highly appropriate symbol to use as a concrete evocation of this native heathendom with its various religious practices. This could well be an explanation of why the sacred author should have chosen the serpent in particular as an imaginative image of the spiritual power of evil. The practical moral of the narrative as far as Israel was concerned is thus manifest enough. The Paradise narrative can be set fairly and squarely in the context of the Law and of the preaching of the prophets. During the whole of Israel's period of geographical stability, Jahwism was constantly being threatened by the danger of syncretism and of Baalism; and Israel was all too much inclined to look to these local gods for salvation. Here, in the narrative, the consequences of this tendency are plain for all to see. Only faith in Jahweh, and obedient observance of His Law, can bring salvation and life (cp. Dt 30:15–20).

For these reasons it is difficult to see the "sexual interpretation" as more than an unproved and somewhat forced explanation of a certain number of loose elements, which, far from being interpreted in the light of their context, are taken as a norm to which the context then has to be made to fit. To do this is to abandon the universal significance of the narrative, which, in itself, demands to be understood as a characterization and designation not of a particular sin but of sin as such.

The views of those who have arrived at a sexual interpretation not by exegetical but by ideological means (e.g., Mayrhofer) have not been considered. Taking in a wide variety of evidence (virgin birth of Christ, circumcision, the fact that original sin is incurred by *generation,* strength of concupiscence in the domain of sex, and such like), the sexual character of the

281

primal sin is deduced by a process of reasoning from the apparent nature of the hurt to that of its cause. A certain type of mind, which is fond of grandiose conceptions and attractively presented syntheses, is extremely susceptible to this kind of thing, and it is as a rule practically impossible to wean such people to any other way of thinking. We need not, indeed, attempt any such thing, since such an argument would no longer have anything to do with the exegesis of Genesis.

26

The Judgment

THE narrative of the temptation and the Fall, with its deep insight into human nature, comes to a new dramatic climax with the equally perceptive description of the meeting between Jahweh Elohim and the sinful couple. The sacred author's awareness of God and his understanding of man now, as it were, join hands. The God of Israel is a living God, from whom there is no escape. It is a terrible thing to fall into His hands, but it is also the only way to save what still can be saved. God does not leave man to pick up the pieces by himself, but comes immediately to the rescue. In the very moment that the power of evil seems to have triumphed, He takes things in hand. Judgment is inevitable. But this judgment is nothing else than a solemn recognition and partial sanctioning of the situation into which man has brought himself by his sin. And it is the sentence of a merciful judge, for our narrative is also a Proto-gospel. The pursuit of man by God's avenging righteousness is not the end of the story; we are already reminded, though it is still in the far distance, of the parable of the Good Shepherd who goes in search of the lost sheep.

God's Midday Walk

The way in which Jahweh Elohim makes His presence felt is not so clear as is often supposed. The most likely translation of Genesis 3:8 reads: "Then they heard the voice of Jahweh Elohim who was walking in the garden in the breeze of the day." Jahweh Elohim does not speak as yet, so that we may suppose that they did not actually hear His voice, but at the most the "sound" of His footsteps: they heard Him coming.

We give preference, however, to the interpretation which would relate the verb which has been translated here as "walk" with "sound." This means abandoning the idyllic picture of Jahweh strolling in His own garden in the fresh breeze which in Palestine as elsewhere often blows in from the sea on sunny days round about midday. According to Vaccari, the sacred author's meaning is to say that God's presence was revealed by a rustling among the leaves: they heard the sound (*qôl* = any kind of sound, including a voice) of Jahweh Elohim which echoed round the garden (*mithallêk* = going here and there, wandering around) in the breeze of the day. There is much to be said in favor of this translation. Such a concrete, imaginative way of indicating Jahweh's presence, while still preserving the hiddenness of His holy Being, is entirely at one with the whole concept of God which the narrative proclaims, and which is both illustrated and confirmed by 2 S 5:24: "And when you hear the sound [*qôl*] of footsteps in the tops of the balsam trees, then make ready quickly, for then is Jahweh going before you." And there is also the theophany which was granted to Elias, described in detail with a definite theological purpose: all of a sudden, Jahweh was going by, but He was not in the strong wind, nor was He in the earthquake (*non in commotione Dominus!*), nor yet in the lightning. "But after the lightning there whispered a soft breeze. As soon as Elias heard this, he covered his face with his mantle, and the sound of a voice came to him which said..." (1 K 19:11 ff.).

The translation: "They heard there the voice of Jahweh echoing through the garden, while the midday wind came up"

(Dutch translation of Van den Oudenrijn), confirms the construction of the phrase which we have proposed, but gives a completely different exegesis by interpreting "the voice of Jahweh" as being a metaphor for thunder, as indeed it is in several Psalms. The trial now follows immediately, first of the man, and then of the woman. Not, be it noted, of the serpent, because its guilt is something that goes without saying; there can be no excuse for it, since it acted out of pure wickedness, standing as it does, in the narrative, for the power of evil and for everything that is ranged in enmity against God. After the trial, there follows, in reverse order, the judgment: first of the serpent, then of the woman, and lastly of the man.

Structure of the Judgment

In the judgment, we are faced once again with the whole problem of the garden of Eden. The time is no doubt not yet ripe for a general solution; for the time being we shall have reason to be well content if we find that we can determine with precision where the difficulty lies.

The judgment contains a number of elements which are apparently intended to have the character of a penalty, and which yet would seem to belong by nature to those who are punished. The most obvious example is death, which appears to be laid upon man, who is mortal by nature, as a penalty. From this one may reasonably conclude to a privilege of immortality; but one cannot treat the whole of the judgment in the same way—it cannot be supposed, for example, that the serpent was once supernaturally endowed with feet! Things that are natural to the serpent—to creep on its belly, to "eat dust," to be a dangerous animal against which man needs to be on his guard ("enmity")—these things are imposed as a penalty. Are we then to suppose that it was once otherwise? St. Thomas considers

285

that this would be a "thoroughly unreasonable" conclusion, "for the nature of the animals did not alter by the sin of man."[1] The Spanish exegete Tostatus (+1455), in whom there is practically nothing here that is not to be found, including the above-mentioned opinion that Jahweh manifested himself in the mid-day breeze, arrives eventually at the following formulation of the difficulty: How, he says, can something which belongs to the *nature* of the serpent be at the same time an *evil?* And amongst a whole series of discursive considerations, he lets fall a phrase which is as succinct as it is to the point: *istud malum magis est in homine quam in serpente,* the evil lies much rather in the man than in the serpent. This is extremely relevant. The sacred author, in order to make it clear what a great religious transformation has taken place in man, shows the whole of nature as having been changed from top to bottom. Moreover (probably with a polemical ulterior motive) he takes the natural characteristics of the serpent and uses them to typify the depravity of the devil. So that what the narrative at first sight appears to present as a physical alteration in the condition of the serpent, is really to be understood as a form of expression which is adopted as a means of conveying something that really lies on the human and religious level.

So far so good. But again, we cannot go on like this. The woman's penalty consists in the pains of childbirth and in subjection to her husband, that of the man in hard work and in death, the latter penalty consisting in the fact that he loses the privilege of immortality. The question which has to be faced is whether the other privileges, too, presuppose a previous state of privilege. In other words, how far did this state of privilege extend?

The structure of the narrative is homogeneous from top to

[1] *Summa Theologica,* I, Q. 96, 1 ad 2.

bottom. At the top we have a divinely willed state of original privilege (immortality), the reality of which is dogmatically certain. It would however be "thoroughly unreasonable" to extend this state of privilege throughout the whole of creation (into the world of the animals for example). So that we are forced to ask where the borderline is to be traced between the doctrinal content of the narrative and its imagery. And what, in particular, is to be said about the privilege of exemption from suffering?

Exemption from Suffering

It is a view generally accepted by theologians that man, in his privileged state, was exempt from sickness and pain. In past times there was no great difficulty in picturing this situation fairly accurately. There was the tree of life, with all its miraculous properties; the peace which reigned in Paradise meant that man had nothing to fear either from his fellow men or from any of the animals, and it formed part of his privileged condition that he had a special gift of knowledge, so that there could be no question of error, mistakes, or unpleasant surprises of any kind. And as if all this was not enough, there was also a special Providence watching over him to guard against accidents. It must be confessed that the whole of this picture of the paradisal situation is determined by an unduly literal interpretation of the biblical text, with the result that a number of these points have gradually tended to be left aside, and insofar as they do still occur in the manuals, it is because they belong to the repertoire, as it were, and are repeated without conviction or further reflection. One gets a strong feeling of having got beyond the bounds of tangible reality with discussions as to whether or not the first man was capable of falling into error, or as to the extent of the knowledge which he possessed as the teacher of the human race and as the inventor of language, both of which, incidentally, are qualities which are recognizably bound up with an untenable exegesis of the name-giving tableau.

A manual of 1950 gives the following four arguments in favor of the privilege of exemption from suffering: *1*) The Paradise narrative shows man as being in a state of happiness and well-being. *2*) In the judgment, pain and suffering are presented as consequences of sin. These two arguments are of course, as such, of no value, inasmuch as they beg the question of the correct exegesis of the biblical text.

3) The testimony of the Fathers. Here it must be noted that the many patristic texts to which appeal can be made in this connection are of no account as long as no consideration has been made of how much of what they say remains once those elements which depend upon an all too slavish commentary on the letter of the narrative have been eliminated.

4) The connection between exemption from suffering and immortality. Nowadays, this would seem to be the main argument. Its value stands or falls with the presupposition that the privilege of immortality corresponded to a previous physical quality which was already possessed by the first man (and which would appear to have been somewhat difficult to get rid of after the Fall, or so it might be thought when one considers the long life enjoyed by the Patriarchs!).

Without wanting to anticipate the results of the theologians' researches, it may be remarked that exemption from suffering is not easy to situate in the world which we know from our own experience. For it to be credible, man's material surroundings would have had to have been entirely different, with a different climate, flora and fauna—concerning which St. Thomas concluded already that they were not different. The point will become clearer as we consider the penalties, in addition to death itself, to which man was condemned.

288

The Penalties

Work does not, in itself, have the nature of a penalty. Not only is it part of man's nature, but it can even be said to have had a place in his life in Paradise. The emphasis in the narrative is on the hardness of the work. But the difficulty remains that it would seem to be part of the natural constitution of the earth that it demands to be worked "in the sweat of man's brow."

Was the earth indeed different in some way before man first sinned? The narrative, quite logically, says that it was: as a consequence of man's sin the earth was smitten with a curse, and it was only then that it began to bring forth thistles and thorns. It is however "thoroughly unreasonable" to take this as if it was meant to be a piece of biological information, and there is then no reason to suppose that human work, considered purely as physical effort, was any different before man first sinned than it was thereafter. "The evil is in the man." It is man who has drawn down a curse upon himself; it is his religious situation that has changed. He now looks at everything in the material world with other eyes; his relation to it is different and he experiences it quite differently. The narrative conveys this in a striking and suggestive way by representing things as if it was the world which then behaved differently in relation to man. But this does not remove the difficulty of how "hard" work is to be reconciled with the privilege of exemption from suffering.

St. Paul does not interpret the teaching of the narrative that the man is the head of the woman as a penalty for sin, but rather as a consequence of the divine act of creation. And since in the narrative itself the woman is said to have been created as a "helper" for the man, it can also hardly be a part of the judgment to have decreed that the natural subordination of the woman to the man is a consequence of sin, i.e, that it is a

289

natural relationship which, before man sinned, was annulled by way of privilege.

The judgment must therefore be interpreted as bearing rather on the degeneration of this relationship into slavery and tyranny, which was so evident a reality in heathendom in general and in the Eastern world in particular. The judgment is therefore recognizing a fact rather than formulating a law, and when it is understood in this way, this part of it presents no further difficulty, since the penalty is seen to lie not in the natural structure itself, but rather in the wounded state of that natural structure.

The reader will no doubt himself have begun to realize by now that as regards the last point which has to be considered in this connection, it is in all probability a false problem to start wondering how the possibility of childbirth without pain is to be envisaged. In any case no exegete will feel able to pass judgment about certain actual situations on the basis of the narrative alone. It is for the theologians to reflect further, and more deeply, about this privilege of exemption from pain, and not, it is to be hoped, along speculative lines alone.

The Basic Problem of the Garden

Meanwhile, as so often, all we can do is to hang on as firmly as possible to the two ends of the chain. One of these is the conclusion of St. Thomas ("thoroughly unreasonable"), confirmed as it is by exegesis, and the other is the dogmatically certain fact that the privilege of immortality formed part of the state of original righteousness. How it is that these two ends, with their respective implications, are in fact joined together in a single chain is something which is not at the present moment entirely clear. To this end a deeper and broader understanding (which will then have to be expressed in an adequate formula) will be required of what precisely the historical or metahistorical character of the events related in the Paradise narrative really is.

In the course of this book, we have already spent two chapters (14 and 15) in getting to grips with the "garden of Eden." In the light of the general line of thought which has been worked out in these chapters, which would now appear to need applying not only to man's surroundings, but also to what the narrative has to say about man himself, it may be that, by way of conclusion, the following consideration is relevant.

Man's existence is characterized by suffering. The privilege of exemption from the latter is the reverse of this actual situation. What the sacred author has done is to choose, from simple experience, the most universal and typical of all man's burdens, and to explain them in terms of a curse which now lies upon the human race in consequence of its primal sin. The narrative is therefore intended first and foremost as a religious exposition and explanation of the present concrete reality. It is entirely in function of this present reality that the sacred author elaborates his account of the past. The important thing is that we should not lose sight of the fact that the object of this account is to throw light on *the present* religious situation. It is a fundamental mistake, still all too common, for the narrative concerning the primal state of things to be considered in isolation, and for it then to be assumed that the essential question is that concerning the corresponding historical state of affairs.

Again and again, we have to force ourselves to return to the most elementary principle of all exegesis: The first condition of any reliable judgment about the Paradise narrative, or any other biblical text, is that our own point of view should as far as possible be the same as that of the sacred author. And his concern here is first of all to convey something about the disastrous present, which is at first sight so difficult to reconcile with the content of his faith in God. In the process of doing this, he is

291

obliged to go back and consider the historical event of man's first sin, which has cut across the line of God's original saving purpose. The picture which he gives of Paradise, as a past reality, is simply a concrete representation of this divine purpose.

The biblical evidence concerning the state of affairs which existed before this first sin does not allow us to make any kind of historical reconstruction of it, since its central point of reference is a judgment of value about *present* reality. All the narrative is saying, in the last resort, is that if things had gone as Jahweh had intended, man and the world in which he lives would have looked quite different. That they are as they in fact are, is not to be blamed upon Jahweh, but on sin, that of the past as well as that of the present. And the believer must therefore see in suffering and death more than a mere necessity of nature.

We have therefore no means of knowing, from the evidence which the Bible gives us, what sort of reality may in fact in the past have corresponded to the "state of Paradise." There is at all events one reality which certainly does correspond to it— God's saving purpose, which is still ever present and active, and still forever being hindered by sin.

It is this divine purpose which gives a meaning and a perspective to man's catastrophic existence, and which will at the last be completely victorious over sin. Then indeed the state of Paradise will be a reality, and indeed far more than the state of Paradise as Genesis depicts it: all that is mortal in man will be clothed with immortality, all things will be made new, and there will be a new heaven and a new earth.

The prophets, who lived in the midst of a wretched and sinful Israel, were enabled to draw from their faith in Jahweh the certainty of the messianic salvation that was to come; to them it was given to fathom the mystery of Jahweh's real and ultimate purpose in His election of Israel. It is because of this certainty that the Paradise narrative has in the last resort a universal significance for the whole of humanity. It is not by chance that Israel's vision of the end of all things is in many ways parallel to its vision of the first beginnings.

If we are not mistaken, the purpose of the description of Paradise in Genesis is to give an assurance that there is hope for sinful and wretched man, and that his present situation by no means corresponds with God's plan for him. This plan will only be fully revealed and brought to its fruition when the old world has come to an end. The Creator, for His part, will not give up; He will bring His saving plan to pass despite all. This is the substance of the faith of which the Proto-gospel is a succinct expression.

27

The Proto–gospel (Gn 3:15)

It is not possible, within the scope of this book, of which this chapter forms the conclusion, to give an exhaustive treatment of the Proto-gospel. Instead of investigating the numberless suggestions that have been put forward by way of solution to the many questions which it raises, we shall simply do our best to provide a concise summary of the relevant evidence and of such of the many available points of view as seem to be sufficiently well-grounded to provide some kind of general basis for the exegesis of this difficult text. It is neither necessary nor desirable that we should answer every question with a definite yes or no; there is no point in trying to put overdefinite questions to a text which is in fact far more the expression of a profound but vague conviction than the formulation of a sharply defined idea. It is, for example, far more important to show that the perspective of the text is that of God's saving purpose, than to determine from it the precise nature of this promised salvation or the manner in which it is to be realized.

The Text

"And I will put enmity between you and the woman and between your descendants and her descendants: he shall crush

294

your head and you shall strike at his heel." That it is not the
woman herself but rather her descendants who are referred to
in the second half of the verse as the opponents of the serpent
is clear from three different pieces of evidence in the original
text: the pronominal subject of the verb "crush" ("*he* shall crush
your head"); the form of this verb; and the pronominal object
of the same verb when it is used the second time ("you shall
strike at *his* heel"). The point is that in all these cases, the
Hebrew language possesses a perfectly good feminine form in
addition to the masculine form which is used here. The feminine
pronoun *ipsa,* which occurs in the Sixto-Clementine Vulgate,
and which is perhaps not even the correct reading of Jerome's
original translation, can thus scarcely be supposed to be based
upon a correct but lost reading of the original.

The same Hebrew verb (*shuf*) occurs in both cases, where
we have translated "crush" and "strike at" respectively. Thus
each of the two protagonists *shuf* each other, the one against the
"head" of its opponent, the other against the "heel." The conclusion has sometimes been drawn from this difference that the
victory of the one over the other is foretold in the text by the
indication of a decisive wound (on the head) being incurred on
the one side, as opposed to a secondary wound (on the heel)
on the other. Christ, and in Him the believer, overcomes the
devil, but at the price of suffering, etc. This conclusion would
seem to be somewhat premature, since the difference in question is a necessary part of the situation as it is presented. The
starting point of the text is quite clearly the duel between man
and the serpent, and in such a conflict it is simply the natural
course of events that the man should seek with all his might
(thus with his heel) to crush the head of the serpent, and that
the serpent should aim its bite (which is equally deadly) at the
heel of its attacker. If it should succeed in this, its victory is
likewise complete. The normal meaning of *shuf* is "to crush."

There is also a related verb *shaef*, which in addition to "crush" can also mean "snap at," or "bite at," and hence, "lie in wait for." Contamination can easily take place between the two verbs, since the second one contains a weak letter (*aleph*) which can be omitted in speech and even in writing, so that it becomes identical with the other verb. In short, since it is the consonants above all which determine the meaning of a Hebrew word, *shuf* lends itself extremely well to the sort of play on words which we know that this author is so fond of employing (*âdâm-adâmâh; ish-isshâh, ârôm-ârum-êrôm*). The precise meaning must therefore be determined by the context in each case, and it seems indeed to be clear here, since it can hardly be said that the bite of a serpent "crushes" a man's heel.

The various translators of this text have naturally enough sought to maintain this play on words. The LXX and those translations which have followed it (among others the *Vetus Latina*) have "lie in wait for" (*têrêo*, [*ob*]*servare*) twice, Jerome and the Dutch "Statenbijbel" have "crush" (*conterere*) twice. Besides these, the Vulgate, with its mixed translation, has a number of predecessors (Aquila, Irenaeus, Cyprian). These variations have had the appropriate enough consequence that the polyvalence of *shuf* has acquired a sort of historical dimension, so that it is now based upon more than a mere philological argument. The image employed by the text itself is indeed an argument in favor of thinking that the Vulgate, while it has abandoned the play on words, has preserved the meaning faithfully enough. We may compare the translation proposed by Lagrange: "lui te *brisera* la tête et toi tu le viseras au talon"[1] And we shall find that a consideration of the wider context provides further confirmation that the sacred author did indeed intend these two meanings one after the other.

[1] *Revue biblique* (1897), p. 352.

The Context

The purpose of the Paradise narrative as a whole is to give an explanation of the situation which man's experience reveals to him as his own. The narrative starts with an idealized and deliberately contrasting picture, and concludes with a delineation of the situation as it now is. And this is where the judgment comes in: it serves as a literary means by which the sacred author can draw this situation in all its characteristic lineaments. Beneath this literary form, what it contains is Israel's vision of the present in the light of its faith in Jahweh. This vision is by no means devoid of hope. Condemnation is never Jahweh's last word. This is clear enough in the preaching of the prophets, which in its inspiration is so closely linked with our own narrative. We may thus expect a priori that the perspective of salvation will be present in the latter somewhere.

Throughout the whole of the history of salvation we find the divine plan being continually cut across by human sin. The Paradise narrative came into being spontaneously as a result of reflection on this fact. And ever and again, Jahweh bends His saving purpose to meet the new situation which sin has created, indeed sin even seems to provide Him with an opportunity for realizing His plan on a higher level still. In terms of the history of Israel in general, this becomes especially clear when Israel draws upon itself, by sin, its own downfall as a nation. Israel's national state of privilege is then lost, but the faithful remnant finds it again on a higher level, even though it continues to experience the loss of the original state of privilege as a real chastisement. In the same way, man's paradisal state of privilege is now irrevocably lost, and the way to the tree of life is barred, but not the way to Jahweh—for how indeed could this be so for someone as deeply committed to his faith

297

as this writer? But it is now for him a way of faith, to be followed under the sign of a real and painful deprivation.

That the above general consideration is not as far-fetched as might perhaps appear, can be seen from a comparison with the rest of the book of Genesis. This latter, in its present form, represents a synthesis of two parallel lines of development.

The so-called Priestly narrative, in whose general canvas a number of larger and smaller fragments of the older Jahwistic narrative have been incorporated by the final author, shows how the Creator formed the cosmos out of chaos, how the chaos then returned as a consequence of sin (the Flood), and how finally the human race was given the chance of a new beginning in Noah, with whom God established a covenant which he later confirmed and further expanded in His covenant with Abraham. In all this, the Priestly writer is doing no more than developing on a broader and more cosmic basis the same essential line of thought that he found in the Jahwistic narrative.

The starting point of the latter was the description of Paradise, from which it then went on to show how sin had brought a curse on the whole of humanity and on the earth, and which continued to work out its effects in the Flood and in the confusion of tongues (Babel), but which was taken away by the blessings given to Sem, to Noah, and to Abraham and his descendants.

Against this background, a number of the details of the Paradise narrative fall into place. That Jahweh Elohim teaches man how to clothe himself is more than a delicate stroke of the author's pen: it shows that Jahweh intervenes not only in order to punish man, but also in order to take positive steps, and to set bounds to the disastrous consequences of sin. His intervention provides a certain breathing space. He does not abandon man to the tempter, but rather comes and takes his part: He puts him back, as it were, on the side of God, over against the serpent who is the *common* enemy. He takes action in the same

way that an angry father might take his child away from the
influence of an older and bad companion with whom the father
had strictly forbidden the child to have any contact. It is the
companion who gets the full weight of his anger, for the child
is innocent by comparison. But as soon as the father has dealt
with the companion, he then proceeds to take the child in hand.
The judgment on the man and the woman recorded in Genesis
does therefore contain an element of pure punishment, while
the judgment on the serpent provides the psychological moment
for a more favorable perspective to enter in.

That this perspective is indeed there is confirmed by the
parallelism between the three condemnations. It is inadequate
to understand the condemnation in 3:15 as saying simply that
all is now up with the paradisal state of harmony between man
and the animal world. The verse would appear to be far more
a reaction or counterpart to the monstrous covenant against God
into which the serpent had enticed the woman. It must therefore be interpreted in such a way that it is seen to be a judgment
on the serpent and on the serpent alone. The woman cannot be
understood as being involved to the same extent. She is mentioned here because it is she, who was the serpent's victim, who
will be the instrument by which he will receive his punishment,
just as in the second condemnation the man is mentioned because it is he, who was led astray by the woman, who is to be the
instrument by which she will receive her punishment, and as in
the third condemnation the man is punished by means of the
earth whose fruits he had misused.

There must therefore be more in the verse than just an expression of the bare fact of experience that the relationship
between human beings and serpents is one of perpetual enmity
and war. Like the condemnation of the man, that of the serpent
ends in a point of climax: the Proto-gospel must needs express
in regard to the serpent a climax of punishment, curse and
humiliation; in other words, *the conflict must end to the dis-*

advantage of the serpent. It was the serpent, in Paradise, who overcame man, and made him into an enemy of God. But God has intervened, and has turned the tables on him, so that he finds that he has drawn the enmity upon his own head, and that it will be man who finally holds the victory.

The Serpent as Camouflage

The sacred author had his own good reasons (the safeguarding of monotheism and of Jahweh's absolute and supreme causality) for not representing in his own spiritual form the evil-intentioned, supernatural being who successfully cuts across Jahweh's plans. He may perhaps also have had certain (polemical) reasons for taking the serpent, in particular, for camouflage in this connection, since he was thereby providing Israel with an incidental warning of the danger which threatened it from native heathendom. This camouflage means that the narrative has the outward form of folklore, which is however merely a literary form of expression which the author has adopted for the sake of the communication of a deeper truth, in the same way that we find done in the story of the Tower of Babel, for example.

The actual verbal expressions which occur in the narrative have thus been chosen in such a way that they do indeed apply to the purely natural relationship between man and the serpent, but also in such a way that at the same time the spiritual relationship with which the author is really concerned appears constantly through the camouflage. This is especially noticeable in the Proto-gospel. For whereas in verse 15a the woman, in Paradise, stands over against the serpent, and in 15b descendants stand over against descendants, in 15c it is the descendants who stand over against the serpent once more. This structure suggests three things: *1*) that the enmity between the two sides will culminate in a *final conflict,* since the head of this one serpent can, after all, only be crushed a single time; 2) that in the enmity between the two lots of descendants, the real antagonist is the paradisal serpent, who is thus envisaged as a *permanently present spiritual power,* who transcends the actual animal of the narrative itself; 3) that the spiritual individual, whom the paradisal serpent serves to camouflage, will be faced, in this last and decisive conflict, with an *individual opponent* over against him.

Thus when the narrative says that in consequence of the primal sin a conflict has arisen between man and the serpent, its purpose is to teach that this primal sin has been the cause of a permanent conflict between man and the devil. In this conflict, the devil will eventually be overcome—this is precisely his condemnation—and this will happen by the intervention of one of the descendants of the woman whom he has deceived. The woman will die, but as the mother of all living things she will have her revenge through her seed, and this through one of them in particular to whom the whole of humanity will owe its victory.

The Seed of the Woman

Israel's cast of mind is totalitarian, and does not make a complete and final distinction between the individual and the community to which he belongs. This comes out very strongly in the case of the Hebrew word for "seed," which frequently refers to an individual (Gn 4:25), but mostly in his involvement in a particular community and as its representative. Compare, for example, the seed of Abraham (Gn 22:18), and the seed of David (2 S 7:12). So that when we find that later texts, under the influence of a more explicit expectation of salvation, begin to carry over the collective aspect of the earlier texts and concentrate it more on to the individual meaning, there is no need to suppose that some heterogeneous element has been introduced, since what has occurred is simply the unfolding of a

301

dynamic potentiality which the original biblical expression already contained. The LXX, for example, translates the subject of "crush" by the masculine pronoun *autos,* even though this in fact refers back to a neuter word (*sperma*). Paul's commentary on the "seed" of Abraham (Gal 3:16) is well known, as also is Matthew's application to Christ of a text which in its original context refers to Israel (Mt 2:15; Hos 11:1). Particularly instructive in this connection is the figure of the Suffering Servant of Jahweh, who is individual in character and who yet at the same time sums up and represents the faithful remnant of Israel.

It follows that when the New Testament finally reveals Christ as being Satan's conqueror, we are justified in seeing a connection between the indications in Genesis and the later reality, and in accepting as a fact that in the expression "seed" the individual and the collective meanings are indeed interwoven. We can therefore say that the Proto-gospel refers vaguely, but according to the literal sense of the text, to the victory which the human race was to gain over the devil in Christ. It is the God of peace who through Christ crushes Satan under our feet (Rom 16:20; cp. Lk 10:17–20).

The question then arises, if it is admitted that "seed" refers in one way or another to the person of the Messiah, whether "woman" may not, in parallel fashion, be understood in a Marial sense. Considered in the light of revelation as a whole —in which the parallel Adam-Eve/Christ-Church (Mary) is one of the principal elements—it would be hard to deny that there is indeed a certain Marial element in the text. But it also needs to be said that an exegesis which would connect the Marial sense with the text of Genesis in a satisfactory manner has not yet been achieved, either according to the literal meaning or by the way of typology. The most recent attempt at proving a literal Mariological sense (Coppens) is not to my mind convincing. Coppens understands "woman" as being a universal term which

302

in the last resort applies to every woman ("on entrevoit que chaque femme aura à lutter"), so that the attention can be directed by the context either to one or to a number of particular women, in this case to Eve as the source of the enmity and to Mary as the mother of the Conqueror in the final stage. The difficulty with this attractive piece of exegesis would appear to be that on the level of the literal interpretation, "seed" refers to humanity as a whole, and thus "woman" must signify the common mother of humanity, which is Eve.

Among the sources from which further light on this matter will no doubt come, we have Apocalypse 12, in which the main figures of Genesis 3 occur once more in New Testament guise: *1*) the great Dragon, the old serpent who is called Devil and Satan; *2*) the Woman; *3*) her Child; *4*) the remnant of her seed. With the independent style which is so typical of the New Testament, and in which the Apocalypse goes particularly far, St. John uses the biblical figures of the first, primeval conflict in his depiction of the last great apocalyptic struggle. It is perhaps for this reason that the precise meaning which he there means to give to the text of Genesis is difficult to pin down, since the literal and the typological are constantly interwoven, and also in some cases appear to have undergone a certain shift in meaning. It is in any case not to be expected that a further unravelling of these elements will necessarily make it possible to establish the Marial characteristics of the apocalyptic Woman and her relationship with Eve with any greater precision.

The Proto-gospel has had its share in the general misunderstandings of the past concerning the primal history which is related in Genesis. It has in consequence too readily been seen as the starting point of Israel's messianic expectations, and as the first link in the traditional series of messianic texts. The result has been that this ancient text has been made the foundation for a construction which is really heavier than it is able to bear. In the exegesis of the Fathers, on the other hand, it most often has a notably modest part to play.

This text is the expression of the vision which Israel possessed, through its faith in Jahweh, about human existence, which is full of sorrow but still not without hope for the future. This vision is the product of Israel's national history and of its national expectation of salvation. It was because of this alone that Israel was able to transpose its faith in a future salvation on to the wider plane of humanity as a whole.

This does not in any way mean that Genesis 3:15 thereby loses its own proper historical and objective content. We may certainly accept it as an authentic interpretation of the situation which really existed at the time of man's first origins. The first men sinned, but God did not simply abandon them because of this, but rather sought out a new way by which to realize the salvation which man had thus gambled away. God continued to concern Himself with man, and on the latter's side there remained both the need and the expectation of this salvation. This is the common human experience, the primal fact of which Israel has given an account for itself in the Proto-gospel.

Text: Genesis 1–3

Creation (1:1-2, 4a)

1 ¹In the beginning God created the heavens and the earth. ²The earth was formless and empty, and darkness lay over the deep. And the Spirit of God was brooding over the waters.

³And God said: "Let there be light." And there was light. ⁴And God saw that the light was good. And God separated the light from the darkness. ⁵And God called the light Day and the darkness he called Night. And there was evening and there was morning: the first day.

⁶And God said: "Let there be a dome in the midst of the waters, in order to form a separation between them." And so it was. ⁷And God made the dome and separated the waters which were under the dome from the waters which were above the dome. ⁸And God called the dome Heaven. And there was evening and there was morning: the second day.

⁹And God said: "Let the waters which are under the heaven come together into one place, so that the dry land may appear." And so it was. ¹⁰And God called the dry land Earth, and the waters which had come together he called Seas. And God saw that it was good.

¹¹Then God said: "Let the earth bring forth vegetation, plants that bear seed and fruit trees bearing fruit each with its seed, upon the earth." And so it was. ¹²And the earth brought forth vegetation, plants that each bear their own sort of seed, and trees which bear fruit each containing its own sort of seed.

And God saw that it was good. [13]And there was evening and there was morning: the third day.

[14]And God said: "Let there be lights in the dome of heaven in order to separate the day from the night, and also to serve as signs to distinguish the seasons, and the days, and the years; [15]and let them be lights in the dome of heaven in order to give light on earth." And so it was. [16]And God made the two great lights, the greater light to rule over the day, and the smaller light to rule over the night, and He made the stars also. [17]And God put them in the dome of heaven, in order to give light on earth, [18]and in order to rule over the day and over the night and in order to separate the light from the darkness. And God saw that it was good. [19]And there was evening and there was morning: the fourth day.

[20]And God said: "Let the waters swarm with living creatures, and let there be birds to fly over the earth across the dome of heaven." [21]Then God created the great sea monsters and all the living creatures that swarm in the waters, each according to his kind, and all kinds of feathered birds. And God saw that it was good. [22]Then God blessed them and said: "Be fruitful and multiply, and inhabit the waters in the sea, and let the birds multiply on land." [23]And there was evening and there was morning: the fifth day.

[24]And God said: "Let the earth bring forth all kinds of living creatures, cattle and creeping animals and wild beasts of the earth, according to their kinds." And so it was. [25]Then God made the different kinds of wild beasts and the different kinds of cattle and creeping animals, each according to its kind. And God saw that it was good.

[26]Then God said: "Let us make men in our image, after our likeness, that they may rule over the fishes of the sea and over the birds of the air and over the cattle and over the whole earth and over all the creeping animals that creep over the ground."

²⁷Then God created man in his image, in the image of God created he him, male and female created he them.

²⁸And God blessed them and said to them: "Be fruitful and multiply and inhabit the earth and subdue it, and rule over the fishes of the sea and over the birds of the air and over all the animals that move upon the earth."

²⁹Then God said: "Behold, I have given you every plant that bears seed in all the earth and every tree that bears seed in its fruit: you are to have them for food. ³⁰And to the wild beasts and to the birds of the air and to all living things that move upon the earth, I have given all green plants for food." And it was so.

³¹And God saw everything that he had made, and behold, it was very good. And there was evening and there was morning: the sixth day.

2 ¹Thus were the heavens and the earth completed, and all the host of them. ²And on the seventh day God finished his work which he had done, and he rested on the seventh day from all his work which he had done. ³And God blessed the seventh day and made it holy, because on that day he rested from all his work which he had done in the creation.

⁴ᵃThis is the story of the heavens and of the earth, when they were created.

Paradise (2:4b-25)

⁴ᵇWhen God had made the earth and the heavens, ⁵there were still no wild plants growing, nor any green herb; for the Lord God had not yet caused it to rain on the earth, and there was no man to till the ground. ⁶But a flood came up out of the earth, and watered the whole face of the ground. ⁷Then the Lord God formed man out of the earth of the ground, and blew the breath of life into his nostrils; and so man became a living being.

⁸Then the Lord God planted a garden in Eden, in the East,

and put there the man whom he had formed. [9]And the Lord God made to grow up out of the ground every kind of tree that is pleasant to be seen and good for food, and also the tree of life in the midst of the garden, and the tree of the knowledge of good and evil.

[10]And a river flowed out of Eden that watered the garden, and it divided there into four branches. [11]The name of the first is Phison; it flows around the whole land of Hevilath, where there is gold, [12]and the gold of that land is good; bdellium and onyx stone are also there. [13]The name of the second river is Gehon; it is the one which flows around the whole of the land of Kush. [14]The name of the third river is Tigris; it flows to the East of Assyria. And the fourth river is the Euphrates.

[15]And the Lord God took the man and put him in the garden of Eden to cultivate it and to watch over it. [16]And the Lord God commanded the man, and said: "You may eat as you will of every tree in the garden, [17]but of the tree of the knowledge of good and evil you shall not eat, for if you eat of it you shall certainly die."

[18]And the Lord God said: "It is not good that man should be alone. I shall make him a helper worthy of him." [19]Then the Lord God formed out of the ground all the beasts of the field and all the birds of the air and brought them to the man to see what he would call them. And whatever the man called every living creature, so is its name. [20]And then the man gave names to all the cattle and to all the birds of the air and to all the beasts of the field, but he found no helper worthy of man. [21]Then the Lord God caused a deep sleep to come over the man, and while he slept he took one of his ribs and filled up its place with flesh. [22]And the Lord God made a woman out of the rib that he had taken from the man, and brought her to the man. [23]Then the man said:

"This, at last, is bone of my bones
and flesh of my flesh.

She shall be called Woman,
for she was taken out of man."

²⁴Therefore a man leaves his father and his mother and cleaves to his wife, and they become one flesh.

²⁵And they were both naked, the man and his wife, and they were not ashamed before each other.

The Fall (3:1-24)

3 ¹Now the serpent was more subtle than all the other wild animals that the Lord God had made. And it said to the woman: "Did God say that you may not eat of any of the trees in the garden?" ²And the woman answered: "We may eat of the fruit of the trees in the garden, ³but of the fruit of the tree that is in the middle of the garden, of that tree God has said: 'You shall not eat of it nor touch it, or you shall die.'" ⁴Then the serpent said to the woman: "You shall certainly not die, ⁵but God knows that, when you eat of it, your eyes will be opened, and you will be like gods, knowing good and evil."

⁶And the woman saw that the tree was good to eat and attractive to the eyes, and that it was desirable in order to gain understanding by it. And so she took of the fruit and ate, and gave some of it also to her husband who was with her, and he ate.

⁷Then the eyes of both of them were opened, and they knew that they were naked. And they sewed fig leaves together, and made themselves aprons. ⁸Then in the cool of the day they heard the sound of the Lord God walking through the garden, and the man and his wife hid themselves from the Lord God among the trees of the garden. ⁹But the Lord God called out to the man and said to him: "Where are you?" ¹⁰And he answered: "I heard the sound of you in the garden and then I became afraid, because I am naked, and I hid myself." ¹¹And He said: "Who told you that you are naked? Have you eaten of the tree from which I forbade you to eat?" ¹²And the man said: "The woman

309

whom you have put with me, she gave me of the tree and then I ate of it." ¹³Then the Lord God said to the woman: "What have you done?" And the woman said: "The serpent led me astray, and I ate of it."

Then the Lord God said to the serpent:
"Because you have done this, you shall be cursed
among all tame and wild beasts;
you shall go on your belly
and you shall eat dust all the days of your life.
¹⁵And I will create enmity between you and the woman
and between your seed and hers;
he shall shatter your head
and you shall shatter his heel."
¹⁶And to the woman He said:
"I will greatly increase your pain in childbearing,
in pain shall you bear children
and you shall long for your husband
and he shall rule over you."
¹⁷And to the man He said:
"Because you have listened to the voice of your wife
and have eaten of the tree of which I commanded you:
You shall not eat of it,
cursed is the ground because of you,
in pain you shall eat of it all the days of your life,
¹⁸and it shall bring forth thistles and thorns for you,
and you shall eat the plants of the field.
¹⁹In the sweat of your brow you shall eat bread
until you return to the ground from which you have come,
for you are dust, and to dust you shall return."

²⁰And the man called his wife Eve, because she became the mother of all living things.

²¹Then the Lord God made clothes of skins for the man and his wife, and clothed them.

²²And the Lord God said: "Behold, man has become like one

of us by the knowledge of good and evil; let him now also not stretch out his hand and take of the tree of life, and live for ever." [23]And the Lord God drove him away out of the garden of Eden, to cultivate the ground from which he was taken. [24]And He drove the man out, and let him dwell to the East of the garden of Eden. And He put the cherubim, and the sword flaming in every direction, to guard the way to the tree of life.

Biblical References

Index

318